THE AMAZING LAW OF INFLUENCE

THE
AMAZING
LAW OF
INFLUENCE

KING DUNCAN

PELICAN PUBLISHING COMPANY
Gretna 2001

*The word "Pelican" and the depiction of a pelican are trademarks of
Pelican Publishing Company, Inc., and are registered in the
U.S. Patent and Trademark Office.*

Library of Congress Cataloging-in-Publication Data

Duncan, King.
  The amazing law of influence / by King Duncan.
    p. cm.
  ISBN 1-56554-861-2 (alk. paper)
    1. Conduct of life. 2. Chaotic behavior in systems—Miscellanea. I. Title.

BJ1581.2 .D785 2001
170'.44—dc21

00-068219

Printed in the United States of America

Published by Pelican Publishing Company, Inc.
1000 Burmaster Street, Gretna, Louisiana 70053

The Amazing Law of Influence is dedicated to four people who have had a defining impact on my life: two grandparents, now deceased—the Reverend G. F. Cox, a Circuit riding Methodist preacher, and Mrs. Anna Armstrong Duncan, a teacher whom I hardly got to know, but whose influence was nevertheless felt; and my parents, Charlton King Duncan, Sr. and Glennie Cox Duncan.

It is also dedicated to eleven people I count on to influence the world in a most positive way: my four daughters, Rebecca, Deborah, Angela, and Selina, their terrific husbands—Stephen, Greg, Bill, and Christian—and my two beautiful grandchildren, Rachel and Sebastian. It is also dedicated to the person who has encouraged me every step of the way: my wife, Selina.

Contents

Introduction

It was a stressful situation. Writer Catherine Ryan Hyde was driving home late one night in a run-down section of Los Angeles. Her aging car began spewing smoke and came to a complete stop. Suddenly, out of nowhere, two men with a blanket ran toward her car. Her instincts warned her that they were going to do her harm. She gripped the steering wheel and tried to prepare herself for the inevitable. To her surprise, the two men did not intend to harm her. Their purpose was to smother the flames that were by now shooting out from under her hood. At the risk of their own lives, they put out the fire.

After the fire was out and she had recovered her composure, Ms. Hyde tried to thank the men, but they were gone. She was left with the emptiness all of us have felt when we find ourselves unable to express our gratitude. So, what do you do if you cannot pay someone back? Ms. Hyde decided the best thing was to pay it forward—to pass the favor on to someone else.

This incident inspired Catherine Ryan Hyde to write the novel *Pay It Forward,* which was subsequently turned into a motion picture starring Academy Award winners Kevin Spacey and Helen Hunt, as well as Haley Joel Osment, the popular child star of *The Sixth Sense.*

Pay It Forward is an inspiring story of a teacher, Eugene Simonet, who gives his seventh grade class their initial assignment for the school year: "Think of an idea that could change the world, and put it into action." One of his students, a serious-minded twelve-year-old boy named Trevor McKinney takes his teacher at his word and comes up with a simple plan: He'll do something really good for three people who, instead of paying him back, will be asked to "pay it forward" by aiding three other people who, in turn, will aid three others ad infinitum. This was young Trevor's plan for changing the world.

In spite of sterling performances by each of the leading actors, *Pay It*

Forward was not a box office success. Nevertheless, the author has done us a great service. Through young Trevor, she has demonstrated how change takes place in our world.

Welcome to *The Amazing Law of Influence*—an exhilarating study of the impact one person can have on his or her world. It is based on one of the central tenets of chaos theory—that tiny, incremental changes that build up over time within dynamic systems can trigger monumental alterations in the way things work in the world. Chaos science deals primarily with physical phenomena, and can be very technical. But this is not a technical book; instead, it is a volume of clear, concise concepts. But when you finish reading it, you will understand as you never have before that tiny, incremental changes in human behavior can also lead to monumental alterations in the way society functions. In other words, a solitary individual can, under the proper conditions, exercise enormous influence in the world as a whole.

Like our physical world, the human community is a dynamic system, and it is singularly susceptible to the actions of individuals. For within this dynamic system is a law—a law that guides many of these incremental changes and allows them to yield results far more impressive than the force of their original stimulus might have indicated. Here is the good news: you and I can harness the power of this dynamic law and put it to work in our families, companies, and communities with the result that we improve not only the quality of our own lives, but the quality of life for everyone.

It's like something Scott Adams once said.[1] Adams is the creator of the wildly popular comic strip Dilbert. The strip is syndicated in thirty-nine countries, which proves that Dilbert is a hero to corporate drones around the world. In an interview in *Time* magazine, Adams says, "I always expect everything I do to change the world, not just because there's something special about me, but because everything in the world *was* changed by one person, if you think about it" (italics mine).

He's right on both counts. Everything we do changes the world and everything in the world was changed by one person. How would you like to change the world? How would you like to be affecting life on this planet centuries from now? Impossible, you say? Not really. What if I could show you in a few simple steps how you really could change the world, beginning with those closest to you? Would you buy into it? Forget for a moment how preposterous that sounds. Forget for a moment the sense of powerlessness that modern life often imposes on us.

Before we begin, let me ask you another question. If you knew that you could exert a positive influence that would result in a changed world, would you really want to do it? That is a critical question. Remember, we live in a very hedonistic world. Many people listen only to one radio station—WII-FM—"What's in it for me?" There is a wealth of material in this book that will benefit you, even if you have no interest in saving the world. You will find ways to more effectively influence people you work with and people you love. But this book is especially written for people who dream of a better world and would like to be a solution, rather than part of the problem. This book is for those who want to do well by doing good. If you are a member of this group, then get ready: you're about to learn how you can change the world.

THE AMAZING LAW OF INFLUENCE

CHAPTER 1

The Most Exciting of Nature's Laws

A noted chemist once said something that really captured my attention. "Raise one of your fingers and wiggle it. When you wiggle that finger, you are tickling every atom in the universe." Wow! I was impressed. All that power in my little finger.

Dr. Donald Hatch Andrews, professor emeritus of chemistry at John Hopkins University, went on to say that the atomic structure of our universe is so incredibly sensitive that a person cannot move a finger without changing the relationships among all atoms in the universe.[1]

Dr. Andrews' words echo the work of the physicist J. S. Bell and his colleagues. Building on the work of the creative thinker Ernst Mach, they have shown that all things are connected—at all times and instantaneously at any distance. Mach pointed out, using gravity, that every tiny movement anywhere in the universe automatically affects everything else.[2] What an exciting concept! Our universe is so sensitive that the movement of one atom affects every other atom. Along the same lines, one of my favorite writers, Frederick Buechner, compares the world to a great spider web. He writes, "If you touch it anywhere you set the whole thing a-moving." Amazing.

Concept #1: Every tiny movement in the universe affects the entire universe.

Hold on to this concept for a moment while we consider another significant insight into how our world works.

Back in the 1960s, the Beatles were captivating the young, bombs were falling in Vietnam, and in a laboratory at M. I. T., a meteorologist named Edward Lorenz had just made a discovery that would forever doom the science of long-range weather forecasting. What he found—quite entirely by accident—was that the tiniest possible movement in the air in one part of the world can produce dramatic changes in weather patterns months later in another part of the world. He called it *the butterfly effect*. What Lorenz discovered was that a butterfly flapping its wings in Malibu might set into motion a series of meteorological events which could, months later, produce a monsoon in Malaysia.

Tiny changes yield enormous consequences. No wonder our meteorologists have so much difficulty predicting the weather. If a butterfly can produce a monsoon, think what a bald eagle might do! Think what you might do!

Concept #2: Tiny actions can lead to dramatic changes.

Wrap your mind for a moment around these two important concepts. Now add a third concept more exciting and far-reaching than either one of these. I call it *The Amazing Law of Influence:* **One life touches another, and potentially both lives are changed; one life touches another, and potentially the entire world is changed.**

Here is the central theme of this book. If you change one life, including your own, then potentially you are changing the world.

CHAPTER 2

One Man Who Changed the World

Have you ever heard of an Englishman named John Howard? Though relatively obscure, he just may be one of the most important people of the twentieth-century because of something that seemed insignificant at the time.[1]

The date was December 13, 1899. The Boer Wars were going on in South Africa. At the time, Howard was an Englishman working near the town of Pretoria. An English journalist who had escaped from a Boer POW camp knocked on Howard's door and sought refuge. Howard took him in, looked after him for a week, and helped him escape back to Europe. Once safely back in England, this journalist wrote a news story about his adventure in South Africa. It was so gripping that it was carried by newspapers around the world. In fact, the story was so widely published that the journalist gained international fame that eventually propelled him onto the center stage of world politics.

The journalist's name was Winston Churchill.

What if John Howard had not been there to rescue Winston Churchill? What if Churchill had not risen to rally the British people in the Second World War? What if Hitler had not been defeated? You and I might be speaking German today.

Staggering suppositions, to be sure. But the point is this: John Howard changed the world. Without his acts of compassion and courage, the world might never have heard of Winston Churchill. John Howard made a difference and influenced the course of history. How? By leading an army? By holding a political office? No, Howard made an impact simply by performing an act of kindness and valor for another human being.

And here is what matters: You and I might not be a Winston Churchill, but we can be a John Howard. We *can* make a difference. How? By the amazing Law of Influence: One life touches another and potentially both lives are changed; one life touches another and potentially the entire world is changed.

CHAPTER 3

Changed by a Smile

In a letter to *Psychology Today* magazine, Dr. Robert Healy, a psychotherapist, wrote of a patient who had come to him for help after having changed his mind about committing suicide. It seems that this patient, a young man, had planned to jump off a bridge when something strange happened.[1]

While driving his car to the bridge, he stopped at a traffic light. Looking toward the sidewalk, he spotted an elderly woman who was smiling at him. He felt himself smiling back. The light changed and he drove on, but the memory of her kindly face stayed with him. He began thinking to himself that maybe life wasn't so bad after all. Before reaching the bridge, he turned his car around, drove home, and entered therapy to get help with his problems.

It was nothing dramatic, just an old woman with a pleasant expression on her face. But she changed this desperate young man's entire psychological environment.

I read this and thought to myself, "What if he had passed *me* on that street? Would the result have been the same?" Powerful thought. One life touched another, and a life was changed. But the process is just beginning. A young man decided to live; undoubtedly he will now touch other lives. Maybe he has family members, friends, and colleagues at work whose lives will be different because of him. His therapist wrote a letter to a national magazine read by millions. You and I now know about that experience, and it may affect our own actions. Perhaps we will treat strangers differently. Ultimately, the possible consequences of this man's decision to live are incalculable.

Suppose that young man has children and one of them performs some significant act—or, for that matter, one of his grandchildren or great-grandchildren. Suppose that somewhere among his descendants is another Winston Churchill? You can see that later generations might be affected by this man's decision not to die, and it all began with an old woman's smile.

I must confess that I thought of omitting this story because it seems like such an isolated, unlikely event—a kindly smile from an elderly woman changes a young man's life. But recently I heard a taped interview with the well-known inspirational speaker W. Mitchell, who speaks from a wheelchair. He was in a motorcycle accident that left disfiguring burns over most of his body, including his face. Later he was in an airplane crash that cost him the use of his legs. Mitchell says that after his motorcycle accident, the most difficult adjustment he had to make was dealing with people who refused to look at him because of the appearance of his face. This was more crushing than the accident itself. But then, he said that one day a woman not only looked at him, but she also smiled. "That smile changed my life," he says. Can a smile do that? You bet it can. Now Mitchell delivers his inspiring message to large audiences all over the world. And every once in a while in those audiences someone is touched in a life-changing way. The ripples of influence go on and on.

The real-life implications of the powerful Law of Influence are amazing. We don't have to be politicians or rock stars to prompt change. We can be an old woman smiling at a passerby on a street or at a man in a wheelchair. We can be John Howard giving assistance to someone in need. Anytime one person encounters another the possibilities are limitless.

A story came across the Internet recently of the owner of a drive-through coffee business in southwest Portland, Oregon. She was surprised one morning to have one of her customers not only pay for her own mocha, but also for the mocha of the person in the car behind her. When the second car pulled up, the owner had the pleasure of telling her that her drink had already been paid for. This customer was so pleased that someone else had paid for her coffee that she bought coffee for the next customer—and that customer did for the next, etc. This string of kindness—one stranger paying for the next customer—reportedly continued for two hours and twenty-seven customers.

When you perform an act of kindness for someone else, you never know where it might end.

I am reminded of some words that have been attributed to South African President Nelson Mandela: "Our deepest fear is not that we are inadequate. Our deepest fear is that we are powerful beyond measure." I believe he is right. Through the amazing Law of Influence, we have enormous power. *One life touches another and potentially both lives are changed; one life touches another and potentially the entire world is changed.*

CHAPTER 4

Lessons from the K.G.B.

So now, how does this law work? To answer that question, it would be helpful to go back about forty years or so.

The Cold War is now a distant memory. In retrospect, the events of that ongoing confrontation between the world's great superpowers seem melodramatic—though for those who lost their lives in conflicts such as Vietnam and Korea, the events certainly were deadly serious.

I have always been an avid fan of spy stories. So I was fascinated to read about a method used by the Soviet espionage apparatus, the K.G.B., during Cold War days to track United States Embassy personnel living and working in Moscow.

According to William Poundstone in his book *Bigger Secrets,* this feat was accomplished using an invisible powder—$NO_2C_6H_4CH:CHCH:CHCHO$ (nitrophenylpentadienal or simply, NPPD). Soviet agents spread NPPD in strategic places that United States Embassy personnel were sure to touch, such as doorknobs or steering wheels, thus ensuring that it would be transferred to the hands of these personnel. They, in turn, would leave traces of NPPD on everything and everyone with whom they came into contact. For example, imagine that the Russians found traces of NPPD in the apartment of one of their own agents. It would be strong evidence that this agent had dealings with the Americans and might be a double agent.[1]

Why NPPD rather than some other chemical? NPPD glows under ultraviolet light. The Russians could have used portable ultraviolet lamps to follow the trail. NPPD is also extremely tenacious once it gets on the skin, as it does not come off with normal washing for a long time.

Now, here is what's interesting. According to Poundstone, no one is sure how well this powder works. Suppose an NPPD-marked person attended a diplomatic reception and shook hands with several hundred people. Would the KGB end up tracking them all? What about the people those people touched? Theoretically, the chain of persons with traces of NPPD on their hands could go on indefinitely.

NPPD and the Law of Influence

Now, imagine that you and I have NPPD on our hands. How far would our sphere of influence extend if we could trace our daily personal contacts using ultraviolet lamps? The answer might surprise you.

In *Pay It Forward,* Trevor McKinney takes the assignment given by his teacher seriously—"Think of an idea for world change, and put it into action." He decides to do something really good for three people who, instead of paying him back, will be asked to "pay it forward" by aiding three more, etc. Beginning with three is a nice, conservative start. Theoretically, however, young Trevor could have thought much bigger. There is a principle called the Rule of 250. It states that every one of us has a constellation of two hundred and fifty people with whom we interact in one or two weeks. Two hundred and fifty is a lot of people, people we come into contact with on a regular basis. The NPPD of influence would be deposited upon these people.

Now admittedly some of these are very casual contacts. They include the cashier at the supermarket, the clerk at the post office, and the greeter at our church or synagogue. But the list would also include our family, co-workers, and friends. While some of these contacts would be casual, others would be quite intense. The important thing is that each contact we make has within it at least the possibility of life-changing, even world-changing influence. Every contact is an opportunity for the ripple effects of influence to begin. This is level one of the Law of Influence—the two hundred and fifty people with whom we have immediate contact. What about the two hundred and fifty with whom each of them has contact? How far would our NPPD be detected if we could trace it to the third or fourth level? Hold on, now things are really getting exciting!

CHAPTER 5

The Small World Problem

He is controversial, but I wonder if there has been a researcher more creative than psychologist Stanley Milgram. Like most psychology students, I first encountered Milgram through some horrific studies he performed back in the 1960s. These studies involved the willingness of people to follow orders from a presumed authority, even when those orders contradicted their conscience.

In these studies, an experimenter in a white coat would instruct subjects to deliver what the subjects believed were high-voltage shocks, not to a rat or a monkey, but to *another human being*. Sixty-five percent complied even though they knew the shocks could conceivably be lethal. (We understand that the subjects in this experiment weren't really getting shocked. They were actors hired to simulate the perception of nearly being electrocuted.) Still, the subjects in this study thought they were administering near fatal doses of electricity, and yet they persisted. Why? Simply because they were told to do so.[1]

This is the stuff of nightmares. However, the studies are important when considering atrocities such as those that occurred in Nazi Germany. People have a tendency to comply with authority regardless of the consequences. We can see how easily the Law of Influence may be used to destroy rather than create. We will deal with that later. In any case, when I think of Stanley Milgram, the association is somewhat unpleasant.

Nevertheless, Milgram also produced a very positive study that is as important as his better known and more "shocking" study on compliance to authority. He called it the "small world problem." It is a study of the phenomenon we know as networking.[2]

Milgram observed the networks of friends, relatives, and business associates that make up society and wondered if a specific individual in one part of the country could get a personal introduction to a specific individual in another part of the country, using only these personal contacts. Could a letter, for example, be passed from a randomly selected individual in Nebraska to some other randomly selected person in Boston using only friends, friends of friends, and friends of friends of friends, etc., to hand deliver the letters? ("Friends" were defined as persons known on a first-name basis.)

Milgram discovered that not only was the answer to this question yes, but it took surprisingly few intermediaries to accomplish the task. *It typically took five or six people (5.5 persons) for two individuals half a continent apart to communicate through a chain of acquaintances.*

This is another amazing concept. Let's imagine that you or I have a problem, a concern, a driving passion, and we want to sit down with someone who is in a position do something about it. Would it be possible to tap into the grapevine of friends we have, and friends of their friends and so on, and get a personal introduction to that individual? The answer is yes, and it would only mean slightly more than five actual contacts.

Perhaps you saw either the movie or the Broadway play, *Six Degrees of Separation.* It is based on a similar idea—that we are only six levels of contact removed from everyone on earth—six degrees of separation. Playwright John Guare explains that this concept stems from the work of the inventor Guglielmo Marconi who surmised that by the time the wireless telegraph connected the country, we'd be able to find anybody on the planet through the interrelationships of 5.83 people.

John Allen Paulos, professor of mathematics at Temple University gives added credence to this principle. He points out that if you sit next to a stranger on a plane, ninety-nine times out of a hundred, if you learn enough about each other, you will discover a link. This connection could be that your sister once dated his brother, your cousin knows his dentist, or that he went to the same school your brother-in-law attended.

To show you how persuasive this concept is, there is now a website operated by MacroView Communications Corporation, (www.sixde-grees.com) devoted to helping people use the six degrees concept to find "people you want to know through the people you already know." Here's how the sixdegrees website works: you go to the site and type the name or e-mail address of the person you want to be connected to, and the system tells you who you know in common. Based on this theory, sixdegrees uses the list of people you know to connect you with those they know and so on. The possibilities are endless. But let's return to Milgram's study.

It Really Is a Small World

How does the "small world" concept work? It's really quite simple, though I may sound like an Amway distributor as I explain it. If you have just 50 friends, and each of those friends has 50 friends, you have 2,500 friends of friends. If each of these 2,500 has 50 friends, you have 125,000 friends of friends of friends, and, if each of them has 50 friends, you now have 6,000,000 friends of friends of friends of friends. Naturally there would be some overlap, so the exact number would be smaller than 6,000,000. However, we did start with just 50. The Rule of 250 says that 6,000,000 might be a very conservative estimate. In fact, maybe it is possible that we *are* only 6 levels of contact removed from everyone on earth.

Or let's approach it from another angle.

If you have ever received a chain letter, then you know the totally irrational fear that if you throw this chain letter away, you may suffer some horrible consequences. According to Don Voorhees, author of *The Book of Totally Useless Information,* you don't have to feel guilty. In fact, there could be dire consequences if you passed it on.[3]

Voorhees contends that if you started a chain letter and sent it to just five people, and asked those five recipients to send the letter to five more people, those five would send it out to twenty-five people, who would then send the letter to six hundred and twenty-five people. In less than fifteen "cycles," the letter would reach over six billion people, and the world's postal systems would collapse. No one would be doing anything but sending and receiving chain letters. According to Voorhees, it could spell the end of civilization as we know it!

It is easy to poke fun at the six degrees concept, but there is enough truth in it to cause us to think seriously about the possibilities. Whether you begin with 5 people or 500 people, the implications of the small world principle are staggering. One ordinary person with a new idea, new product, or a deep passion about some cause or another, could theoretically send out ripples of influence to 50 people, then 2,500 people, then 125,000 people, and finally 6,000,000 people; thus, within a relatively short time, to the whole world.

As a concrete example of how rapidly this can happen, notice how fast humor spreads across our country. A joke can start on the floor of the New York stock exchange (the site, according to some sources, of a significant body of humor) on Monday, and a week later be told around water coolers in Los Angeles. This is the power of networking. If you want to have an impact in the world, you don't have to buy a television station or a newspaper or get elected to a political office—all you have to do is put this incredible power to work.

Henry Drummond once observed: "Every atom in the universe can act on every other atom, but only through the atom next to it. If a man would influence other men, he can do it best by influencing, one at a time, those he comes into contact with." One at a time. It is not the only way influence spreads, as we will show later, but it is astoundingly effective. Anytime we touch someone else's life, we are setting off a chain reaction that may never end. Of course, if you add the power of personal influence to the power of modern technology, you end up with real power.

CHAPTER 6

The Wonders of Technology

This is a small world, and it's only getting smaller. Add the power of personal networking to the information explosion—or more properly the technological explosion—and almost anything is possible.

Consider Ted Turner, an adman in Atlanta. Although he is a somewhat bizarre individual, according to the people closest to him, we should look at what he has done for our world. Not too long ago Turner was selling billboards. Then he purchased a UHF television station, channel 17, in Atlanta. He sold commercials by telling potential customers that their commercials would stand out on his station because they would be the only things in color. Later, Turner used that humble, independent station to launch a satellite into the sky, effectively creating the first TV super station. Then he started an all-news cable channel. As a result, during the Gulf War we beheld the spectacle of our Pentagon watching CNN to check the progress of our troops. General John Shalikashvili, Chairman of the Joint Chiefs of Staff, was even quoted on the cover of *Military Review.* "We don't win," he said, "unless CNN says we win." Amazingly enough, Turner changed our world with his technology. But that's just one aspect of the amazing influence of the powerful new tools at our disposal.

Don't you think it was extraordinary that Chinese dissidents during the 1989 siege of Tiennamen Square were getting news out to the world by *fax*? Totalitarian societies all over the world are threatened by the rapid advance of communications technology. To paraphrase the old World War I song, "How are you gonna keep them down on the (communal) farm when they can see Paris?"—and New York and London—via modern communications?

Technology is rapidly changing the world. Some scholars believe the transistor tape recorder brought about the overthrow of the Shah of Iran because tape recorders brought the speeches of the Ayatollah Khomeini to the people of Iran. Some commentators claim that radio broadcasts and computers contributed to the fall of the Soviet Empire. Iron curtains or bamboo curtains are no match for modern communications. A revolution is taking place—a revolution fought not with guns and planes, but with telephone lines and communication satellites. A by-product of that revolution, interestingly enough, is that Western values are taking root in every country in our world.

In a survey some years ago, a sampling of Chinese people were asked to name three famous Westerners. They chose Jesus, Nixon, and Elvis. The Chinese—that most closed of societies over the past half-century—knew about Elvis? Oh, yes, they knew. In fact, in a story on a United States-China summit sometime back, the *New York Times* reported that President Jiang Zemin, visiting the Philippines in 1996, initiated a duet with his host, President Fidel Ramos, in which the two sang "Love Me Tender" in English.[1]

Technologies of various kinds are spreading influence, both positive and negative, around the world. Leaders of oppressive regimes surely realize that they cannot forever shield their people from unpleasant and dangerous information. With the explosion of satellite communications, fax machines, and all the goodies our engineers are producing for us, the world is shrinking exponentially.

A few years ago, my wife and I went to visit our daughter in Vienna, Austria. We toured Southern Europe while we were there. We stayed in small budget hotels so that we could extend our tour as long as possible. We were understandably anxious about making reservations by telephone since we speak no Italian or German, and only a negligible amount of Spanish and French. Then we noticed that many of these establishments listed a fax number. No longer did we have to worry about language problems in arriving at a price—it was spelled out in black and white on a paper copy that we could fold up in our suitcase! Sometimes I wonder how the world existed before the humble fax machine.

And then there's the Internet. The revolution is just beginning. The Internet gives us the ability to touch the entire world almost instantaneously, and people who understand how to use this new, powerful communication tool are not only getting rich, but are also making a difference.

Consider the phenomenon known as "viral marketing," a method of using the Internet for the purpose of hyping new products. Viral marketing was pioneered by Hotmail, the free Internet e-mail company. The founders of Hotmail wanted to stir up word-of-mouth publicity about their new service, so they added one little line at the bottom to their e-mail program: "Get your free e-mail at Hotmail." Every time a Hotmail customer sent e-mail to anyone in the world, it carried that little line at the bottom. This instant advertisement served the same purpose as word-of-mouth advertising, but on a phenomenally larger scale. Within a year and a half, Hotmail had over 12 million subscribers. Hotmail founders dominated the free e-mail business having spent only $500,000 dollars on advertising. Compare that to the $20 million in advertising that their next biggest competitor, Juno, spent to garner fewer subscribers.

Now other businesses are learning how to use the principles of viral marketing to their advantage. When hot new pop singer Christina Aguilera hit the music scene, her agents used viral marketing techniques to create interest in her music. Even before Aguilera's first album was released, her publicist hired an Internet marketing firm to visit teen chat rooms and talk up her music. It also paid some teens in these chat rooms to spread the word in other chat rooms. Soon, the country buzzed with news of Christina Aguilera. With this new and incredibly fast form of advertising, she was on her way to superstardom before her record even came out.[2]

If you receive stories and humor from friends via e-mail, you have probably been the recipient of a very benign form of viral marketing—one you could put to use yourself. For example, suppose you were to write several heart-tugging stories, the kinds that are likely to be widely circulated. With the Web's enormous appetite for stories, I guarantee you that your stories, if they are any good at all, will be widely circulated. At the bottom of each story you submit to these e-zines, you might place the address of your own website. It is conceivable that millions of people will forward these stories to their friends. Some of these people are likely to visit your website. Within a very short time, and at practically no cost, you can be touching lives around the globe.

People in business, government, education, etc., are making contacts every day all over the world via the Internet, the fax machine, and all the other tools of modern technology. When you add the fact that English is rapidly becoming the dominant world language—making it easier than ever to communicate across national borders—you can easily see how one person can make a difference. Indeed, this may be the most opportune time in history for one individual to influence the fate of planet earth.

The January-February 1996 issue of the *The Futurist* carried this prediction:

The rate of global change—technical, social, and cultural—will continue to accelerate, creating innumerable surprises and dangers.

In today's world, more change occurs in a decade than occurred in an entire century in times past. Moreover, the tempo of change promises to get faster because of the rapid deployment of infotech: few people write formal letters anymore, preferring phone calls or spur-of-the-moment e-mail messages.

One consequence is that the social order becomes more subject to The Butterfly Effect, much discussed in Chaos Theory. Just as a butterfly flapping its wings in Europe might set off a chain of atmospheric events leading to a typhoon in the Pacific, a small event in today's highly networked world may be magnified into big events elsewhere. The growing integration of the world and the rising speed of communications increase the likelihood that small chance events will have major consequences in the future. For this reason, the world may experience more surprises, and have less time to decide how to deal with them.

This is a turbulent time, a critical time. As we face a new millennium, we stand again at the proverbial crossroads. Does humanity continue its march of progress or do we take steps toward our own destruction? We are often told that the Chinese figure for crisis consists of both danger and opportunity. Wise people will make this time in history a time of opportunity.

CHAPTER 7

Riding the Ninth Wave

Businessman and writer Max De Pree tells the hilarious true story of an owner of a small company who made it a practice to approach people personally after they had worked for the company for a year. He would walk into the plant, give a short speech to the employee, and then present him or her with a velvet box containing the company's logo on a sterling silver tie tack. One day he presented this gift to a gentleman who had recently completed his first year. The young man opened the velvet box, took out the sterling silver tie tack, and said, "Gee, that's beautiful!" Then he calmly inserted it into the lobe of his left ear.[1]

The world is changing. Have you noticed? In the movie *Back to the Future,* Michael J. Fox wanders past a 1950s gas station and is shocked at the sight of four smiling attendants converging on a car to fill up the tank, clean the windshield, check the oil, and even polish the chrome. Most of us would be shocked at such service today.

Supposedly Adam turned to Eve and said as they left the Garden of Eden, "My dear we live in a time of transition." You and I live in a time of transition. As someone has noted, those of us over age fifty were born before credit cards and computers—dishwashers and dryers—electric blankets and electric typewriters—freezers and Frisbees—moon landings, Mars probes, microwaves, McDonald's, Michael Jackson and Madonna—penicillin, polio shots, pantyhose and the Pill—television and tape decks—and, of course, Xerox. It has even changed the way fathers talk to their sons. Dads used to say, "When I was your age, I had to walk five miles to school in the snow." Today's dad is stuck with boasting, "When I was your age, I had to walk clear across the room to change the channel."

The explosion of knowledge and information has been overwhelming. Reliable estimates suggest that more information was produced in the thirty years between 1965 and 1995 than was produced in the entire five thousand-year period from 3000 B.C. to 1965. It is said that a single edition of the *New York Times* carries more information than the average seventeenth-century British citizen would encounter in a lifetime. It has been calculated that, at present, knowledge doubles every two years. However, some experts predict that human knowledge will double every seventy-three days by the year 2020. How much change are human beings capable of enduring?

Fred Race of Cleveland, Ohio tells of stopping at the Road Runner Market in Quartzsite, Arizona in the late 1980s. A sign on the counter read: "Your patience is appreciated. New electronic cash register, same old ladies."[2]

That's the problem, isn't it? Technology is changing faster than our ability to absorb it all. And if the problem was vexing a decade ago, think how impossible it must seem to many people today. My seventy-seven year-old mother has asked me more than once, "What are these 'dot-coms' I keep hearing about?" You try explaining such phenomena to a person who knows nothing about computers, the Internet, etc.

Change Is Accelerating

Alvin Toffler brought it home to us in his book *Future Shock.* Toffler reduced human life on earth to eight hundred lifetimes—a lifetime being a little over sixty years.[3]

The first 650 lifetimes of man's sojourn on this planet were spent living in caves. It took 730 of our 800 lifetimes before we could write. The printing press was developed about eight lifetimes back. We have only had electric motors for the past two of these 800 lifetimes, and the majority of material goods and services we use today have been developed in the present lifetime. The one thing you can say with authority about change is that it is accelerating.

When the Voyager II spacecraft traveled into deep space, sending back information and pictures from Saturn, Uranus, and Neptune a few years back, it carried six computers on board with 32K of memory altogether, much less than one one-thousandth of the capacity of today's average desktop word processor. Why was such a sophisticated spacecraft equipped with only 32K of memory? Because it left this planet in 1977, when the desktop and the laptop were only dreams of the future, when the pocket calculator and the silicon chip were very new news.[4]

Coping With a World in Transition

I read recently that the men who served as guards along the Great Wall of China in the Middle Ages were often born on the wall, grew up there, married there, died there, and were buried within the wall. Many of these guards never left the wall in their entire lives.

Our grandparents may have lived lives not much different from those cloistered men. Even today, in my area of the country, we might run across someone who has never been outside the mountains of east Tennessee. But all of us have seen the Great Wall of China via television. Visually and vicariously, at least, we have all walked on the moon. We have seen more and we know more than any generation that has ever lived.

We live in a fast-changing world, but rapid change is disconcerting. Studies show that the majority of us are uncomfortable with change; instead, most of us prefer stability.

When trains were first introduced, naysayers predicted that passengers would get nosebleeds because the trains would be traveling more than fifteen miles per hour. Real concern was expressed that travelers might suffocate when going through tunnels. Obviously, change is not always easy.

Radio Preacher Chuck Swindoll tells about a youth worker many years ago in an ethnic church with Scandinavian roots. Because he was an optimistic and creative young man, this worker decided he would show the teenagers in his church a film about foreign missions. Within an hour of showing this black-and-white, 16 mm, thoroughly safe religious film, the church leaders called him in and asked him about what he had done. Without trying to be argumentative, the youth worker recalled that at the last missionary conference, their church showed slides. One of the church officers stopped him with these words: "If it's still, fine. If it moves, sin!" Now you know the definition of sin.[5]

This reaction is similar to that of a woman in our church. Our pastor installed video screens and brought upbeat music into our worship service. After one service, this woman walked toward the pastor who stood waiting at the sanctuary door. She complained, "Reverend, if God were alive today, He would turn over in His grave at the changes in this church!"

Change is difficult, and yet times of change are times of great opportunity.

The Ninth Wave

In their book, *The Third Wave,* Alvin and Heidi Toffler described history as "a succession of rolling waves of change." They listed three great waves of change. The first was the agricultural civilization that lasted several thousand years. The second was the Industrial Revolution, which lasted about three hundred years. Now we are in the Third Wave, the Information Age. Some people give it a life span of about two decades. Some say it has already ended and has been succeeded by a fourth wave, the Biogenetic Age.

Robert D. Dale, in his book, *The Leading Edge,* gives us a very helpful additional concept which he calls the Ninth Wave.[6]

The Ninth Wave grows out of a superstition of ancient mariners, who made their living on the sea and spent the better part of their lives on water. They knew the wind and waves intimately, and held a superstition that inevitably one wave comes along that is greater than anything that has preceded it. They called it the Ninth Wave. Somehow from time to time, the sea and wind team up to create this unique force. The seafarers further believed only those who planned carefully and timed their actions precisely were able to catch the Ninth Wave's crest. If they did, however, these enterprising seafarers could ride this wave farther than they had ever gone before.

There have been many Ninth Wave times in history, i.e. the fall of the Roman Empire, the invention of the printing press, the Protestant reformation, the advent of democracy, etc., not to mention the dawning of the third millennium. I believe we are living in a Ninth Wave time, a time of both incredible change and incredible opportunity. Let's think of some Ninth Wave individuals.

Bill Gates is not even fifty years old, yet he is the richest man in the world. His wealth stands in excess of seventy billion dollars (depending on the current value of Microsoft stock). Do you know how much seventy billion dollars is? Let's imagine that you began spending a thousand dollars a day on the day Christ was born two thousand years ago. If you kept spending at that rate for a thousand more years, you would spend *one* of those billions. Now imagine spending seventy times that much. If you are earning any interest at all on that money, forget it. You would never be able to spend it all! Bill Gates didn't inherit one penny of his wealth. Instead, he caught a vision of a new world and he gave himself to it completely. You might say he decided to *own* it completely. It is interesting to watch Gates now emerge as the greatest single philanthropist in the world. Perhaps charity is the wave of the future for the fabulously wealthy. But who can argue that Bill Gates is a Ninth Wave individual?

Ted Turner. Say what you will, but he parlayed a run-down black and white television station into one of the most influential television empires on the face of this earth. I have enormous admiration for the man. In his mid-forties, he changed from an ultra-conservative to a person seeking to exercise a positive global influence. Even before the fall of the Berlin wall, Turner was promoting cultural exchanges such as the Goodwill Games to foster greater cooperation between the Soviet Union and the United States. In fact, Turner will not allow anyone at CNN to use the word "foreign." He wants his people to know that we are all in this thing together. Ted Turner is a Ninth Wave individual.

Nelson Mandela. Would anyone have ever predicted that this man who spent over twenty years in a prison would one day be president of the very country that imprisoned him? But there was a freedom in Mandela's soul that prison bars could not destroy. Regardless of your political inclinations, you have to wonder if he was ever really a prisoner of the South African government. How does a man maintain such dignity, grace, and ability to articulate the concerns of his people after being confined for so long? His body may have been imprisoned, but not his mind, his heart, or his soul. Nelson Mandela exerts moral influence over a nation undergoing turbulent change. But like any great person of influence, Mandela's shadow extends beyond national borders to encompass the world. Nelson Mandela is a Ninth Wave individual.

Obviously this list could contain thousands of names. Many would not be recognized outside their own community, but they are people whose presence in our world guarantees that this will be a time not only of many challenges, but also many opportunities.

I hear other middle-age people say that they would not want to go back to their teen years or earlier—they're insane. I look at my grandchildren, Rachel, ten, and Sebastian, three, and I get excited about the changes they will experience in their lifetimes. I'm also a little envious, for I am an optimist at heart. I believe there are enough caring, Ninth Wave people, and I believe the future will offer more positives than negatives. Do you know two hundred and fifty people? How about fifty people? Do you have a vision for a better world? Then you are well on your way to being a Ninth Wave person of influence.

But wait. Thus far we have only been dealing with one generation of influence. Influence never stops with one generation! So hold on, because the news gets even more exciting . . .

CHAPTER 8

Making a Difference
Through the Centuries

One of the cultural peculiarities Americans have to adjust to while traveling in Europe is topless beaches. It is a cultural thing, of course, not really a moral one—though I will say, as a relatively objective observer, that American women on the whole are much smarter in preserving a little mystery and decorum in this one area of their lives. Since my wife and I have made several trips to Europe, I hardly notice this particular difference between the two cultures any more. Honestly, I would not even mention it except I want to share with you a most amusing incident that occurred last summer on the Greek island of Santorini.

Santorini is not the most visited of the Greek isles, though it certainly ranks as one of the most beautiful. It is far to the south of the Greek mainland, near the island of Crete. We arrived for our stay in May, which is considered the off-season. While we were there, a few hundred people were lounging on beach chairs scattered along the coast for maybe half a mile.

Not far from us was a group of six college girls on holiday from the United States. A couple of them promptly removed their tops and began putting on sunscreen. I decided to go for a walk down the beach, which my friends and family will tell you is one of my favorite things to do. I walk miles at a time. The rhythm of the waves and the soft breeze off the ocean relax me as nothing else can. As I made my way back to my chair after this particular walk, I noticed one of the college girls. Her back was to me, but as I passed her, I noticed that she was sitting straight up, her face was very white, as if she had seen a ghost, and she was talking very intensely with a young man. Oh, yes, the top to her bathing suit lay on the ground beside her, but she was tightly clutching under her arms a towel that completely covered her chest.

As I sat down, my wife said, "The funniest thing just happened. I heard a young man's voice say quietly, 'Lisa, is that you?' Then I heard one of the young women almost scream, 'David?'" My wife said she had never seen anybody move as quickly as did that young woman grabbing a towel to cover herself. It seemed that Lisa and David attend the same small college in Michigan (I thought mischievously, probably a small church college). Evidently, exposing yourself on a public beach occupied by a few hundred strangers is not the same as exposing yourself to someone you know from back home.

Now I ask you, what are the odds? Here this young woman was probably doing the first daring thing in her life—removing her top on a public beach. She was in the middle of the Mediterranean on a small island where few of the people were even Americans. It was the off-season. Only a few hundred people were there that day—and one of them just happened to be a young man from her small college. What are the odds? St. Paul's words might be apropos: "Be sure your sins will find you out."

Let me give you another example of a strange coincidence that is even more mind-boggling. This really happened to a friend of mine just the way I am going to tell it—though I have changed all the names for obvious reasons.

George and Helen Schmidlapp live in Phoenix, Arizona. George has a brother in Baltimore, Maryland named Ted Scmidlapp whose wife is named Marilyn. They have a son named Brian. The Schmidlapps have a sister living in Knoxville, Tennessee whom we will call Nancy.

One day Ted and Marilyn's son Brian was visiting a small college in Pennsylvania. His purpose was to decide if he wanted to go to school there. He met another student who was from a small town we will call Nowheresville, Pennsylvania. The other student introduced himself. When Brian told him his name, the other student replied, "Schmidlapp is an usual name. Would you happen to be related to a Helen Schmidlapp?" Brian replied, "Well, I have an aunt in Phoenix named Helen." Brian's new friend said, "Well I'm from Nowheresville, Pennsylvania. It's a small town where everybody knows everybody else's business. Before I left for school, I heard that a Helen Schmidlapp is moving to Nowheresville. It seems that her family has some property there and she is moving there to take it over."

Brian said, "I'm certain my aunt and uncle aren't planning to move from Phoenix. There must be another Helen Schmidlapp somewhere in the country."

A week or so later, Brian called his Aunt Nancy in Knoxville and told her about this conversation. Aunt Nancy assured him that she had heard nothing about George and Helen leaving Phoenix. They decided it was all a strange coincidence.

Later that day, Aunt Nancy decided to call Phoenix. It was absurd, of course. The last she heard, George and Helen loved their home in the Southwest. But her curiosity was aroused. After all, there are not that many Schmidlapps in the United States. And so she dialed their number.

Helen answered the phone and she was angry at George. She had not related this to anyone else up to this point, she told Aunt Nancy, but they had been having marital difficulties for years. "One of these days I'm going to disappear from here," Helen said forcefully, "and no one will know where I am!" Aunt Nancy resisted the temptation to say, "I know exactly where you will be. You will be in Nowheresville, Pennsylvania."

What are the odds? Again, be careful what you plan. You think you can hide, but as the Bible warns in another place, "What is whispered behind closed doors will be shouted from the housetops."

I have always been fascinated by coincidence—or luck—or Providence—whatever you choose to call it. How many times does it happen in our lives: two seemingly unrelated events somehow converge to produce a surprising result? Scientists working with quantum physics speak of non-locality—two independent but similar phenomena occurring at the same time that apparently have no link. Some people talk of synchronicity, a similar phenomenon. Harold Fritzsch of the Max Planck Institute describes it as "a system in constant interaction with all other objects in the world. Nothing is or can be completely isolated." We are a part of a system of constant change. Within that system, we observe phenomena we refer to as coincidental. *A* happens and then *B* happens. Then *A* happens again, and *B* returns as well. We look for a link between the two events, but none seems apparent. Then it happens again. When we find no obvious explanation, we call it coincidence. Perhaps coincidences occur as random, inexplicable phenomena, or perhaps not. I contend that many "coincidences" can be explained by applying the Law of Influence.

A few years ago our family visited Bermuda. As you know, Bermuda is a beautiful island that sits about five hundred miles off the coast of North Carolina. Bermuda was named for a Spanish explorer, Bermudes, who was thrown off his course in the 1500s. He thought he had landed in the New World like Columbus, but actually he still had about five hundred miles to go to get to the mainland. As far as we know, he was the first explorer to land on that island now known as Bermuda.

Bermudes' ship was carrying live animals—hogs and goats—on board. They didn't have any refrigeration, so they carried live animals to eat. This makes sense, if you think about it, though the ambience on board the ship must have left much to be desired.

It turned out the journey wasn't as long or as bad as Bermudes thought it would be. As a result, he let some of his hogs and goats loose on the island because he didn't need to carry them any farther. Now, prior to this event, there had been no animals on Bermuda that we know of. Birds would fly in from time to time, but no land animals.

Forty or fifty years pass and British Admiral George Sommers is sailing his fleet across the Atlantic to Virginia. A terrible storm comes up, separating him from his fleet, and the admiral is shipwrecked on the little island of Bermuda. Nobody else, as far as we know, has landed on Bermuda between the time that Bermudes was on the isle and Sommers' accidental incursion.

Sommers loses all of his supplies in the shipwreck and is able to salvage only some tools. But here is his real problem: the ship carrying food for him and his crew is on its way to Virginia. Does Sommers starve? Of course not. He discovers hogs and goats on the island of Bermuda. Why? Because forty or fifty years before a Spanish explorer landing on the same island had too many goats and hogs and released them. Once released in Bermuda, these domesticated animals prospered because they had no natural predators.

Now is that luck or what? Cruising along in the Atlantic, Sommers and his crew are shipwrecked on this tiny island, and there just happen to be hogs and goats because some other explorer forty or so years before had an oversupply of livestock and released some of them.

Life is full of such coincidences, but they don't happen in a vacuum. In Sommers' case, at least, there were some extenuating circumstances. This was an age of exploration, particularly in the New World. The likelihood of such an event occurring was increased by the number of ships that were making transatlantic crossings. So, in a sense, there was a hidden relationship between the two events, however slight.

Now let's apply this information to the Law of Influence. A man is headed toward a bridge to commit suicide just as an old woman smiles at him. Because of that smile, he changes his mind. Let's press the matter further. His great grandson becomes a research scientist who discovers a cure for cancer. Without that old woman's smile, millions of people would suffer and die. What is the hidden link? *It is our shared humanity.* Each of us has a need to reach out and connect to others. When we reach out, we discover what we call coincidences.

Some of us stifle that natural urge to connect with other people. We shrink back when we should be reaching out. Perhaps we have had painful experiences in the past that make us wary about interacting with others. Maybe we are just shy. Whatever the reason, we cheat ourselves out of rich experiences when we fail to connect with others.

The Power of an Open Heart

I am convinced that one of the secrets of bringing good things into your own life is to develop an openness to others. Like-minded persons are drawn together when the element of mutual openness is present.

My wife, Selina, had a "small world" experience quite recently. She went blueberry picking near the foot of the Great Smoky Mountains with our youngest daughter (who is also named Selina). In the party was our son-in-law, Christian, who is a native of Vienna, Austria—our grandson, Sebastian, and a delightful seven year-old child from Burundi named Paulin. Our daughter Selina works for Bridge Refugee services, resettling refugees in the area around Knoxville. This is how she came into contact with Paulin and his mother, who had been in this country about six months after a horrifying escape from their native land. A friend of Selina and Christian, named Helen, who had recently moved to Austin, Texas, joined them for the blueberry experience.

Helen grew up in Africa and spent many years working there as an adult. Interestingly enough, she spoke Swahili, young Paulin's native tongue. Paulin does well in English, but you can imagine his joy at finding someone with whom he could communicate in the language of his homeland.

During the afternoon, an older couple happened by. Coincidentally, they had recently come back from Austin, Texas, having visited their daughter and her family. They connected immediately with Helen. As the conversation ensued, the couple volunteered the fact that they had spent many years in Vienna, Austria. In fact, the husband had been an American ambassador in Vienna. Son-in-law Christian's ears perked up. Now he had someone with whom he could compare experiences. It made for an enjoyable afternoon for all.

Amazing coincidences, you might say. Not really. First, these people all shared two things in common—an openness to others and a mutual interest in international relations. They were drawn together by these shared attributes. We would find many such "coincidences" occurring if we were more willing to open our lives to those around us.

Contrast this experience with one I had a few years back. I was spending several days in a Comfort Inn in Amarillo, Texas. I noticed a distinguished older couple, also guests at the hotel. I overheard a conversation with a desk clerk. The couple had come to Amarillo for the wedding of a niece.

I knew that I should introduce myself. After all, we seemed to be the only guests staying for more than one night. The rest of the guests appeared to be oil workers or migrants brought in to work on nearby ranches. The couple appeared to be quite amiable. I knew we would find many things in common. But I am a shy person, and my shyness has cost me dearly over the years. Later, in talking with one of the hotel employees, I discovered that the distinguished-looking man was one of the translators of the Revised Standard Version of the Bible. As such, he had made an important contribution not only to human knowledge, but also to the spiritual growth of millions of persons. As soon as I returned to Knoxville, I opened my copy of the RSV Bible. Inside the front cover was this gentleman's name.

What an opportunity I had missed to share experiences with a person of great stature because I had given in to reticence. When we reach out to others, we discover common ground and many amazing "coincidences" occur. What if we also knew that by reaching out we could make a difference in someone else's life, and that by reaching out we could change the world?

We *can* change the world by reaching out to others. But not only for this generation. Like Bermudes and his hogs and goats, we can benefit people yet unborn. It might be through our influence on a child, our influence on a stranger, or our influence on a community. As an unknown philosopher has said, "Every action of our lives touches some chord that will vibrate in eternity." Let's look at the influence of one man on his community—an influence that continues to affect your life and mine more than one hundred years later.

CHAPTER 9

A Life Changed—A World Changed

When I was thirteen years old, someone gave me a book that deeply affected me. I was brought up in a very religious family and this book touched a chord deep within my soul. It was a very simple novel written over one hundred years ago called *In His Steps*.

In His Steps is the story of a somewhat complacent church congregation that is goaded by a tramp into taking seriously their mission in the world as followers of Jesus. When the tramp dies, the deeply moved congregation commits itself to living for one year with the constant question, "What would Jesus do?" Every action or decision the congregation makes is based on this question, "What would Jesus do?" It's not an easy year for the congregation, but they stay true to their commitment, and in the end have a powerful influence on the surrounding community.[1]

In His Steps sold millions of copies in its day, is still in publication, and is considered one of the most popular books in the world. In fact, I read recently that one the best-selling items in religious bookstores at this time is a little bracelet with WWJD ("What Would Jesus Do?") engraved on it.

The author of this simple but moving story was Pastor Charles M. Sheldon. Sheldon strove to live out the message of his idealistic novel, and in doing so made many contributions to each of the communities in which he lived. However, one contribution Sheldon made is still affecting your life and mine one hundred years later.

Charles Sheldon and his wife moved to Topeka, Kansas during a time when the town was suffering through a depression. Sheldon dedicated himself to identifying with struggling people in his community. For example, he dressed as a laborer, and spent a week traveling through the town looking for work, just to find out what unemployed people were facing. The experience of walking in the shoes of those living in adverse circumstances so moved him that it became a regular part of his life.

Throughout each week, Sheldon worked side by side with laborers, lawyers, doctors, and students. He developed a great compassion for those around him, and each week he would share his experiences with his prosperous congregation. Charles Sheldon's zeal for identifying with his fellow man even led him to spend a week in a prison. This experience stirred him to work for prison reform. Yet, there was one particular experience Sheldon had that not only changed his life, but changed the lives of all Americans—though he did not live to see it.

Sheldon lived for three weeks in an African American community called Tennesseetown, which was located just outside of Topeka. Tennesseetown was composed of freed slaves and their families. Sheldon was struck by the difficulties under which these people lived. For one thing, slaves had been forbidden to learn to read and write, which obviously put them at a terrible disadvantage. Sheldon wanted to help, so he founded a kindergarten in Tennesseetown, one of the first in the country. It was a very fine, high quality school that soon began training kindergarten teachers for schools across the country.

One of the graduates of the Tennesseetown kindergarten was a young man named Elisha Scott. Scott was a bright, energetic child who showed tremendous potential. Sheldon encouraged Scott though elementary school, high school, and eventually through college. Sheldon even helped him to go to law school—a rare accomplishment for an African American in that day and time. Scott was so grateful to Sheldon for his help that he named one of his sons Charles Sheldon Scott. Charles Sheldon Scott followed in his father's footsteps and became an attorney too. In fact, Charles Sheldon Scott was the attorney who argued the 1954 Brown vs. the Topeka Board of Education case that successfully ended school segregation in the United States. It gives me goosebumps to even think about it. Race relations were forever changed because back in the 1890s a humble pastor took an interest in a bright, energetic African-American child and helped him get the education he needed.

You never know when you touch another person's life where it all might end. This is particularly true when it is a child's life that is affected. As someone has said, "To the world you might be one person, but to one person you might be the world." Teach a child to read, to appreciate science, or to develop a deep curiosity about life and stand back. You might, quite inadvertently, produce a George Washington Carver, Madame Curie, Albert Einstein, or a Charles Sheldon Scott, and the world will be forever blessed.

Influence Never Stops With One Generation. It Continues For Centuries.

Just as Sommers profited from Bermudes' stop on Bermuda years before, we profit from the actions of persons like Charles Sheldon who lived and died, perhaps in obscurity, before we were even born.

Some of the ancient bricks of Egypt and Babylon exhumed by archeologists reveal the print of a dog's foot. Undoubtedly, thousands of years ago when these bricks were put out to dry, this unknown dog stepped on some of the wet bricks. Now, centuries later, its ancient presence is still felt. So it is with our lives. *We bear the imprint of persons who lived hundreds and thousands of years ago.*

Now we can easily see how this is true of famous people. Writers through the centuries have dealt with what has often been called the "immortality of influence." Traditionally, this has meant that some great person lives on in the work he or she has done.

I understand that in Yosemite National Park in California there is a bronze plaque attached to a huge boulder. The plaque features the outline of a man under which these words are inscribed: "Stephen Ting Mather. Born July 4, 1867. Died January 22, 1930. He laid the foundation of the National Park Service, defining and establishing the policies under which its areas shall be developed and conserved for future generations. *There will never come an end to the good he has done*" (Italics mine).[2]

People live on in their work. As the late R. G. Lee put it: "Every telephone ring says that Alexander Graham Bell still lives. Every cotton gin says that Eli Whitney still lives. Every airplane says that Orville and Wilbur Wright still live. And every light bulb burning says that Thomas A. Edison still lives."

Ralph Waldo Emerson was once visited in his home by a local farmer. The farmer saw a book by Plato in Emerson's library. He asked to borrow it. When he returned it, Emerson asked how he liked it. The farmer replied, "I liked it. This Plato has a lot of my ideas." The farmer had no understanding that one reason he had those ideas is that Plato has so influenced the thought of Western culture. In the same way, Shakespearean thought and language have enriched our culture. Many of the phrases we use in everyday life can be traced back to the immortal bard. The examples, of course, are legion. Emerson himself had enormous influence on American values and thought. It is amazing how many of our best ideas today are ones that Ralph Waldo Emerson plagiarized—in advance.

In his book *When Iron Gates Yield*, Geoffrey Bull, an English missionary, tells of his capture by Chinese communists. They tortured him unmercifully. But one day Bull heard a familiar sound coming over a radio somewhere outside his prison room. It was Beethoven's *Emperor Concerto*. Even under such cruel conditions, writes Bull, Beethoven was still speaking from centuries earlier. Great people live on through their work—through their music, their plays, their novels, their inventions, etc. (Comedy writer Woody Allen says he doesn't want to achieve immortality through his work; he wants to achieve immortality by not dying!)

Allen's witticism aside, the Law of Influence says that you and I can be in that esteemed company of Bell, Whitney, the Wright brothers, Edison, and Beethoven. We can leave *our* imprint on history. And we don't have to write a sonata or invent a new widget in order to have a lasting impact on the world. Maybe all we have to do is offer an encouraging word to a stranger. Maybe, like Charles Sheldon, all we have to do is make a difference in the life of a child.

CHAPTER 10

Avoiding a Noose
and Beginning a Downline

In 1930, a young black man named James Cameron was wrongly accused of robbing and murdering a white couple. While in prison, Cameron narrowly escaped being hanged by a lynch mob that stormed the jail. As the men struggled to get the noose over Cameron's head, a woman's voice called out from the crowd, protesting that Cameron had not been involved in the crime. Incredibly, the mob took him back to jail and left him there. Cameron had no idea who had called out and saved him from certain death.[1]

Four years later, James Cameron was pardoned and released from prison. A 1979 visit to Jerusalem's Holocaust memorial inspired him to establish an institution commemorating slavery and the civil rights movement which he called the Black Holocaust Museum. Among the items in this museum is a piece of the rope that was almost used to end James Cameron's life.

Obviously, James Cameron will touch many lives through his museum. But what about that unknown woman who intervened with the mob to save his life? Isn't her contribution to the world as significant as that of James Cameron? After all, if she had kept silent, Cameron would not be alive to do the work he is doing. In fact, in a sense this woman has more opportunity for doing good than Cameron himself through the application of the "small world" phenomenon; for she not only influenced Cameron, but over a lifetime, she will probably influence many others—her family, friends, co-workers, etc. Her influence is multiplied through the lives of every person she touches.

This is the genius of so-called "network marketing"—a controversial phenomenon that became a remarkable force in retailing over the past two decades.

Network marketing, sometimes referred to as "multi-level" marketing, is basically person-to-person marketing. One person—we'll call her

Sally—recruits several others to sell a particular product and Sally gets a small percentage of each of these persons' sales. These persons, in turn, recruit others to sell the product. They profit from their recruits' sales as did Sally. Meanwhile, Sally not only profits from her recruits' sales, but also from her recruits' recruits. She also receives a commission on any of the sales of their recruits ad infinitum. Sally's return on each level will be smaller than on the first level, but because her downline involves so many more people, her overall profit is far greater.

People often demean network marketing as a modern variation of the time-honored pyramid scheme, but some of our most reputable and successful companies today are based on networking principles. I myself am part of a network marketing company which serves professional trainers and seminar leaders. At our annual conventions, it is common to hear the question, "How many people are in your downline?" Good question. How many people are in *your* downline?

Let's think of the woman whose cry from the crowd saved James Cameron's life. Let's imagine that he is on level one of her downline. She touched his life. If there were a way to credit influence like network marketing companies credit recruits, this woman would not only get credit for touching Cameron but also for all the people Cameron touches, etc.

Surely, though, there are other persons beside James Cameron on level one of this unknown woman's downline. There may be hundreds of others whose life she impacted over a lifetime—family, friends, co-workers, etc. She touches their lives, they touch others, and voilà!—the entire world is moved by one woman's courage and willingness to get involved. Theoretically, through the years her influence could extend to millions of persons, and so could ours. It is not a crass question at all: How many people are in your downline? You and I can make a difference. Never let it be said that any one person's life is of little importance. A smile at a stranger, a voice from a crowd, or a word of encouragement. Who knows where it all may lead?

CHAPTER 11

Tracing the Ripples Through the Ages

Some children are up against it from the beginning. She was dropped off at the Tewksbury almshouse, then nearly blinded by a childhood infection. No wonder she was sullen and withdrawn. Today she would be heavily medicated and placed in a special education program. But not at Tewksbury. And not at the Perkins Institution, where she was later admitted.

Many of the nurses marked Annie off as hopeless and gave her minimal attention. Only one nurse cared, but sometimes one is sufficient. This nurse brought the troubled child cookies and love, and saw her through to the day when she was well enough to leave the institution and make it on her own. The old nurse's kindness was rewarded many times over. Little Annie grew into an adult with a passion for helping others as she herself had been helped by her devoted nurse.

It was Little Annie, Anne Sullivan, who brought light into the dark world of Helen Keller. Sullivan, like the nurse who rescued her, saw potential in a little blind, deaf, and rebellious child no one else could deal with. Sullivan loved Keller and worked with her. Keller in turn became an inspiration to the entire world, and was an extraordinary writer, speaker, and friend of world figures, including President Dwight David Eisenhower. It began with the elderly nurse, then Anne Sullivan, then Helen Keller, and finally every person who has ever been influenced by the example of Helen Keller. The chain of influence goes on forever.

The Making of an Evangelist

Before my wife and I started our communications company nearly twenty years ago, I spent a decade in the ministry. The religious community is one area where you can easily trace a line of influence down through the generations.

In 1858, a Sunday school teacher in Chicago named Ezra Kimball became interested in the spiritual welfare of a young shoe clerk in his town. After debating what to do about it, Kimball started down toward Holton's shoe store where the young man worked. After walking by the store once, Kimball finally mustered up his courage and went in. Finding the young man in the stock room, Kimball proceeded to talk with the young man about his faith. The shoe clerk was named Dwight L. Moody. Kimball got through to Moody, who went on to become the greatest Christian evangelist of his day. But, of course, this is just the beginning of our story.

Moody preached a crusade in England, and in 1879, awakened the heart of Frederick B. Meyer, then pastor of a small church. Meyer went on to become a renowned theologian. In fact, later Meyer was preaching in Moody's school in Northfield, Massachusetts. A young man in the back row heard Meyer say, "If you are not willing to give up everything for Christ, are you willing to be made willing?" Those words transformed the ministry of the young man, J. Wilbur Chapman, who became a YMCA worker, back when it was still a religious institution.

Among those Chapman recruited for his ministry was a former professional baseball player, a remarkable man named Billy Sunday. Sunday went on to become the greatest evangelist of his generation. Later at a revival in Charlotte, North Carolina, he so excited a group of local men that they began an ongoing prayer group. Later they engaged an evangelist named Mordecai Hamm to come to their town to keep the revival spirit alive. In the revival with Hamm, a young man heard the gospel and made his profession of faith. This man's name was Billy Graham.

It's remarkable, isn't it? When Billy Graham stands before a worldwide audience, he bears the traces of NPPD of influence of a Sunday school teacher nearly one hundred and fifty years ago who did nothing more than talk to a shoe clerk about his faith.

The Making of a President

The line of influence running through history is awe-inspiring. No one gets to where they are by themselves. Always in the background is the power of someone's influence.

David McCullough, in a biography of former President Harry Truman,[1] notes how much Truman's life seemed to be influenced by the life of another great leader, Confederate General Robert E. Lee. Truman once read a biographical essay about Lee that contained a letter Lee wrote to his young son in 1860. In the letter, Lee urged the boy to always be frank and honest with people. He encouraged his son to keep his word. Then he added this great line: "Above all, do not appear to others what you are not."

"He never did that," notes McCullough. "Like him or not, he never did that."

Harry Truman was touched by the life of Robert E. Lee.

Influence never dies! The word "amazing" is inadequate when we talk about such a phenomenon. If you are a member of a church, you are in a chain of influence that began with a humble carpenter two thousand years ago. If you are in a synagogue, you trace your spiritual lineage back another one thousand years, while our eastern friends can go back even farther than that. What a legacy! But it is true in every area of life. Every generation of scientists is indebted to the generation before it. Jonas Edward Salk, who developed the vaccine against polio, said, "The work I have been able to do depended on the research of men and women whose names remain unknown but whose labors make possible my work." Sir Isaac Newton put it quite eloquently when he said: "If I have seen farther than others, it is because I have stood on the shoulders of giants." Several generations earlier, Bernard of Chartres said something similar. He said we're all like dwarfs mounted on the shoulders of giants. He said that if we can see more than they did, if we can see further into the wide future, it's not by virtue of any sharpness of sight on our part, or any physical distinction, but it's because we're carried along, high and raised up, by their giant size.

Giants Among Us

Giants among us have left an indelible mark on civilization. Without them, the world would still be lumbering along in darkness and confusion. Some of these giants were scientists.

The year was 1951. Inventor Charles H. Townes[2] was struggling with the problem of producing high frequency radio waves. Was there a way to make these waves so tiny that they could go to the very core of matter and show the inner workings of things? It was a challenge that gnawed at him constantly, and even disturbed his sleep.

One restless night, Townes wandered downtown to a local park. He had just sat down on a park bench when he had a revelation. Suddenly, he knew how to solve the problem of producing high frequency radio waves! This revelation led to the discovery of the laser—a device that is revolutionizing the practice of medicine.

Later, Townes discovered that the bench he sat on when he received this epiphany faced the historic home of the great inventor Alexander Graham Bell. Bell had been the first inventor to show that light could carry information, a discovery that made possible the whole idea of lasers in the first place. Would it sound too mystical to say that the spirit of Alexander Graham Bell lives on in Charles Townes?

Some of those giants were scientists, but others made their contributions in the arts.

Beethoven's Kiss

Andor Foldes was one of the most gifted classical musicians of the twentieth-century. A native of Budapest, Foldes was already a skilled pianist by age sixteen, but he was troubled due to conflict with his piano teacher. At this critical juncture in Foldes' life, a renowned pianist, Emil von Sauer, came to his city to perform. Von Sauer had the unique heritage of being the last surviving pupil of Franz Liszt.

At von Sauer's request, young Foldes played for him some of the most difficult works of Bach, Beethoven, and Schumann. Afterward, von Sauer kissed Foldes on the forehead and told him his teacher Hans Liszt had kissed him on the forehead when he was a student. Liszt was passing on a kiss he had received from Beethoven, who had been moved on one occasion by Liszt's playing. Von Sauer felt Foldes deserved the honor of preserving this heritage. Can you imagine what it meant to young Foldes to receive a kiss that came directly from Beethoven?[3]

Dr. Albert Schweitzer, on the other hand, was a man of great talent and intellect. Not only was he a professor of philosophy and theology, but he was also a medical doctor and an esteemed musician. However, in 1913, Dr. Schweitzer turned his back on a successful career and comfortable life in order to dedicate himself to working among the poor in Africa. He and his wife spent the rest of their lives as medical missionaries in Gabon.

Norman Cousins, a close friend of the Schweitzers, once noted that their example has served as the inspiration for many other works of mercy.[4] Many hospitals and at least one orphanage in Africa were built by people who heard the Schweitzers' story and were inspired to give of themselves in service to others. Their story still calls people to selflessness today. The poet Henry Wadsworth Longfellow wrote: "Lives of great men oft remind us that we can make our lives sublime and departing leave behind us footprints in the sands of time."

We are grateful for these giants who strode across the landscape of human existence. Nevertheless, the Law of Influence says you don't have to be a giant. You can be a schoolteacher who takes an interest in a small child, a salesperson who tries her best to improve her customers' lives, or a police officer who apprehends criminals and tries to rescue people who are headed down the wrong path.

"I shot an arrow in the air," said the poet. "It fell to earth I know not where." We cannot know how far the ripples of our influence may extend. The tiniest act of kindness or the most innocuous words of encouragement may still have positive effects generations later. "How wonderful it is," said Anne Frank, "that nobody need wait a single moment before starting to improve the world."

CHAPTER 12

A Debt to Many Strangers

It is a great luxury to be able to take our freedoms for granted. Courage is no longer a prerequisite for publishing a controversial article, or speaking out against government corruption. Nevertheless, behind every one of our basic human rights there is the story of someone, sometimes many persons, who struggled and suffered to increase freedom for future generations.

Elijah Lovejoy was a newspaperman in Missouri and Illinois in the early 1800s. He was also an abolitionist, and his paper carried articles opposing the institution of slavery. Many times, angry mobs broke into Lovejoy's office and destroyed his printing press. But one night, the angry mob went a step further and killed Elijah Lovejoy.

News of Lovejoy's murder inspired a young Bostonian named Wendell Phillips to give up his law practice and to dedicate his life to ending slavery and securing basic freedom and human rights for all people—a dream he realized in his lifetime.

In Alton, Illinois, there stands a statue of martyred newspaperman Elijah Lovejoy. In Boston, you'll find a statue of Wendell Phillips, the man who carried on the cause. One man's life and death inspired the other man to take a stand, and the sacrifices the two men made are still felt down to current generations.[1]

Contributing to the Process

Former Surgeon General C. Everett Koop writes in his memoirs of his desire to attend medical school at Columbia University's College of Physicians and Surgeons. When he went to Columbia for his admissions interview he felt very much at home. The discussion with the admissions panel seemed to go well until one of them asked Koop, "Do you ever expect to make any major discoveries in medicine?"

"It was a stupid question then; it is a stupid question now," Dr. Koop writes. He answered by saying that discoveries in the field of medicine are made by those who are building upon the efforts of many who preceded them. Then he added, "I would like to be the one who makes a major discovery, *but I will be content to contribute to the process.*" (italics mine.)[2]

The admission interviewers decided that C. Everett Koop didn't have the stuff they were looking for at Columbia's College of Physicians and Surgeons. He was devastated. But he still feels that he gave a good answer. He *did* give a good answer. We are all contributing to the process. That is our chief role in life. Perhaps fate will put us in a position where we will make a major breakthrough and our contribution will be spotlighted in the world of public recognition. But for the most part, we will build on the foundations others have laid. And in doing so, we will be laying a greater foundation for those who come after us.

Touched by an Angel

Many businesspeople are discovering that, in order to succeed, all they need is to get in touch with an angel. Angels, in the new parlance, are extraordinarily wealthy individuals who put their money to work by investing in start-ups of new businesses. According to an article in Smartbusinessmag.com (June 2000), angel money is America's fastest-growing pool of risk capital. In California, angels finance at least twenty times more companies than conventional venture capitalists.

Why should already wealthy people like Bill Gates, Paul Allen, and Jim Barksdale expose themselves to such risks to help beginners? I would like to say they do it out of the goodness of their hearts, but it is more apt to be the result of certain quirks in our tax system. If they sell accumulated stock in their companies, they have to pay the government twenty-eight percent. If they plow the money into a promising startup, it is taxed at a lower ten to twenty percent capital-gains rate. These wealthy individuals not only save money they would otherwise send to Uncle Sam, but they may strike a new fortune with their investment to boot.

What a country! See how wealth could be created in a ever continuing ripple effect? Angels breed angels! But that is not only true in the world of finance, it is true in all of life, which brings us to the one thing we cannot do.

CHAPTER 13

The One Thing We Cannot Do

A man tells about growing up on a farm where they raised hogs. Occasionally, he and his brothers would try to catch all of the hogs in order to treat them with an awful concoction that was designed to keep off critters like ticks and fleas. His father would always say, "Now, boys, remember there will be some of them you cannot catch, so put an extra dose on those you do catch. Sooner or later they will rub up against the others."[1]

What is true of hogs is also true of humans. We are constantly "rubbing up" against other people. In fact, it's becoming ever more difficult *not* to rub up against others. It seems that we are constantly surrounded by people—in traffic, at the supermarket, at work.

Once while driving to my mother's home in a semi-rural area just outside our hometown of Knoxville, Tennessee, I noticed a couple in a pickup truck approaching from my left at an intersection. I had the stop sign and they had the right-of-way. Evidently they had taken a wrong turn somewhere because they seemed determined to turn around in the intersection by making a left turn, then backing up, and heading back in the opposite direction. Conscious of their predicament, I was willing to wait while they accomplished this maneuver.

Unfortunately, Murphy's Law wasn't willing to cooperate. Before they could even begin to back up, six cars converged on them. Here was an intersection that a few years ago would see scarcely a dozen cars in a day, and now six cars were converging at the same time. It is more difficult than ever to avoid contact with other people.

Broadcaster Paul Harvey[2] once told about a criminal who had all his fingerprints removed from his fingers so that he could pursue his life of crime without being detected. He went through a long, painful ordeal in order to accomplish this—all to no avail. Now he is all the more easily caught when he commits a crime because he is the only man *without* fingerprints. Our influence is like that. It cannot be stopped or silenced. The one thing we cannot do is *not influence*.

T.S. Eliot's *J. Alfred Prufrock* asks, "Do I dare disturb the universe?" The Law of Influence says that it does not take much to disturb the universe. Each new poem, song, work of art, or even smile, word or deed can do the trick. We live in a dynamic universe. Everything we do influences someone else. And that influence may be surprisingly long-lasting. Who knows when a random act or word may have a staggering impact on somebody's life?

Now, perhaps this is a greater burden of responsibility than you would like to bear. Telling a friend about the intent to write this book, he said, "How are you going to overcome the 'Look out for Number One' mentality in our society? Most people today don't care about the greater good; they're interested only in themselves."

A fair statement, even though I don't agree with it. There are many people who are concerned about the greater good. There are people who are concerned about the environment, concerned about their churches, synagogues or mosques; people who do volunteer work carrying meals to the elderly and ministering to AIDS victims. The list of caring acts that occur every day in this world would be endless. Even if these were caring acts simply within the home, they add up to millions of acts daily. People do care. Even more importantly, the whole thesis of this book is that people can be influenced to care.

Lois Lowry, in her inspiring book, *Number the Stars*, set amidst the Nazi occupation of Denmark, tells about a Christian girl who, moments before Nazi soldiers arrive, tears a gold chain bearing a Star of David from a Jewish friend's neck and clenches it in her fist. By the time the soldiers have left, an impression of the Star of David is imprinted in her palm.[3]

A fourth-grade teacher read this book to her fourth grade class. As she read this particular story she passed around a chain and a Star of David similar to the one described in the book. And while she was reading she noticed that one student after another pressed the star into his or her palm, making an imprint.

The battle to imprint compassion on today's world is not over by any stretch of the imagination. People do care. Examples of their caring are multitudinous.

People Who Care

Snow lay on the ground on the cold December day in Milwaukee when fourteen year-old Frank Daily boarded the Number 10 bus after school.

Soon after, the bus stopped for a very pregnant woman who grasped the handrail, struggled aboard and plopped into the seat behind the bus driver with her feet raised. But for a pair of torn stockings, her feet were bare. When the bus driver asked where her shoes were, she explained that after making sure her eight children had them, she had no money left to buy herself a pair. She'd gotten on the bus just to warm her feet, she said, and would ride around for a while if he didn't mind. Knowing she needed his shoes more than he did, Frank glanced down at his new Nike basketball sneakers, then pulled them off, and handed them to the woman as he got off the bus. The driver called after him to ask his name and told Frank that in twenty years of bus driving he'd never seen anything to match what Frank had done. Frank maintains that what he did that winter's day was no big deal and says, "We all have the potential to be heroic in some way."[4]

Jeanne Van Velkinburgh is a single mother who lives in a poor neighborhood in Aurora, Colorado. It isn't easy raising two active young boys by herself. It's even harder for Jeanne, because she has to run her household from a wheelchair. On November 18, 1997, Jeanne tried to intervene in a racially motivated attack on an African immigrant. Her heroism earned her a bullet in the spine. She is paralyzed from the waist down. But Jeanne's hardships don't get her down; she keeps an upbeat attitude, in spite of living in constant pain. She teaches her boys to think positively and to set goals for their lives. Jeanne plans to open her own business someday, as soon as she's saved up enough money. She doesn't dwell on the injustices of the past, but focuses instead on the good times in the future.[5]

In every community you will find heroes. The news media focuses on those who are destructive, violent, and coarse. We need to remind ourselves that the overwhelming majority of people are law-abiding, caring folk who are willing to help if they see a need.

I've read that the late Fred Herman would begin his speeches by asking audiences: Who was Jim Thorpe's coach, who taught Einstein arithmetic in the second grade, who was Paderewski's piano teacher in the 6th grade? Pop Warner was Jim Thorpe's coach. I have no idea who influenced Einstein and Paderewski. But somebody was there making a difference in the lives of these two splendid individuals. We are what we are because of the influences in our lives.

The problem is that it is easy to get discouraged, and discouragement is our worst enemy. Caring is contagious, but so is apathy. Human beings are great imitators; if we see someone doing something noble, our own behavior is drawn toward nobility; if we are in a situation in which people are responding passively to a situation, then we become passive too.

A Revealing Experiment

It's like a classic experiment that Dr. Robert Cialdini tells about in his book, *Influence.*[6] An unsuspecting person walks by when someone yells "Rape!" Nearby are two other people who are in on the study and have been told to ignore the cries for help and keep walking. The subject doesn't know whether to respond to the pleas or not, but when he sees the other two people act as if nothing is wrong, he decides that the cries for help are insignificant, and ignores them as well.

Cialdini points out that our response to another person's plight is often determined by how other people respond. This is our cue about whether the situation merits our involvement. In other words, the most important person in any situation in which compassion and courage is involved is the first person to act. After one person acts, then others are prone to respond as well. People do care, they simply need a little prompting. They need someone to step out from the crowd and go first.

In the classic motion picture *Casablanca,* Rick, played by Humphrey Bogart, is asked by a desperate man arrested by the Nazis, "Why didn't you help me?" Rick answers cynically, "I don't stick my neck out for anyone."

Many people today don't want to get involved. Involvement carries many risks. Someone has to set an example to get the process underway. Someone has to be the first one to show caring. The problem is that we think of caring as an emotion. It may begin as an emotion and it may be fueled by emotion, but true caring is an action.

It's like something that happened the first time the immortal star of the old Brooklyn Dodgers, Jackie Robinson, stepped out on a major league ball field. Robinson was a phenomenal baseball player. He set records for stolen bases and for fielding as a second baseman, and earning the title of league MVP in 1949. But he was an even greater individual.[7]

After his baseball career was finished, Jackie Robinson was an outspoken champion of civil rights. In 1963 he traveled to Birmingham to be with Dr. Martin Luther King, Jr. after the bombing of the church in which four little African-American girls died.

Jackie Robinson influenced many young people—particularly young people of color, not just in our country, but around the world. In fact, retired Archbishop and Nobel Peace Prize winner Desmond Tutu once described what Jackie Robinson's breaking the color barrier meant to him as a boy thousands of miles away in South Africa. "It gave me an inspirational life," said Tutu, "to know black people could do such a thing."

Dr. Robert Curvin, a black political scientist, wrote in the *New York*

Times how the example of Jackie Robinson changed his life when he was a youngster: "I was enriched by my attachment to him; the level of my expectations was raised by his example." We all have been enriched by Jackie Robinson's example. Throughout his career, Robinson faced unbelievable abuse and opposition. Through it all, he remained at all times a gracious gentleman and an ideal for persons of all races all over the world. But this is important: Jackie Robinson didn't make it alone (no one does). When Robinson first put on a Brooklyn Dodger uniform in 1947 and walked onto Ebbetts Field in Flatbush, you could hear people booing in the stands.

Peewee Reese, the Dodger shortstop from Louisville, ran out to Robinson and stood next to him. The boos began to diminish. Eventually, the entire Brooklyn Dodger team strode to Robinson and stood by him as well. In minutes, the cheers and applause drowned out the boos. Jackie Robinson was the beneficiary of Peewee Reese's act of decency and courage. And, as they say, the beat goes on. Feelings are contagious. People need to see someone else step out from the crowd; then they are encouraged to step out from the crowd as well.

In the movie *The War*,[8] the character Stephen Simmons tells his wife that he doesn't want their kids growing up thinking they're powerless. He tells her that he wants them to know that everything they do in this world has a consequence. He is heartened by the fact that the children still believe in miracles; they still believe anything is possible. He concludes by saying, "And as long as they believe like that they're going to be something. They're going to make a difference, and that means I've made a difference."

We can make a difference if we are willing to step out from the crowd.

Laughing Through the Tears

I have been reading with enthusiasm about Bob Zmuda, the founder and president of Comic Relief,[9] a yearly charity telethon in which the country's best comedians raise money for the homeless. Since its start in 1986, Comic Relief has raised over thirty-five million dollars. A few years ago, Bob toured a women's shelter that received support from Comic Relief. His guide told him of a particular woman whose life had been changed at the shelter. When this woman had arrived, she had been a violent alcoholic. Thanks to the care and training available at the shelter, she was now sober and employed. Bob Zmuda was moved by the story and asked to meet the woman. The guide looked him in the eye and said, "You're talking to her."

In a hundred different ways, each of us can make a difference in someone's life and thus make a difference in our community and subsequently in our world. But because both caring and apathy are contagious, one person needs to step out and lead the parade. One reason that our stepping out can sometimes make a difference is that attitudes are not always set in concrete. Sometimes a person will say he feels one thing, and then turns right around and does something completely different.

In 1934, a man named R. G. LaPiere toured the southern half of the United States accompanied by an Asian man and his wife.[10] Racial prejudice was a part of life in the 1930s, including intense prejudice against Asian people. This was long before a ban was placed on discrimination in interstate commerce. Nevertheless, LaPiere and his companions visited hundreds of hotels, restaurants, and tourist establishments of all kinds. Ninety-nine percent of the places they visited admitted the Asian couple, and almost all did so without a hassle. Many were even quite gracious in their behavior. That doesn't sound all that surprising until you discover that six months later LaPiere sent out letters to the managers of the hotels and restaurants they had visited. In his letter he told them that he was planning to tour the south with two Asian companions and he wanted to know ahead of time whether they would be served. Ninety-two percent of the businesses replied that they did not serve Asians and that LaPiere could save himself considerable embarrassment by not showing up with such undesirables!

Interesting! Their actions were more civil than their attitudes. They were opposed to people of color in the abstract, but when confronted with a particular couple of another race, they were not nearly as antagonistic as one might suppose. We will deal with racial bigotry in another section, but the battle to change society through positive acts of kindness is not a hopeless one. In fact, I am quite optimistic about the future of humanity because when any one person meets any other person, change may occur.

CHAPTER 14

Moments of Interface

Television personality Ben Kinchlow tells about an interview he had with that grand old actor Charles Coburn. Kinchlow asked a stock question: what does one need to get ahead in life—brains, energy, or education?

Coburn shook his head. "Those things help. But there's something I consider even more important: *knowing the moment.*"

Kinchlow stared at his guest, pencil poised. "What moment?"

"The moment," Coburn answered, "to act—or not to act. The moment to speak—or to keep silent." Coburn went on to describe the importance of timing in the theater. It was his strong feeling that timing is the key to life as well.

He is right, of course. "Knowing the moment. Timing is . . . all-important . . . "[1]

I remember studying the concept of "teachable moments" back in educational psychology—those moments when people are particularly susceptible to new information. Perhaps you have experienced one of those moments: you are sitting in the same seat in the same classroom, listening to the same professor speak on the same old topics, when, all of a sudden, something she says sets your mind racing. "Aha!" you think, "now I understand." The professor has caught you in a teachable moment. At any other time, that same information would have whizzed through your mind without even stopping to catch its breath. But this particular moment, you were ready.

Businessman Paul Stern[2] has noticed that the same phenomenon occurs anytime people interact. He calls it "the moment of interface." Stern, president of Burroughs Corporation, uses the analogy of the great tennis player, Bill Tilden.

Tilden was a great student of the game of tennis. He photographed other players in action and analyzed them. Finally, he concluded that the great difference between players that determined their success or failure was the position of the racquet as it made contact with the ball—the moment of interface. If the racquet face was both vertical and rising when it met the ball, the stroke would be effective and accurate; otherwise, it would not be. Applying this insight to a business audience, Stern comments that a similar phenomenon takes place in business: the critical issue is what happens at the moment of interface between customer and company.

This is the critical issue in all of life—the moment of interface between others and ourselves. What happens in that moment? Moments of interface are unpredictable and potentially life changing. At any other moment in history, an old woman's smile would not even have registered with a young man driving by in a car, but this particular moment found him vulnerable and therefore open to influence.

Psychologist Carl Jung put it this way: "The meeting of two personalities is like the contact of two chemical substances; if there is any reaction, both are transformed."

Just Forty-five Minutes

There was a fascinating column in *Parade* magazine about actor Dabney Coleman.[3] The column took us back to 1957 when Coleman was twenty-five and unsure of himself. At the time he was married to Ann Courtney Harrell, a marriage that lasted just two years. But it was during this union that Coleman met a well-known celebrity. That encounter changed his life, literally overnight. "The reason I became an actor," Coleman explained, "was because Zachary Scott visited our apartment in Austin for forty-five minutes."

Scott, who died in 1965, is best remembered for playing opposite Joan Crawford in the movie *Mildred Pierce*. "He came to my door," Coleman went on. "I'll never forget the way he stood and asked if my wife was at home. He had style. In that moment I knew I wanted to be an actor, to be like Zachary Scott. The next day I got on an airplane and flew to New York."

I wonder if Dabney Coleman ever told Zachary Scott that forty-five minutes in Scott's presence changed his life? Amazing, isn't it? One life touches another life, and in that moment of interface, life is transformed. Do such life-changing experiences happen in the real world? Yes, they do. They happen all the time to all kinds of people.

I had a daughter who nearly starved herself to death because a family member who hadn't seen her in a while greeted her by saying, "My, haven't you become a little butterball?" That one playful remark nearly ruined my daughter's life. More about that later, but teachable moments happen. For better or worse, people can have their lives changed in what seems at the time to be the most innocuous of encounters. We don't completely understand why this should be so. If you're like me, you can remember events in your own life that seemed trivial at the time, but still you retain a vivid picture of them in your mind. You hear the hurtful or encouraging words as if they were happening in the present moment. You feel the pain or the pride, the rejection or the affirmation, that you experienced. Out of proportion to the time involved, these innocuous events have been formative in building your character. It doesn't take a major, ground-shaking event to make a difference in our lives. Sometimes a simple sentence will do the trick.

The Majesty of a Simple Sentence

Any theologian would finger Joe as a walking example of the concept of total depravity. Kicked out of school at the age of twelve for "vandalism, incorrigible behavior, and brutality to other children," Joe's life followed a downward spiral from there. Stints in reform school didn't seem to soften his character. He became a habitual thief, and his behavior was marked by constant violence and recklessness. Much of his time in the reform school was spent in solitary confinement, locked away in a cramped cell without light or human contact.[4]

Joe's crimes condemned him to two long stints in prison, where his violence earned him many more months in solitary confinement. But prison did nothing to reform Joe's character. He seemed hardened to morality and normal human behavior.

When he was finally released, Joe moved to the small town in Wisconsin where the famed psychiatrist Dr. Milton Erickson spent his childhood. Joe's experience had a profound effect on Erickson's later career in therapy. Something happened to Joe that radically transformed his life.

One day in town, Joe crossed paths with Susie, a local farmer's daughter. Susie worked alongside her father helping him to run his large farm. Susie was quite pretty and many young men had tried in vain to woo her. Joe was struck by Susie and asked if he could take her to the weekly Friday dance. Susie replied, "You can if you're a gentleman." The next day, Erickson reports, many storefronts found themselves blocked by boxes of previously stolen goods, mysteriously returned.

To make a long story short, Joe was hired to work on Susie's father's farm, proved himself to be a model worker, and eventually won Susie's hand in marriage. Later they inherited the farm and Joe earned a reputation as a good and helpful neighbor.

Erickson closes his story like this: "And one day Joe went to the local reformatory and offered to hire their newly released boys to work on the farm. His good treatment and the honest work reformed many a young man starting out on the wrong road in life."

The evidence suggests that the ripples of influence from Joe's acts, like all deliberate acts of care and concern, still continue. But here is what interested me: Milton Erickson made this telling comment about the remarkable change in Joe's life: "All the psychotherapy Joe received was, *'You can if you're a gentleman'*" (italics mine).

One simple sentence changed a young man's life. Of course that simple sentence was part of a very important relationship. Still, there is an awesome grandeur in seeing the changes that can transpire when one life comes in contact with another. "A helping word to one in trouble," said Henry Ward Beecher, "is like a switch in a railroad track . . . an inch between wreck and smooth, rolling prosperity."

Now, please notice that, at this point, we are not talking about dramatic, carefully constructed acts of influence—cornering people on the street and confronting them with their need to change. We are talking about small, almost imperceptible changes that occur anytime two human beings make contact. As Tim McGraw has said, "We all take different paths in life, but no matter where we go, we take a little of each other everywhere."

The Trimtab Factor

Sometime ago, Harold Willens wrote a book titled *The Trimtab Factor: How Business Executives Can Help Solve the Nuclear Weapons Crisis.*[5] To understand what a trimtab is, picture a large oceangoing ship traveling at high speed. The mass and momentum of such a vessel are enormous, and great force is required to turn its rudder and change the ship's direction.

In the past, some large ships had, at the trailing edge of the main rudder, another tiny rudder—the trimtab. By exerting a small amount of pressure through the trimtab, which in turn exerted pressure on the larger rudder, one person could easily turn a giant ship. In short, Willens contends, a small amount of leverage can produce a powerful effect.

So it is in the process of human relations. **The Law of Influence states that the tiniest change in a person's life can yield great results.** Such changes may be imperceptible to the person exercising the influence. Still, in the end, the effect may be revolutionary. As Francois Mauriac has said, "No love, no friendship can cross the path of our destiny without leaving some mark on it forever."

Imagine a ship heading from New York to Europe. Only a few degrees of variation at the point of embarkation can put the ship in South Africa rather than Europe. A big mistake we often make is assuming that because we cannot make big changes in the way people respond to us that we are having no impact at all. Nothing could be further from the truth. The cumulative effect of tiny changes can be staggering.

This principle was graphically illustrated by a scientist who hung two spheres from the ceiling—one made out of iron and weighing one ton, and a tiny one made out of cork, which was many times lighter and attached only by a thread. Then he set up an electrical mechanism that kept the cork ball swinging slowly, each time hitting the iron ball.

After several days of uninterrupted swinging, the iron ball began to swing back and forth in rhythm with the cork ball. Gradually, its motion increased until its arc was quite wide—all because of the constant impact of the tiny cork ball. Small influences can yield major results, especially when pressed with persistence.

One hundred thirty years ago, the great nineteenth-century reformer Sojourner Truth was speaking out on behalf of women and children. She was accosted by a heckler who told her she was no more significant than a tiny flea. She responded: "If a flea bites often enough, even a big dog has to scratch." A person's influence should not be measured by his or her stature in society.

According to the National Bureau of Standards, a dense fog covering seven city blocks of one hundred feet is composed of less than one glass of water. Obviously, a little water goes a long way; so it is with acts of influence. We may think to ourselves, "What I say, what I do doesn't matter. My influence isn't even one little drop in the bucket." As someone else has noted, it depends on what the drop is and what's already in the bucket.[6]

As any committed terrorist knows, one little drop of water falling into a bucket of acid may cause an explosion. One drop of germ culture may threaten an entire population given proper conditions. Conversely, one drop of cleansing disinfectant may neutralize a whole bucket of poisonous material. A speck of yeast introduced into dough will leaven the entire mix. "A drop in the bucket" isn't at all unimportant. It may be of very great importance in the results it achieves. That you and I are responsible citizens is evidence that tiny acts of influence accumulating over a lifetime can make a profound difference. A simple sentence can change a life, and the startling fact is that we may not even be aware that we are having any effect at all.

"I beg of you to remember," said Booker T. Washington, "that whenever our life touches yours we help or hinder; wherever your life touches ours, you make us stronger or weaker, there is no escape—man drags man down, or man lifts man up."

The Influence of a Millionaire

I am a member of the National Speakers Association, a professional association of some of the premier speakers in the nation. My life has been touched by people like Cavett Robert, the founder of the association, Bill Gove, Zig Ziglar, Nido Quebein, Jeannie Robertson, Robert Henry, and dozens of other magnificent modern orators. Many people are in the speaking profession today because they were touched by one of these great speakers. Each of these speakers will tell you in turn that somewhere along the way, someone else influenced them. If you have read any of Tony Robbins' books or attended any of his seminars, you will find that he credits the influence of speaker Jim Rohn for his success.

Jim Rohn, in turn, gives credit to a Mr. Shope, a wealthy man who took him under his wing when Jim was twenty-five years old and going nowhere professionally and financially. As Rohn puts it, he had pennies in his pocket, nothing in the bank and creditors were hounding him continuously. By following Mr. Shope's advice, Jim Rohn was a millionaire by the time he was thirty-one. Mr. Shope made Jim Rohn promise to share his principles of success with others, and Jim Rohn has undertaken to keep that promise. Every successful person I know tells about someone somewhere who touched his or her life.

I heard a woman on National Public Radio tell how when she was five years old, a concert pianist visited her home. "She had red hair just like mine," she said, "and when she sat at the piano it was wonderful. I made up my mind right then that when I grew up, I wanted to be her." And that young woman did go on to become a concert pianist of some renown. It is a story repeated time and time again.

Garrison Keillor had an influential cowboy singer named "Rambling Jack" Elliott on his *Prairie Home Companion* radio show. Keillor quizzed Elliott on an incident that had an enormous impact on the world of rock music.

One day many years ago, Elliott had some time to kill waiting on a train in Rochester, England. Some young boys were playing around on the railroad platform, so Elliott decided to take out his guitar and entertain them. One of those boys was named Mick Jagger. Jagger was so impressed with Elliott's playing that he decided he was going to go home and learn to play the guitar. Speaking for millions of parents, I'm not certain that "Rambling Jack" Elliott did the world a favor that day, but he certainly had an impact on one young man, and thus on the world.

Touched by "The Man in Black"

There once was young man who had been looking for trouble ever since his father died when he was nine. Finally, he found himself in prison after an attempted robbery. One day, country star Johnny Cash gave a concert at the prison. That day, the young man turned from his hard living and set his sights on becoming a singer. After his release, the young man went on to record dozens of hit records and win numerous country-music awards. And who is this ex-con who was inspired by a jailhouse concert? None other than the "Okie from Muskogee," Merle Haggard.[7]

Moments of interface occur almost daily. And sometimes the consequences are spine tingling.

He Didn't Even Remember

In the book *A Second Helping of Chicken Soup for the Soul,*[8] Nancy Moorman tells of the day her friend, Charlie, an art teacher, stopped by to see her. One of his former students, a young lady named Angela, paid him a visit that had visibly affected him. Angela had talked to Charlie about her husband, new baby, and promising career. But she also had a more meaningful reason for visiting.

In high school, she had dealt with an abusive stepfather. Frightened and ashamed, she thought suicide was her only escape. One weekend when her parents were gone, she planned a way to kill herself with carbon monoxide. She taped up the windows and areas of ventilation in the garage and wrote out a letter to her mother. Her plan was to go to school the next day, then come home that evening and kill herself.

But the next day in art class, Charlie gave Angela some encouraging words about her artwork followed by a friendly pat on the arm. These small gestures made Angela feel someone cared for her. So she went home and wrote her mother a goodbye letter. Then she packed up her belongings, called her minister, and left her parents' home never to return. She built a successful and happy life for herself, and she felt she owed it to Charlie.

Charlie was amazed. He never dreamed that something so small could have such an impact, especially since he had no memory of this major turning point in this young person's life.

A small amount of leverage, a slight variation in direction—this is how the Law of Influence works. A kind neighbor, a thoughtful friend, an understanding pastor or teacher, a compassionate judge—the list of persons who may be there at precisely the moment of greatest need is endless. We can make a difference. We *are* making a difference.

The amazingly insightful psychologist William James once said: "I am done with great and big things, great institutions and big successes. I am for the tiny, invisible, molecular, moral forces that work from one person to another, creeping through the crannies of the world like soft rootlets, or like the capillary oozing of water, yet which, if you give them time, will rend the hardest monuments of man's pride."

That's the kind of influence this book is about, "like soft rootlets, or like the capillary oozing of water." Maybe some day you will write a best-selling book or compose a beautiful sonata that will still be bringing hope and insight to people generations later. But, in the meantime, there are thousands of tiny actions or words that you are sending out that may have an impact just as long lasting.

Just as I was finishing this chapter, I sat behind a car at a traffic light. On one end of its bumper was a sticker that read: "Commit random acts of kindness and senseless deeds of beauty." On the other end of the bumper was a sticker that read, "Visualize whirled peas." I like the sentiment and the humor.

An encouraging word to a child, a smile at a stranger— "random acts of kindness and senseless deeds of beauty" that are amplified into world changing events. Mahatma Gandhi said it best, "Almost everything we do is insignificant. But it is very important that we do it." There is the world's best hope—to realize that what we say and what we do does make a difference.

CHAPTER 15

Mr. Holland's Opus

Many people were inspired by the movie *Mr. Holland's Opus* starring Academy Award-winning actor Richard Dreyfuss. The film portrays several decades in the life of Glenn Holland, a composer turned high school music teacher, and the impact he had on his students. Mr. Holland was struggling to compose a symphony even as he sought to inspire his young charges.

The most touching scene in the movie was when Mr. Holland was forced to retire owing to cuts in the music budget. Hundreds of his present and former students gathered in the school auditorium to pay tribute and to hear his symphony performed for the first time. He received a standing ovation not only for his symphony, but also for the contribution he had made to these young lives. One of his former students put it best: "Mr. Holland, you have written the symphony, but we are your music."

An interesting aspect of the movie was the real life influence a teacher had on Richard Dreyfuss' life. Dreyfuss didn't win any awards as a student. "I lived in the principal's office," he admits. "They had a special seat for me there. I talked back," he says. "I always had an attitude. I refused to be ignored."[1]

Fortunately, Rose J. Landau, drama teacher and acting coach, saw some potential in the young man that he didn't see himself. Dreyfuss says he thought of her often during the making of *Opus*. "I finally figured out what it was that made Rose J. such a great teacher," he reflects. "She really believed that we were as great as we thought we were. I can still see her face the night we did the play *The Zoo Story*. She looked at me like I was God's gift. And because she felt that way, I was."

I wonder if most teachers are aware of the difference they make in young lives. I know there were two teachers in high school to whom I am eternally indebted. They saw potential in me even when I saw none myself. One was a choral director, Mrs. Corrine Rhodes, and one was a

Speech and English teacher, Mrs. Irene Reynolds. I can still see Mrs. Rhodes—slender, excellent posture, energetic, always optimistic.

Mrs. Reynolds was a worrier. I can picture the distressed look on her face as she tried to get me to focus on my commencement address. "You're going to disgrace the whole school," she cried. Since I was much more interested in spending time with my girlfriend than I was in saving the reputation of the school, Mrs. Reynolds finally ended up writing most of my address herself. She and Mrs. Rhodes must have despaired many times that their influence on me would ever produce dividends. Now I'm more grateful to these two women than mere words can express. The accumulation of their small acts of encouragement have made a real difference in my life.

Teachers have an enormous opportunity to apply the Law of Influence. Get a copy of the book *Mentors, Masters, and Mrs. MacGregor.*[2] It is filled with true stories of teachers who have touched people's lives. Take the one about Barbara Bennett, for example, a typing teacher in Hardin, Montana in 1965. Like most teachers, she struggled to make ends meet on a salary that was nowhere near commensurate with the responsibilities of her job. One of those responsibilities was protecting the typewriters from vandalism. The school administration was cracking down on school vandalism, and they told Barbara that she would have to pay for any typewriters that got vandalized in her classes unless she could find the culprit. Rickety, unstable typing desks and heavy, unwieldy typewriters made for an accident waiting to happen.

One day, a certain kid was goofing off and accidentally sent his typewriter crashing to the floor. Barbara's heart sank when she saw the culprit. She knew little about his family, except that he lived with his grandparents, and he probably couldn't afford an expense of this kind. Silently, Barbara prayed as she picked up the typewriter and placed it on his desk. Lo and behold, it worked perfectly! Turning back to the rest of the class, Barbara never gave the incident another thought. Over the next few years, the young man involved in the typewriter incident got into all sorts of trouble and eventually dropped out of school.

Many years later, however, this young man visited one of Barbara's classes. He wanted her to know that she had said something to him that had affected his life. When she had come running back to his desk to pick up the typewriter, he had been scared. But when the typewriter worked, Barbara had commented that everything was okay, and that he must have been born under a lucky star. For some reason, that comment really touched the young man.

A few years back, his grandfather died, and he had gone through some tough times. So much so that he began considering suicide. One day while out driving, he decided to drive off a highway overpass. But the first overpass he came to was clogged with cars. Not wanting to jeopardize anyone else's life, the young man decided to try the second overpass. At both the second and the third overpasses, there was heavy traffic. Suddenly, he remembered Barbara's comment so many years ago, that he had been born under a lucky star. He began to think that maybe he wasn't meant to die yet.

This young man went on to earn his G.E.D. and to create a better life for himself. He had just come back to thank Barbara for a casual comment she made years ago that saved his life. You never know. What we do know is that teachers are in a unique position to create a better world.

Consider the story of Kenny Wheeler.[3] Wheeler grew up in east Los Angeles where gang-related deaths are an epidemic. While in high school, Wheeler looked and acted like a gang member, but he didn't actually join a gang. He was fortunate enough to have a teacher who looked out for him. One time, Wheeler skipped school and this teacher called his home. Wheeler's parents went out and looked for their son, found him, and took him back home with them. Says Wheeler, "The other guys laughed for a week—but now some of them are junkies or in jail. It was worth the week that they humiliated and teased me!" Today Wheeler is a gang counselor in Los Angeles.

In the book *Growing Up Country And Liking It!*,[4] Jean Ollis Honeycutt tells how her sixth-grade teacher positively influenced her self-esteem. Jean's teacher, Mrs. Hampton, signed her yearbook that year, "Love and Admiration, Mrs. Hampton." Jean wasn't sure what "admiration" meant, so she looked it up in the dictionary. Here is the definition she found: "Admiration—to regard with wonder and delighted approval. To have a high opinion of." From that day on, Jean became an excellent student, always striving to live up to Mrs. Hampton's assessment of her. In her senior year, Jean was named class valedictorian.

There Was a Teacher . . .

In his autobiography, *Breaking Barriers,* syndicated columnist Carl Rowan tells about a teacher who greatly influenced his life.[5] Her name was Miss Thompson. Miss Thompson read to Rowan a quote attributed to Chicago architect Daniel Burnham which read: "Make no little plans; they have no magic to stir men's blood and probably themselves will not be realized. Make big plans, aim high in hope and work. Remember that our sons and grandsons are going to do things that would stagger us."

Thirty years later Rowan gave a speech in which he said that Frances Thompson had given him a desperately needed belief in himself. A newspaper printed the story, and someone mailed the clipping to Miss Thompson who wrote to Rowan. She told him that he had no idea what that newspaper story meant to her. For years, she endured her brother's arguments that she had wasted her life—that she should have married and had a family. She put the clipping in front of her brother in which Rowan gave her credit for helping to launch his career. After her brother had read it, she said, "You see, I didn't really waste my life, did I?"

No, and Carl Rowan did not waste his life either. You see, there was a teacher . . .

Years ago a college sociology class gathered case histories on two hundred young boys in the Baltimore slums. In almost every case, the students in this class predicted grim futures for these boys. But a follow-up study twenty-five years later found that one hundred and seventy-six of the boys had achieved astounding success. In this second study, each of these men pointed to one certain teacher who had inspired them. What was her secret teaching method? According to the elderly teacher, she had loved the boys, that was all.

In the midst of the teacher-bashing that is going on right now in our society, we who are parents need to be reminded that *Mr. Holland's Opus* is being lived out daily in hundreds of thousands of schools all over this nation. Henry B. Adams put it this way: "A teacher affects eternity, he can never tell where his influence stops."

There is a legend about a king who set aside a special day to honor his greatest subject. He was to select a winner from four finalists—a philanthropist, a doctor, a judge, and an old woman. The philanthropist had given most of his wealth to the poor. The doctor had spent his career healing the sick. The judge was known for his wisdom and compassion. Yet the king chose the old woman as the winner. When people questioned him, the king replied, "You see the philanthropist, the doctor, and the judge? Well, she was their teacher!"[6]

I have a soft spot for teachers, and it shows. But teachers are not alone in wielding an awesome influence. Healthcare workers can make a dramatic difference in people's lives. So can salespeople, police officers, cab drivers, and you and I. Joyce Eyman put it this way, "A hundred years from now it won't matter the kind of house I lived in, what my bank account total was, or the kind of car I drove. But the world may be different because I was important in the life of a child."

James Caan is instantly recognizable in his more than fifty films. He often plays a tough guy, a role that may seem unusual for a man with such a soft side. A few years back, Caan took a six-year sabbatical from acting. During that time, he began coaching Little League sports.[7]

One of his players, Josh, was not naturally athletic, so Caan spent extra time coaching him. Near the end of the season, Josh finally hit the ball. Caan recalls that as he waved Josh around the bases, he saw tears well up in the child's eyes. When Josh reached home plate, he jumped on it with both feet, threw his arms in the air and looked up to Heaven. As James Caan says, "Nothing replaces that—nothing in the world. I mean, to literally change a kid. That was the best time of my life." You and I can relate to that, can't we? What greater privilege can there be than to make a difference in some child's life?

A Little Child Shall Lead Them . . .

Of course, influence is a two-way street. There are also young people who can serve as a model for adults.

Jim Stovall was only seven years old when he was diagnosed with juvenile macular degeneration, an eye condition that would eventually result in his total blindness.[8] In spite of his deteriorating eyesight, Jim focused on living as normal a life as possible. When he first set his sights on college, he didn't realize just how much of a disadvantage he faced. He dropped out after a short while, but finally returned, determined to succeed. In his free time between classes, Jim volunteered at a local school for the blind. There he was assigned to a boy named Christopher, who was four years old, and blind and brain-damaged due to a cerebral hemorrhage. The teachers had no hope of Christopher ever learning anything. They just asked Jim to keep the boy's shoes tied, so he wouldn't trip, and to keep him away from the stairwell so he wouldn't fall.

But Jim had loftier dreams for Chris. From day one, Jim told Chris that he would learn to tie his own shoes and to climb the stairs without help. Chris kept saying to Jim, "No, I won't. No, I won't," but Jim wouldn't listen. Those were his two goals for the child. Every day they practiced shoe tying and stair climbing, and every day Christopher was sure he wouldn't be able to do it. Back and forth they argued, with Christopher saying, "No, I can't" and Jim insisting, "Yes, you can."

During this time, Jim was finding it harder and harder to keep up with his classes. He received no help from the university. He was having to work ten times harder than the other students in order to learn his material, and he wanted to give up. The day came when Jim decided to drop out of college and give up his volunteering at the school. He called together the principal and Christopher's parents to announce his decision. As soon as he finished, the first words out of little Christopher's mouth were, "Yes, you can." Now it was Jim's turn to start saying, "No, I can't," but Christopher wasn't taking it. "Yes, you can," he insisted. And Jim Stovall decided at that very moment that he had better start believing what he had been telling Christopher all along.

Three years later, Jim Stovall graduated from college with highest honors. And little Christopher learned to tie his shoes and climb the stairs all by himself. Not long after Jim's graduation, Christopher suffered another cerebral hemorrhage that killed him. At his funeral, one of the speakers remarked that it was a shame that no one would ever know what Christopher could have accomplished if he had lived. But Jim Stovall had to set that person straight. As he said, "(Christopher) has made his contribution because anything I do from this day forward I owe to him." Jim Stovall went on to found a television network that is carried over thousands of cable stations around the world. He is also a successful speaker who travels the country giving motivational speeches. Everywhere he goes, he tells the story of Christopher, and how Christopher changed his life.

Influence can come from almost any direction. Sometimes, it takes a little child to lead the way, and sometimes, it takes a teenager.

In the 60s, Patty Perrin and her family were living in Afghanistan while her husband served a stint in the Peace Corps. Patty was miserable in Afghanistan. She wanted the comfort and familiarity of home. She didn't know the language and she didn't have a purpose. She became increasingly isolated, and began turning to alcohol for comfort. She needed a purpose, a vision, maybe even a personal revival. What she got was Margaret.[9]

Margaret was a fourteen-year-old whose parents were also Peace Corps volunteers. Their remote area of assignment had no schools for older children, so Margaret came to live in the larger city of Kabul, with Patty, her husband, and daughter. Where Patty had become passive and helpless, Margaret was incredibly active and driven. Where Patty longed for the familiarity of home, Margaret wanted to live the Spartan existence of the average Afghan family, in order to toughen herself up.

Margaret was constantly setting goals and challenging herself in new and different ways. She was a go-getter and a risk-taker, and she was painfully honest. Right away, Margaret ascertained that Patty was drinking too much, and she confronted her about it. In spite of her resentment of this awfully forward child, Patty did stop drinking. When Patty was talked into accepting a part in a local theater production, Margaret followed her all over the house, practicing lines with her. Patty couldn't even escape her little drama partner when she went to the bathroom. Margaret relentlessly drilled her on her lines, and on opening night Patty did a perfect job. Her self-esteem began to rise.

Margaret moved out after a year, determined to live with an Afghan family and to learn their ways. But by then, Patty had taken an interest in life again. She became more involved in her community, and began volunteering her time on some Peace Corps missions. Margaret's stubborn, ambitious, daring, honest, active approach to life had revived in Patty her own spirit of adventure and accomplishment. She was ready to embrace life again.

It would be ageist, indeed, to assume that only adults have something worth passing on. There are many committed, character-driven young people. Many have much they can teach us. Still, the primary burden is on those of us who have passed out of young adulthood. Surely one of the chief reasons we are allowed to take up space in this world is to build a better world for those who come behind.

Tracing Our Influence

A company was in a battle with the city administration. The company wanted to expand, but there was opposition in the surrounding community. So the company adopted an interesting strategy: They began paying their employees in silver dollars. Suddenly, silver dollars were everywhere. They began flowing over counters in stores, filling stations, theaters and refreshment stands. Where silver dollars had been all but forgotten, they were now everywhere. People began to see just how important the company was to the community, and opposition to its expansion dried up.

I wish it were as easy to trace the ripples of influence each of us sends out as it was for that company to trace its impact on its community. Maybe we need a guardian angel to show us what our lives contribute.

You were probably touched as I was the first time you saw the heart-warming film *It's a Wonderful Life*. George Bailey, the lead character, never felt like his life counted for much. He had dreams of becoming a famous architect. Instead, he feels trapped in a humdrum job in a small town. Then a crisis occurs that strains his every resource. He is on the verge of losing the bank his father established and he is faced with unjust criminal charges. Although he has a fine family and many friends in the community, the injustice of the situation plunges him into despair. Faced with this crisis, George Bailey goes to a bridge to end his life. It is there that he has an encounter with Clarence, his guardian angel.

Clarence takes him to town to show him what his community would be like if he had never been born. It is not a pretty picture. The town is a different town with many sordid wrongs. The angel shows George how his work has benefited many families and how his kindness and thoughtful acts have changed the lives of others. In short, he showed him that the world is a better place because of George Bailey.

It would be nice if an angel could show us the consequences of our acts of kindness so it would be possible to trace the ripples of our influence. It would add a tremendous amount of hope and zest to life. Obviously, that's not possible, however, and sometimes we despair if we are really making any difference at all.

On the tombstone of a famous English poet are inscribed the words, "I have plowed the water." In a similar vein, a cynical Greek philosopher put his thumb in a pail of water. Then upon removing it, he asked his students, "Where is the hole that my finger once made?"

If only we could see our influence at work. Once a teacher said to me in despair, "Sometimes I get so discouraged. I can't see that my work is having any impact on the young people I'm teaching." But the Law of Influence says that each of us is having an effect every day of our lives—although some of those effects may not be visible for generations. Who knows what that small child you offered encouragement to may one day do with his or her life? Who knows where that teenager may yet end up, due to your support?

Of course, there is another side to influence—the dark side. For every Einstein there is a Timothy McVeigh. Sometimes the influences that are exerted on our lives are negative and destructive. There are those who have been hurt, exploited, even permanently damaged by the thoughtless actions of another—a fact we need to deal with honestly and in some detail.

CHAPTER 16

The Dark Side of Influence

In the seventies, we all agreed with the Carpenters that "What the world needs now is love, sweet love." But in the new millennium, the word *love* can take on a different meaning. In May 2000, a computer virus nicknamed the "Love Bug" invaded hard drives and shut down many businesses around the world in only a few days.[1]

This ingenious bug worked like this: recipients found in their e-mail either a message with the appealing title "I LOVE YOU" or an e-mail attachment titled "love letter for you." Who could resist peeking at a message with such an appealing tag? When the e-mail message was opened, this insidious virus spread through the user's address book. Instantly, messages were sent out to persons in the address book that also said "I LOVE YOU." In a very short time, millions of computers were infected. In a matter of hours, major corporations all over Europe had to shut down their e-mail systems to fend off the Love Bug. Even the State Department in Washington was infected. Investigations led to a young man in the Philippines as the likely suspect.

Imagine that—a solitary individual on the other side of the world with no bombs, no automatic weapons, no deadly biological agent could still strike terror in the hearts of men and women around the world using a simple e-mail message: I LOVE YOU.

There is a flip side to the Law of Influence that says that in a world as interrelated as our world is, one person can do unimaginable evil as well as unimaginable good. It doesn't take long. It doesn't even take much in the way of resources. A computer and an e-mail account will do the trick. There have always been people with a reckless disregard for the greater good. Unfortunately, in today's world their mischief-making can be even more lethal. Although people may intend no evil, tragedies can occur just because the world is so interrelated.

A Much More Tragic "Love Bug"

Could there be a more perverse example of the Law of Influence than the spread of the AIDS virus? It is difficult to imagine that this deadly bug was not recognized in this country until 1979. In an astoundingly short time, thirty-five million people have been infected worldwide. In South Africa, a stunning twenty percent of the population is infected with the HIV virus. In Africa as a whole, one-third of fifteen year-olds will die long before achieving adulthood from this scourge.

According to the *Christian Science Monitor* there will be an estimated forty million "AIDS orphans" in Africa by 2010.[2] But what kind of social structure will await them, even if they survive this epidemic? In some countries there are now more people in their seventies and eighties than in their forties. How can the social and economic fabric of a nation survive without adults in their prime to carry the burdens of society? The heartbreak this disease has introduced into so many individual lives, families, and even nations in a relatively short time is simply incalculable.

Consider the attributes of this crafty killer with regard to the Law of Influence. It must be spread person to person. Once infected, it is entirely possible for a person to live a decade or longer with no knowledge that he or she is infected. The symptoms may resemble a mild flu that may disappear entirely, only to reappear at a later time. Meanwhile, the infected person may be spreading the virus to an untold number of other persons who themselves may be totally unaware that they have been exposed. And they, of course, may spread it to still others. Thus, with each person-to-person contact, a new round of infections may be begun, ad infinitum. Some people have discovered they are infected only because they had a routine blood test. Only then did the HIV virus reveal itself in all its ugly horror. No wonder thirty-five million people worldwide have been infected. Could there possibly be a more demonic plague to torture the human race? Could there be a more compelling argument for the divine wisdom of monogamy?

All human life is connected to all other human life. This means that we are responsible for one another. I am at heart a child of the sixties. I much prefer peace to war, love to hate, and equal opportunity to bigotry. I can sing, "Where have all the flowers gone?" with the best of them. But I am continually impressed with the impossibility of living in a world where people have no other philosophy than "doing your own thing." Without a sense of responsibility for one another, all human enterprise is endangered. It is not enough to do one's own thing. Eventually comes a time of accountability. Then we will realize the importance of buckling down and doing the right thing.

One Woman Who Did Her Own Thing

Five feet, six inches tall, blue-eyed, with blonde hair, Mary Mallon could have been pretty. However, she was always somewhat overweight, and she was decidedly sullen and uncommunicative. Her withdrawn personality seems strange when you consider her main vocation in life—she loved cooking for other people. Amazingly, this somewhat benign interest caused her to spend a large portion of her adult life confined in institutions. In fact, her final arrest would occur as she was taking food to a friend.

If you haven't guessed by now, Mary Mallon was better known as "Typhoid Mary."[3] For at least six years before she was discovered by health authorities, she worked as a cook in the northeastern United States, spreading typhoid everywhere she worked. A 1904 epidemic on Long Island was traced to her, but she disappeared before she could be quarantined. Later her irresponsibility surfaced at other places, but at each new outbreak, she moved on. In 1907, Mary was taken into custody against her will and forced to submit specimen samples to be checked for typhoid germs. Her body, it turned out, was a veritable typhoid factory! Mary herself was immune to typhoid fever, but as a carrier, her effectiveness was deadly. She never broke any laws, but she had citizens in a panic and the police combing large areas for her. She was never convicted of murder, but she left a wake of destruction and death behind her.

Informed that she could not go on cooking but could work most other jobs with a few basic precautions, Mary refused to cooperate. She seemed to feel that she had a right to cook and was being persecuted. As a result, Mary remained in custody until 1910, when the health department in New York City decided to give Mary her freedom on the condition that she not work as a cook and that she report to health authorities every three months. Almost immediately Mary skipped the area and disappeared.

It appears that she tried other jobs at first. However, those didn't pay as well, and Mary liked cooking. So, for the next five years she spread typhoid and moved on from each job before being suspected. One of her last locations was at a hospital in New York where she practically wiped out mothers, babies, and staff. She meant no harm, she contended, but nevertheless managed to infect at least fifty-one people. Not until 1915 was she finally apprehended, and then she was kept in custody until her death from a stroke in 1938, with her name living on in infamy.

The case of "Typhoid Mary" is an odd one. She could have lived a normal life, even as a carrier of typhoid. But as a woman who had no concern for how her actions affected others, she proved to be a deadly menace and spent over half her life in the confinement of health institutions.

I've known a few "Typhoid Marys" in my time, haven't you? I'm not referring to people who spread life-threatening germs, but people whose negative attitudes and destructive lifestyles affect everyone around them.

Zig Ziglar once told about a tree called the Upa Tree that drips poison on everyone who sits under it. Ziglar went on to compare that tree to people who spread negative thinking to everyone they meet. We all know people who are centers of negativity. We've seen the harm they do to their children, their co-workers, and their community. Even more sadly, not only do they spread their infirmity to those within their immediate influence and to the community, but the impact of their attitudes and their actions often will be transmitted for generations. Some of these people are the nicest folks you would ever want to meet.

Leaving aside for a moment people who have obviously destructive lifestyles, I am convinced there are nice people, good people, people who would not deliberately harm another human being who do undue harm because of their unhealthy attitudes. Their influence spreads just as surely as the positive influence we described in the earlier chapters. They plant seeds of fear, doubt, suspicion, and resentment in the world; and out of that fear, doubt, suspicion, and resentment grow the weeds of bigotry, hatred, and self-doubt.

The frightening thing is, the people who contribute to this kind of negativity in the world are not even aware of it. They think they are doing the right thing—they are guardians of the faith, keepers of that which is noble and righteous, protectors of traditional ways of doing things. But instead of spreading joy, hope, peace, and love in our world, they spread the deadly bacteria of fear and distrust.

Each of us needs to ask continually whether we are contributing to the positive or the negative. The Law of Influence says that we are making a difference—every day in hundreds of different ways—for better or for worse.

Stray Voltage

Imagine for a few moments that you are a dairy farmer. It's not an easy way to make a living under the best of circumstances. But suddenly things start going haywire. You find up to ten cows a day on your farm dead. Your milk production, your primary source of income, is plummeting. Calves are being born with gross defects. You even have cows with exploding udders! No one can figure out what is causing these bizarre events.

Then your cats and dogs start dying of heart attacks. Then you start suffering severe electrical shocks yourself. Finally, electricians are dispatched. They identify the problem as stray voltage. Think about that concept for a moment—stray voltage.

On Sunday, April 7, 1991, the television program *60 Minutes* produced a fascinating story about stray voltage and the dairy industry. Most farm areas, it seems, are supplied electricity through above ground cables that can be up to fifty years old. General wear on the cables causes them to be less receptive. In addition, most of these cables have to supply more energy than they were designed for, due to increased local demand. The result is that extra electrical energy that the cables cannot receive is spread through the ground surrounding the electricity poles. Most of these poles are in fields and on farms. Animals, particularly cows, are highly sensitive to electrical current.

Most of the farmers had to sue the state utilities before they would replace the cables. Some sued and were awarded restitution, but still lost their farms in bankruptcy because the utilities took years to make repairs. Most utilities have known for years about the danger of stray voltage, but they have avoided the expense of upgrading their cables.

Is there any stray voltage in your life? Any unintended damage caused by your failure to be aware of the awesome power of influence? It is something for all of us to consider. Like ripples in a pond, influence exudes from us whether we are conscious of it or not. My boss is in a foul mood. He takes it out on me. I go home and take it out on my wife; she on the kids; they on the dog; the dog on the cat; the cat on the canary, etc. There is no end to it.

What kind of energy is radiating from you? Is it positive energy or negative? Is it affirming or hostile? The sad thing is that many people seem capable of radiating only negative influence because that is what they received at critical times in their lives. How doubly sad for those who must live with and around them. Sadder still is the result of stray voltage in the surrounding community.

You can't always predict when this stray voltage is going to strike next. I read about a Polish soccer club that is looking for ways to combat hooliganism among spectators. Soccer is becoming a violent sport around the world—not on the field, but in the stands. This particular club hopes to remedy this situation by packing the stands with young priests. They signed a deal with church authorities in the southern Polish city of Krakow to give free tickets for the club's matches to seminary students. Team officials believe the presence of the priests in the stadiums will discourage rowdy behavior by other fans. Clearly, the success of that plan will depend on the ability of the priests to contain their own feelings. After all, men and women of the cloth are people just like everyone else; for example, I can remember being in a seminary lounge in 1968 during the riots at the Democratic Convention. I can remember hearing fellow seminarians cheering on the police as they beat on students with their clubs.

We all have to be cautious that we keep our baser emotions in check if we want to contribute to a positive world environment—"a kinder, gentler world"—as former President Bush dubbed it.

Garbage In—Garbage Out

I am told that if you were to ascend twenty miles above the Earth over the eastern seaboard of the United States, you would see the largest object made by modern man. It would not be the World Trade Center or the Empire State Building; it would be Freshkills, the landfill produced from the garbage of New York City.[4]

Is that not an apt metaphor for human life in the twenty-first century? Landfills like Freshkills play an important role in our society. Our garbage has to go somewhere. But Freshkills reminds us of that dark side of human nature that causes untold suffering to many who are the unfortunate victims of other people's irresponsibility.

Why is it important for us to set out to create positive ripples of influence? It is because, in the absence of such ripples, psychological, moral, and spiritual entropy sets in. Human garbage has to go somewhere, but sometimes garbage dominates the landscape of human society.

Let's talk about garbage for a few moments.

There is a law of human nature that says the bad drives out the good. Why are neighboring businesses so hostile when a so-called "adult" bookstore moves into the community? It's because once the tide turns in a community, it is difficult to reverse it. Why has New York City worked so hard to drive the peddlers of pornography out of Times Square? Is it because the Big Apple is filled with puritanical busy bodies? Hardly. It is because of this almost inviolable law: the bad drives out the good.

It's like the man who wanted to teach the sparrows in his garden to sing instead of chatter. So he bought a canary and hung its cage in his backyard. The canary sang enthusiastically for a while, but soon became discouraged and it began to imitate the clicks and squawks of its neighbors. The canary had lost its song. Meanwhile, the sparrows continued as before.

Have you lost your song? I hope not. In a society where the ripples of moral decay are stronger and more numerous than the positive ripples of love and responsibility, people can be stripped of their values, and thus their humanity.

A woman tells of walking in her spacious backyard when her attention was caught by the sight of an older man with spray paint lurking near their family's full-grown elm trees. She discovered the man was marking diseased elm trees to be disposed of in coming weeks. The man marked four of their elm trees with sickening circles of fluorescent orange paint.[5]

"What would happen if our family could not dispose of the trees that soon?" her mother asked the tree inspector.

The inspector sadly replied, "In time, all of your elm trees would get the disease from the already diseased ones." That's the problem, isn't it? Disease spreads. Alcoholism and drug abuse, physical and sexual abuse, psychological abuse—all leave scars that may not heal for a lifetime.

Psychological and social disease spread just as surely as disease spread by germs both in the home and in society. Why should we be concerned when one television show exceeds the bounds of good taste? It's because the bad drives out the good. Soon other shows follow suit. Rather than writing thought provoking scripts which require hard work and originality, the writers of these shows will settle for exploiting our baser instincts. Television programs like *Survivor* and *Big Brother* are perfect examples— cheap, easy television with few positive values, but wide popular appeal.

The Law of Entropy

The Second Law of Thermodynamics is the Law of Entropy—that processes tend to move from order to disorder. In William Butler Yeats' phrase, "Things fall apart; the center cannot hold, mere anarchy is loosed upon the world." Entropy refers to a physical phenomenon, but it is also an apt description of what can happen in a company, a family, or a society.

At a meeting of financial analysts, corporation president Max DePree was asked an important question: "What is one of the most difficult things that you personally need to work on?" "The interception of entropy," DePree answered immediately. He went on to explain that anything left unattended to has a tendency to deteriorate.[6] Therefore, an effective leader is one who recognizes this tendency and intervenes to halt this deterioration.

Entropy is a good description of what is happening in our society. In some areas of our corporate life, we are falling apart. Like Max DePree, we need to see that the interception of entropy is our most important task.

In 1993, a disturbing report on American youth was compiled by a commission of educational, medical, political and business leaders. Titled "Code Blue," the study concluded: "Never before has one generation of American teenagers been less healthy, less cared for or less prepared for life than their parents were at the same age."[7]

In their report, they pulled no punches: suicide among adolescents has increased three hundred percent since 1950. Teen pregnancy has risen six hundred and twenty-one percent since 1940. Homicide is now the leading cause of death among fifteen to nineteen-year-old minority youth; drug abuse claims younger victims every year.

We are reaching critical mass. Younger members of our society have had enough garbage dumped on them to fill a million Freshkills. Is there a way to reverse such deterioration? Yes, it's not too late. But it will take people who are committed to change, people who are conscious of their influence in the greater community, and people who are willing to self-consciously exercise the influence they have.

Like the law of entropy, the concept of critical mass is an idea from the physical sciences that has been co-opted by sociologists. Sociologists use the term in a hopeful sense. How many people are necessary to adopt a new practice, product, or belief system before it becomes a chain reaction that in time persuades most people to adopt the practice or product? Critical mass refers to a turning point. And in some ways we may be at a turning point. In spite of the well-publicized problems of our young, there has been a recent drop in teen pregnancies, teen violence, and even drug usage. But these are societal issues as well as individual issues. What is needed are some paradigm shifts concerning values in our society.

In his well-known book, *The Structure of Scientific Revolutions*, Thomas S. Kuhn describes how each age creates paradigms, or conventional models of reality. These are often so widely agreed on that we accept them as reality that can't be changed. Paradigm shifts occur when the model we hold is displaced by another. For example, we went through a seismic paradigm shift in the 1960s that has drastically affected our life as a people. And I say this not pejoratively, but simply as a concerned observer.

I was in theology school in 1967 in Washington, D.C. when I first encountered the word paradigm. I remember how struck I was by how effortlessly our society had discarded the notion of moral absolutes under the intellectual leadership of such people as Dr. Joseph Fletcher and his very influential book, *Situational Ethics*. Almost overnight, it seemed, so-called "thinking" people were rejecting even the possibility of the existence of absolute truth. It was not so much that I was a rabid defender of moral absolutes; it was more that I was offended by the suddenly fashionable idea that such absolutes could not possibly exist. So I mentioned the fact to a philosophy professor, Dr. Harry Taylor.

"How do we know," I asked with both pain and indignation, "that there are no absolutes? Just because it has become fashionable to say so doesn't make it so. And yet that seems to be the underlying assumption of higher education today."

"Oh," said Dr. Taylor, "You mean the paradigms by which society operates."

So I learned a new word. "Paradigm." And it caused me to devote hours and eventually years of thought to the question of how paradigms, once entrenched, can be changed. Perhaps two examples from societies much different from our own will best illustrate the concept of the paradigm.

There is a parasitic disease called schistosomiasis that affects more than two hundred million people in the tropics and subtropics.[8] This disease, caused by flatworms that attach themselves to the walls of the bladder, is contracted in contaminated water. A symptom of this disease is blood in the urine. In the areas where this disease is most common, most school kids—especially boys, who are more likely to play in contaminated water—are infected. Consequently, their urine turns red at about puberty. Some ethnic groups in this area believe this blood in the boys' urine is the equivalent of menstruation in girls and that its absence would be abnormal. As these children grow older, their contact with water becomes less frequent, and they become "cured." They are not aware that these symptoms are not healthy because that condition is the only one they're familiar with. If disease is normal in your society, you accept it unless you've had some experience that shows you that it's not normal.

You have to wonder if some of the things we have learned to accept as normal in our society are really sick. But before we speculate, let's consider one more example of a paradigm.

Mary Roach, writing in *Discover* magazine in an article titled, "Why Men Kill" (December 1998, p.100, 102, 105), notes that the root of most violence in primitive societies is the fight to obtain food. So what, she asks, explains the astonishing rates of violence among the Achuar people of Ecuador?

A 1993 survey among the Achuar people found that fifty percent of male ancestors in that society had been murdered. But anthropologists note that food is plentiful in the Achuan region. Instead, these anthropologists believe it is a matter of status. The Achuar society is based on warriorship. The more successful a warrior is at defeating his enemies, the more status he gains in his society, and the more people who align themselves with him. Higher status means more power and influence. Violence is so prevalent among the Achuar that anthropologists report that a traditional Achuar greeting is "Pujamik," which is translated, "Are you living?"

This attachment to violence is a paradigm, no matter how dysfunctional, by which the Achuar society operates. It would be quite a shift for them to accept the idea of living in harmony and goodwill, but who would argue that such a shift is desirable?

It is time for our society to examine many of the paradigms by which we operate. For example, we are certainly one of the most materialistic societies on earth, and one of the most hedonistic. We worship success, glamour, and celebrity. Surely the rash of violence in our schools is related to the perception that if you are not one of the beautiful people, your life has little value. That is a paradigm sorely in need of reconsidering.

Here's another: It is time to declare as a society that violence is not an acceptable solution to conflict. The 1960s radical Stokely Carmichael contended that violence is as American as apple pie. Well, it's time for a paradigm shift. We need a cultural assumption to permeate every aspect of our life as a people that says "no" to violence. It will require the efforts of the police, of the courts, of the mass media, of parents, of kindergarten teachers—in short, of our entire society. But someone has got to say enough is enough! Perhaps it is time to restore one of those much-maligned absolutes, "Thou shalt not kill."

I will get off my soapbox now. These are but two of the paradigm shifts that would benefit our society. You have your own list, but there are areas that require a group effort.

We Truly Are a Small World

Did you know that dust from the Sahara Desert can be carried by strong, persistent trade winds across the equatorial Atlantic Ocean to

Florida, sometimes forming a thin coating on cars and other surfaces and making it hard for some Florida cities to meet federal clean air standards?

We live in a small world, and all our problems are interrelated.

We're told that significant deposits of DDT and PCBs have been discovered in remote areas of New Hampshire's White Mountains, even though the use of these toxic chemicals has been banned in the United States for close to two decades. How could this happen? It happens because toxic chemicals like DDT are still used in other areas of the world, such as Mexico, Central America, India, and Eastern Europe.[9]

Yale University forest biologist William H. Smith, commenting on this global tragedy, says: "Our study is just another example of why countries cannot independently develop environmental protection policies. What one country does can have an impact on the entire world." What one country does, what one community does, and as we have already seen, what one individual does affects us all.

Like Typhoid Mary, some of us are unconsciously sending out poisonous messages of hostility and fear, exploitation and moral decay. Is it possible to move beyond stray voltage to purposeful ripples of positive influence? Are there steps by which we can make an enduring impact on our world, an impact that contributes to a more peaceful, a more nurturing, in short, a kinder, gentler world? Yes there are, but each of us must look within to see if we are part of the problem or part of the solution.

CHAPTER 17

Role Models

The inspiring movie *Chariots of Fire* tells the story of a young Scotsman named Eric Liddel. Liddel, a great runner, entered the 1924 Olympic Games. The race for which he was most famous and was favored to win fell on a Sunday. Because of his deep religious faith, Eric Liddel refused to run. This caused a furor, and he was greatly criticized. In order to represent his homeland faithfully, Liddel subsequently entered a race that he had never run before, the two hundred meters. He won.[1]

Back in Scotland a young man followed this story in the newspaper and was deeply influenced by it. His name was Peter Marshall. Marshall went on to become chaplain of the United States Senate and the subject of a best-selling book, *A Man Called Peter*. Peter Marshall said that Eric Liddel's example played a big role in his own religious conversion.

Imagine that. An Olympic athlete remained true to his convictions and look at the results: a major motion picture inspired millions; a nationally famous pastor converted; and a best-selling book inspired millions more. It would be amazing indeed if we could trace the impact on individuals around the world that grew out of this singular act of commitment. It certainly produced one of the most memorable theme songs to come from a motion picture. I find myself humming it in my mind even as I write.

It is tempting to conclude that they don't make role models like they used to. Maybe so, maybe not. The story of Eric Liddel is a dramatic one. But there are still plenty of celebrities who are concerned about their influence on others.

Fans of comedian and talk show host Rosie O'Donnell love her quick wit and warm personality. It might surprise them to know that her empathy and sense of humor spring from a deep sadness in her life, the death of her mother. Rosie had been very close to her mother, who died when Rosie was only four years old. Rosie knew when she was four years old that one day she would be in show business. Her mother was in part responsible. Her mother had a great sense of humor as well, which she displayed at such places as the local PTA. Rosie loved making her mother laugh.[2]

When her mother died, Rosie's father was unable to help his children process their emotions, or to fill in the role that their mother had played in their lives. Fortunately Rosie was not without some female role models; two women in her life provided her with acceptance and encouragement. One was the mother of her best friend, Jackie Ellard. Bernice Ellard opened her home to this distraught little girl, giving her a glimpse of normal family life that she had lost with her mother's death. Rosie never forgot the warm, inviting atmosphere of the Ellard home. Every year, she sends Christmas and Mother's Day cards to Bernice Ellard, as a way of thanking her for her kindness so many years ago.

Another woman who receives a yearly Mother's Day card from Rosie O'Donnell is her junior high math teacher, Patricia Maravel, who offered Rosie tremendous encouragement and caring. She tried to help Rosie see her potential and believe in herself. She even made herself available after school to spend time with her. Since early childhood, Rosie O'Donnell had dreamed of being an actress, but in junior high she almost changed her mind. Maravel's influence was so positive in her life that, at least for a short while, Rosie dreamed of being a teacher instead.

Rosie O'Donnell didn't become a teacher, but she still has a deep concern for children. When she is working a comedy gig, it is not at all unusual for her to change her routine to protect any kids in the audience. If she spots little ones from the stage, she will leave out her more adult material to keep the show clean for the kids. She takes her responsibility as a role model very seriously.[3]

Few issues have been as hotly debated in our society over the past three decades as the responsibilities of so-called role models. Many people hunger for sports idols like Eric Liddel. But the world has changed. For one thing, there was a time when there was a benign conspiracy by owners of sports teams, Hollywood production houses, and even the press to portray the people our children idolize in the best, favorable light. That day is past. Imagine if John Kennedy had to deal with the scrutiny that has haunted Bill Clinton.

Even more disturbing, many of our most accomplished entertainment idols have learned to exploit their notoriety by being as naughty as they can, because naughty sells and because nobody gets their picture in the paper by being nice. Teens are drawn to anything that drives mom and dad up the wall. Does it all make a difference? Well, yes and no.

Are young people affected by the behavior of their cultural icons? Yes, to a degree. But not as much as by the behavior of their parents and their friends. Can having the wrong role models be dangerous? Yes, if there is not the proper support system in place at home and school to counterbalance the negative messages that popular heroes transmit.

In one of the most famous shoe commercials of all time, basketball superstar Charles Barkley once protested, "I am not a role model." Karl Malone of the Utah Jazz, responded: "Charles, you can deny being a role model all you want, but I don't think it's your decision to make. We don't choose to be role models, we are chosen. Our only choice is whether to be a good role model or a bad one."

Newsweek carried an amusing quote from Barkley sometime back: "I heard Tonya Harding is calling herself the Charles Barkley of figure skating," Barkley said. "I was going to sue her for defamation of character, but then I realized I have no character."

Later, in a more serious vein, Barkley said he's a better man since a 1991 basketball game in which he accidentally spat in a little girl's face. Barkley took full responsibility for the spitting incident. He was aiming at a heckler, he says, but hit the girl. "What does that say about me that I let a basketball game—a game!—get to me so much that I want to spit on another human being?" he said. "It was my fault . . . after that I started to be a better person."[4]

Charles Barkley is not a bad man. In fact, I have been a fan of Barkley since he was known as "the round mound of rebound" at Auburn University years ago. Whether he likes it or not, though, he influences others.

Having said that, I think it is unrealistic to expect young ball players, many of whom have been catered to all their lives, to suddenly emerge as model citizens. It is absurd that people look to someone for moral authority who has only distinguished himself or herself on a ball field. But that seems to be the way the world works. People are disproportionately affected by the actions and attitudes of celebrities.

People Are People

There are some principles we need to keep in mind when thinking about role models. The first is that people are people. It is always a mistake to elevate any living person to the level of sainthood. This book is about people who are making a positive difference in the world. It is not about people who are perfect. There has only been one perfect person and we got rid of him while he was still in his early thirties. Welcome to the real world. Perfection is too heavy a burden to lay on a president, a teacher, a pastor, a parent, a spouse, or anyone else. People have hurts that no one else can see that cause them to act out in sometimes horrendous ways. This is not a rationalization; it is a reality. But there is more good than bad in most of us, and that is our hope. It does not hurt our young to understand that people are people. They accept the truth about Santa Claus and the Easter Bunny. They can stand the truth about their sports and entertainment heroes.

Who, by the way, is your hero? How do you decide what constitutes a hero? David Granger, editor of *Esquire* magazine, decided to tackle just such a subject recently. He wrote to over two hundred prominent people, asking them about their ideas on heroism. Most of those who wrote back claimed that they weren't even sure what a hero is. Actor Paul Newman wrote, "I'm embarrassed, but I have no heroes that I know of. Everybody that I know or have read about is seriously flawed. Including myself." The best he could recommend was a good role model. For that post, he chose his dog, Harry. Harry's best qualities, according to Newman, are that he's "funky, curious, (and) always of good humor."[5]

Reality Bites but It Also Balances

Let me say without equivocation that I deplore the exploitation of sex and violence by our entertainment media. People focus on violence as the primary evil but, in the long run of things, I suspect we will see more damage from the ravaging of traditional family life than we will from the glorification of murder and mayhem. There is an order to nature, whether bestowed by a benign creator or by evolution. Children need an intact loving home with two parents. The devaluation of sex in our society has robbed us of one of the binding elements in that arrangement. Having said that, however, I am not in favor of most forms of censorship. If people know the truth about their idols' lives, they will not be drawn to emulate their lifestyles.

It's like something comedian Damon Wayans said at a roast by his peers honoring Richard Pryor for his trailblazing comedy career. Wayans said that Pryor was his inspiration. "I wanted to be just like him, except for the drug habit, the failed marriages, and the guns." I suspect that back-handed accolade was only half in jest. What reasonable person would want to emulate the self-destructive lifestyles of some of our superstars?

But you protest: "My teenager is not reasonable." Perhaps not, but the final record has not been written. Given the right kind of love and support and supplied with balanced information, most young people will muddle through. As time goes by, role models have less and less influence. Even positive role models—and that's not altogether bad.

Young people, especially girls and minorities, are often encouraged to emulate people who have succeeded in the fields they wish to enter. However, new research from the University of Waterloo reported in *Psychology Today* suggests that in some cases the use of role models could harm as much as it helps.[6]

Ziva Kunda, Ph.D., designed a study in which the accomplishments of extremely successful teachers were described to first-year and graduate students at her university (all of whom hoped to become professors themselves). She found that the freshmen were indeed inspired by the teachers' example since they felt they had years of schooling before them to achieve what their role models had. The graduate students, on the other hand, felt their self-esteem and motivation drop after they heard a story about a successful peer. They felt bad about the comparison, they told researchers, because they had not achieved as much, and time to do so was now running out.

We probably make too much of the power of role models. When Elvis hit the scene in the late fifties, I was an impressionable high school sophomore. Like many other teenagers, I learned to imitate the famous Elvis sneer and swagger. But I would never have been tempted to adopt his self-destructive lifestyle. Who would, except someone who was already very needy emotionally and socially? In any case, such a person would likely fall under the influence of someone else close by with equally destructive habits. The clue to keeping it all in perspective is the free flow of information. Reality bites, but it also balances.

There Are Plenty of Positive Role Models

If a parent wants to find celebrities who are positive role models, they are out there in abundance. One of my favorites is Mike Schmidt of the Philadelphia Phillies: "I could be a drinker and a hell-raiser," he says, "but it's important to me that I'm not. I won't go places where you'll see me talking with a bunch of women. I think of it this way: if a kid has a Mike Schmidt poster in his bedroom, I'd want his parents to be happy about it."

One of my favorite role models for young girls is professional basketball star, Jennifer Azzi. Maybe it's because she grew up in our neighboring town of Oak Ridge, Tennessee. Women's basketball is big in this part of the country thanks to the sterling influence of Pat Head Summitt and her four-time national champion Lady Vols. Jennifer, though, escaped from Big Orange country and subsequently led Stanford University to the national title in 1990. She has played professionally in Italy, France, and Sweden and is now a star in the WNBA. But she also played for Athletes in Action, a Christian team that plays exhibitions and shares its faith. Jennifer realizes she's a role model: "I read in a daily devotional about how you never know when little kids' eyes are on you. They're going to try and follow a lot of things you do. That's a role that I gladly accept. God has really blessed me."[7]

People are people, and that includes athletes, Hollywood stars, and politicians. For every spoiled star who believes he or she is accountable to no one, there are many others who live positive, responsible lives. The most important truth about role models is that they can only influence in a vacuum. A kid who is surrounded with love and positive values will be able to sift the wheat from the chaff.

CHAPTER 18

The Media

Influence comes from many quarters. I have long been of the opinion that America's most important export is its entertainment media. American values (or lack thereof) have been exported to countries all over the world, sometimes with devastating influence on personal and social mores. No wonder fundamentalist Moslem nations look at us as the Great Satan—the culture clash is astounding.

Now to be fair, much of the media's influence has been positive. How do you keep oppressing women when you see women who have rights and live freely modeled in movies and television programs? The flip side, however, is that the media is as likely to exploit women as it is to exalt them as human beings. So, are our media moguls saints or sinners? The truth is that they are both. It is not my purpose to bash the entertainment media, but to merely point out that they play a special role in influencing society. For example, I am very concerned about the message of violence that many of our motion pictures project.

I will never forget being in a Central American country back in the early seventies when racial tensions were at a fever pitch. Most of the audience was comprised of young black men. We were watching a very violent American movie. Tension in the theater was almost palpable. Between showings of the movie, a speaker addressed the audience. He began by raising his fist in a "black power" salute. I became uneasy, suddenly conscious of being one of the few whites in a theater. I wondered if the violence of the movie might spill over into the real world situation of the audience's growing awareness of their disadvantaged position. I realize now that this was probably a subtle form of racism on my part. As it turned out, I had nothing to fear. The men in the audience seemed to hold no ill will toward me. Still, I will never forget how uncomfortable I felt. In my mind, at least, the movie was graphic enough to provoke violence in the viewers. And I wonder if our entertainment media have not increased the likelihood of violence in areas of the world where the movie theater is still the primary source of community entertainment.

Movies do influence around the world and in our country as well. Examples abound.

Clark Gable took off his shirt in the comedy, *It Happened One Night*, revealing a bare chest underneath, which caused undershirt sales in this country to plummet overnight. Years later, the motion picture *Coma* featured a hospital where patients were murdered so their organs could be harvested and sold. The following year organ donations dropped a reported sixty percent in United States hospitals.

Movies influence people. That can be scary, but it can be also a source of encouragement. Hollywood will always exploit. For some producers, movies are simply a way of making money. They have no scruples about the damage they may be doing to society through unhealthy portrayals of persons and situations.

However, not everything Hollywood produces is exploitative. Just when I am ready to throw up my hands in despair over the irresponsible fare that the sultans of celluloid produce, along comes a project like Steven Spielberg's *Shindler's List* to remind us that Hollywood can have a positive influence. This stirring movie about Oscar Schindler and his courageous act of rescuing Jews from Hitler's death camps vividly portrays what can happen when evil is allowed to run unbridled. It also reminds us of the good that can happen when one person takes a stand.

I am a Spielberg fan, by the way. Who can forget the sensitive and moving account he gave of the tragedy of slavery in his film, *Amistad*? Hollywood has its share of saints and its disproportionate share of sinners. But, quite obviously, movies do influence. So does television, which plays a major role in our lives. My children learned to read and do math at an early age with the help of *Sesame Street* and *The Electric Company*. Television, like motion pictures, has a wonderful ability to inform, enlighten, and inspire.

Take a young man named Archie McNealy as a good example. If life were like baseball, and we were each allotted only three strikes against us, Archie McNealy would have been off the team at birth. He was born into a very poor family. His mother abandoned the family soon after Archie's birth. His dad, a local drug dealer, died when Archie was in his teens. No one in his family had ever finished high school. But from a young age, Archie pushed himself to excel. He is currently a business major at Florida A & M University. He credits family members with inspiring him in many ways. But Archie claims his desire to attend college came from watching *The Cosby Show*, the 1980s sitcom that featured a close-knit, upper-class, African-American family. The children on *The Cosby Show* were all expected to attend college. Archie took that family as his role model as he worked his way through school. If Bill Cosby knows about Archie, surely he is pleased.[1]

Or consider what has happened in Brazil. Soap operas, or *telenovelas*, have apparently brought down the country's birth rate—something the country's family planners had been unable to achieve. Researchers believe that the "subliminal message" delivered constantly during the day via the *telenovelas,* that a small nuclear family is good, has made large families socially unacceptable. [2]

In case you don't think that television impacts your kids, just stop and reflect on how MTV, the rock music network, has changed everything our kids think about sex, violence, and the meaning of life. Sociologist Tony Campolo said that when some colleagues in his field asked one of the top executives of MTV how much influence his network had on teenagers, he answered, "We don't influence teenagers! We own them!"

Does television influence? Why do companies spend billions on advertising if not to influence us? Want a concrete measurable example of the power of television to influence? There is a study that indicates that for each hour of television we watch in a week, we are apt to spend an additional two hundred and eight dollars annually. According to this study, sitting in front of the television five hours a week will raise your yearly spending by about one thousand dollars. Just watching *Who Wants to Be a Millionaire* can set you back a few hundred bucks. Quit watching the tube altogether, and you might yet be a millionaire. Does television influence? Of course it does.[3]

There is a silly story of a market research interviewer who was stopping people in the grocery store after they picked up their bread.

One fellow picked up a loaf of Wonder Bread, and the interviewer asked him, "Sir, would you be willing to answer a couple of questions about your choice of bread?"

The man responded, "Yes, I'd be happy to."

"Fine," the interviewer said, "the question I'd like to ask you is this: Do you feel that your choice of Wonder Bread has been at all influenced by their advertising program?"

The fellow looked shocked and said, "Of course not."

"Well then," said the interviewer, "could you tell me just why you did choose Wonder Bread?"

"Of course I can!" the man replied. "Because it builds strong bodies twelve ways!"

Television influences. That is a scary thought when you consider how much television the average child absorbs by the time he or she leaves high school. Young impressionable minds cannot help but be adversely affected by some of the more exploitative material on television. And p-u-l-l-e-a-s-e do not hide behind the widely accepted mantra that parents should be responsible for the shows children watch. The children most at risk are children who do not have responsible parents. I have to tell you (and it's only happened a few times) I have yet to be in the home of a family in the lower socio-economic bracket that did not receive HBO or some other premium channel. And my observation is that even very young children are being exposed on a daily basis to the crude, dehumanizing fare offered by such media outlets.

A study of viewing habits in Connecticut[4] showed that despite the overwhelming view in that state that parents, not the government, should control what their children see on television in terms of sexual content and violence, few parents make the effort. Researchers found that barely half of the children under eighteen had any time restrictions on viewing, and almost two-thirds had no content restrictions.

Leave it to parents? I wish we could. But people in the entertainment field are going to have to be won as well. Media moguls need to remind themselves of their responsibility to the greater good. Many of these people are highly indignant when confronted with corporations that pollute our physical environment. There is a moral environment in society that is as real as the physical one, and perhaps even more important. People in the entertainment business have a choice to make: whether they are going to be part of the problem or part of the solution.

It is hard to believe now, but when the play *Peter Pan* first premiered in London in 1904, the author, Sir James Barrie, began to hear from parents upset with the play.[5] In the original version of the drama, Peter Pan told the Darling children that if they believed strongly enough that they could fly. Apparently, many children took Peter's word literally and hurt themselves attempting to fly. Without hesitation, Barrie altered the script. Peter would still tell the children that they could fly, but only if they had first been sprinkled with "fairy dust." Since most stores did not carry fairy dust on their shelves, children no longer injured themselves.

Do you mean a mere play could have such influence on children? Even more importantly, would a writer, actor, or producer change a script out of concern for its effects? Maybe Hollywood and New York need to be reminded of Sir James Barrie's example.

Of course, as we have already noted, not all of television's influence is detrimental. Television has great power to sensitize us (as well as desensitize us) to evils in our society. It has the power to replace destructive images in our brain with wholesome, productive images. Used responsibly, television has great power to build a better society.

Movies influence. Television programs influence. It will be interesting to see what sociologists a century from now will say about the impact of the media on our culture. To a certain extent, this has been not only the information age, but also the media age. We have never had a generation as bombarded with influences over the airwaves as the current generation. Has it made us a better people, or has it robbed us of some the values that make life worth living?

And we dare not ignore the influence of the print media—magazines, newspapers, and, of course, books. By choosing to read this published work, you have chosen to open yourself to the possibility of change via the printed page.

Is the printed page powerful? For one hundred years, there was a book that influenced American life, and it had nothing in it but advertisements. It was the Sears Roebuck catalogue. Sears sent catalogues to troops during World War I to "remind them of what they were fighting for." The catalogues were even smuggled into the Soviet Union during the Cold War to demonstrate the affluence of the United States. And in this country the Sears catalogue caused poor boys and girls to dream great dreams. Imagine that, though—influence flowing from a book filled with nothing but advertisements. Books have enormous power to impact lives.

Time magazine was granted an interview with Tim McVeigh's father and sister.[6] After the interview, they were befuddled how Timothy McVeigh, coming from this background could have become the monster that he appears to be. One possible answer is that McVeigh became obsessed with a book: *The Turner Diaries* by Andrew McDonald. Never underestimate the power of the written word.

Og Mandino's Story

Og Mandino was one of the most gracious men I've ever met, and he was a great storyteller. His book, *The Greatest Salesman in the World,* has sold fourteen million copies and is still selling one hundred thousand copies every month. Many of his other books have also sold in the millions. But Og Mandino wasn't always a success.

For two long years, Mandino was a derelict, an alcoholic, and in his own words, a bum. He lost his job, his home, his wife, and his little girl. At one point he passed a pawn shop and saw a gun in the window for sale for twenty-nine dollars. He had thirty dollars in his pocket. He said he was sorely tempted to buy that gun and end it all, but he did not have the courage.

It was at this point that he wandered into a library. He found himself in a section containing so-called success books—books by such people as W. Clement Stone and Norman Vincent Peale. He sat down and began to read, and what he read there changed his life! Og Mandino owed his success to persons he had never met—except through their books.[7] Nonetheless, their influence changed his life. But the story does not stop with Og Mandino.

Drew Carey's Story

Although actor and comedian Drew Carey now gets the last laugh, there was nothing funny about his life before stardom. Carey was only eight when his father died, and a year later he was molested. As a college student at Kent State, he attempted suicide one night at a fraternity party. He returned to school, but earned such poor grades that after five years he left without a degree. After drifting across the country and attempting suicide again, he began reading self-help books in order to find a purpose for his life.[8] Among these was—get this—Og Mandino's *University of Success*. Reading these volumes, he says, helped turn him around. You didn't know there are traces of the NPPD of influence all over most of the books you and I read, did you?

The printed word does not have to be perfect bound, of course, to influence. Arnold Schwarzenegger found his role model, Reg Park, in a bodybuilding magazine.[9] Park was the most powerful person in bodybuilding at that time, and Arnold dreamed of having huge muscles like his. Arnold learned everything he could about Park—his training routine, diet, and lifestyle and put what he learned to good use. Movies influence. Television influences. Books and magazines influence.

Indeed, our world is alive with the power of influence, both direct and indirect. The question we want to address is, how do we go about leveraging the influence we have so that the world is made better because we have lived? The rest of this book is devoted to ten steps that will prompt us to impact life in our homes, at our jobs, and potentially in the world community as a whole.

CHAPTER 19

Step 1: The First Person You Influence

I have four beautiful daughters for whom I'm exceedingly thankful. But living with five females is not without its challenges. Our cabinets are filled with coffee mugs that have slogans such as: "Whatever a woman does, she must do it twice as well as a man to be considered half as good." Then in bold letters it says, "Luckily, this is not difficult."

My daughters are grown now, which saddens me in some ways. But the good news is that they are much finer people than I deserve to have as daughters—which reflects the influence of their mother, who is a person of character. All are engaged in some way in making a difference in the world. As already noted, our youngest daughter helps resettle refugees. Our oldest daughter is a teacher. She and her husband drive into downtown Chattanooga, Tennessee each week to be involved in an inner city ministry where their daughter, Rachel, can experience an interracial atmosphere. One daughter is married to a minister and does religious writing. And one daughter is a hotshot MBA working in corporate life. We are embarrassed about her. Just kidding. We are just as proud of her as we are her sisters, but I need to tell you her story.

A few years ago, I became convinced that Deborah, our second daughter—a bright, beautiful girl—was suffering from anorexia nervosa. About this same time singer Karen Carpenter died from this terrible affliction.

Few diseases in the world are more demonic than anorexia. Generally it affects girls who are high achievers or perfectionists. The disease affects their perceptions of themselves. They become obsessed with their bodies and particularly with the idea that they are overweight.

Now that's not too unusual in our culture. Many of us become obsessed at some time or another with our weight. But girls with anorexia have their perceptions totally distorted. They become convinced they are overweight even when they are not, and there is nothing you can do to change that perception. Some of them will literally starve themselves to death in order to look thinner. For a parent there can be no greater hell. You show your daughter a picture of herself looking like an Ethiopian starvation victim, only to hear her say, "I think I'm too fat."

I can't tell you how many sleepless, terror-filled nights I spent watching my beautiful eighteen year-old daughter grow slimmer and slimmer until her rib cage protruded. I would talk and talk with her, but it did no good. She not only developed bizarre eating habits but exercise habits as well. She would spend hours each day on an exercise bike. Every night I would kneel beside my bed and pray, "Please God, help me reach her before it's too late."

Finally, we went for family counseling. We told the therapist about Deborah's situation. He didn't seem concerned in the least. "Oh, my son is into exercise in a big way, too," he said. "He lifts weights." I wanted to grab him and shake him and say, "You dummy. Look at her. She's skin and bones." Fortunately I didn't, but that's how I felt. But going to a counselor was a good move. We confronted some issues that needed to be confronted.

Three days after our counseling session came the most important night in my life, thus far. I was sitting in the living room of my mother-in-law's house. We were having an evening meal there. Deborah came through the living room, stopped for a moment, looked in a mirror, and said something that I simply could not believe. They were words that melted my heart. "I think," she said, "I'm losing too much weight." I went home that night and wept like a baby. I knew that anorexia's grip had loosened itself from her life.

Deborah is doing great now. She went on to graduate from college magna cum laude. Then she earned her MBA, and has worked several years in management positions in large corporations. And beyond her work credentials she is making a difference. While working for Saturn Corporation, she was publicity chairperson for her county's United Way campaign.

Her eating habits and exercise habits still seem a little extreme to me (I'm one of these people who thinks that if God meant for us to touch our toes, He would have put them farther up on our bodies). But she has more energy than anyone I've ever known. Still, that experience convinced me of the futility of trying to directly influence those closest to us. As Jacob M. Braude once said, "Consider how hard it is to change yourself and you'll understand what little chance you have in trying to change others."

There is an old joke about a nervous bride seeking counsel from her pastor prior to her wedding. "Relax," said the pastor, "You'll do just fine if you follow a few simple rules. First, as you come into the sanctuary, ignore the crowd. Keep your eyes down and focus only on the aisle down which you will be walking.

"After you've begun walking, raise your eyes a little in the direction of the beautiful altar of our church. You've been a member of our church for many years and seen it many times. As you near the altar, raise your eyes a little more until they make contact with the eyes of this young man you love so much and whom you intend to wed. Can you remember that? First the aisle, then the altar, then him?"

The bride thought she could follow that progression. So the day of the wedding arrived, and the bride looked beautiful and poised as she began her journey toward the front of the church. Still, it was disconcerting to guests to hear her muttering under her breath, "Aisle . . .altar . . . him. Aisle . . . altar . . . him."

Most brides learn to their sad dismay that very few males "alter" after the vows are said.

Three Options: One Solution

What do you do if you are in an unhappy situation, be it an unhappy marriage or an unhappy job? There are three possible options.

Option One: Change the Situation

For example, you could get a divorce, quit your job, move to a different part of the country, even change your name, make a clean break with your past, start completely over. This option is always the easiest, one that many people will choose. It's always easier to change jobs than to change ourselves. For some people it's easier to change spouses than to change themselves.

I was amused to read about a man named John Micofsky who felt confident his life would be greatly improved once he was rid of his wife. His dream came true on January 20, 1993, when his divorce from Maryann was finalized. Unfortunately for John, this was not the end of the story. On January 21, Maryann claimed the $10.2 million jackpot in the New Jersey Pick-6 Lottery. When the press asked about John Micofsky's condition, his attorney replied, "Very upset, I think that's the word I would use."[1]

Upset, indeed! That is the route many of us take, however. We change jobs, we change spouses, *yet often the problems remain*. Why? Because we take our problems with us to the next spouse or the next job. But that is the first option—change the situation.

Option Two: Change the Other Person

This is what many people would like to do—alter their spouse, alter their teen-aged children, alter their boss, etc. But usually we are spectacularly unsuccessful when we try to change someone else. I read recently what I believe to be an amazing insight into one of the most intractable problems in marriage: *women expect men to change and they don't and men expect women to stay the same and they don't.* Wow! Somebody could write a book about that!

I have counseled women whose husbands have had problems with alcohol abuse. Often I've had to say to them, "Look, you are not changing him. You're only driving him deeper into his shell." It's very difficult to intentionally change the behavior of a spouse, especially one with a chemical-abuse problem.

It is equally difficult to influence the behavior of one of your offspring, especially after they have entered the teen years. In fact, something demonic often happens when we try to exert influence directly on teenagers. They respond exactly opposite from what we intended. Nothing demonstrates this difficulty more graphically than a phenomenon that psychologist Robert Cialdini tells about called the "Romeo and Juliet Effect," named for the young lovers in Shakespeare's drama who committed suicide because their love was doomed by a feud between their families. Their parents' abhorrence toward their union seemed only to fuel the fire of their romance. That's not unusual, according to Cialdini.[2]

Cialdini cites the work of researchers who studied the relationships of one hundred and forty Colorado couples. The researchers found that couples whose parents object to their relationship viewed one another more critically. However, when parents tried to interfere, it caused the pair to feel greater love and to become more—not less—determined to marry. As parental interference intensified so did the love experience; and when the interference weakened, romantic feelings actually cooled.

What's a Parent to Do?

Implications of the Romeo and Juliet Effect are horrifying to a parent caught in this trying situation. The parent sees danger in a relationship and tries to intervene, but instead of helping actually makes the situation worse. This same phenomenon can be seen in youth involved in cults or gangs. When the parent brings up objections, the young person begins rationalizing the commitment that he/she has made to the group. The very fact of providing a rationalization gives the young person an even greater emotional investment in the stand he/she has taken. This, in turn, leads to a hardening of attitude that makes it very difficult for them to back away.

The best advice I can give to parents of teens is, *don't overreact.* When parents react too strenuously, they usually do more harm than good. I've seen parents become so emotionally overwrought in dealing with a young person's problems that they forever damage their ability to relate to that young person.

Having said that, I confess my wife and I have never had to deal with some of the problems that many parents face, problems with drugs, sex, violence, depression, peer pressure, even attempted suicides. I don't mean to stick my head in the sand. Teenagers can do some dumb things. And the loving parent in today's world will be forever diligent. Still, it's very difficult to change the behavior of any other person, especially those closest to you.

By the way, what is true of teens is also true of adults. By forcing a person to defend a position, we actually strengthen their commitment to that position. One of my favorite nonfiction books is by a British sales expert named Geoff Burch. It is titled *The Art and Science of Business Persuasion.* In his book, Burch suggests we test this hypothesis by finding a friend who is truly politically committed, and going up to him and saying: "Hello, friend, I am going to change your political view," and then proceed to challenge and belittle his beliefs.[3]

After a little while, says Burch, we will have changed his political views. He will be even more committed to his point-of-view. Without even realizing it, we will have moved him in exactly the opposite direction that we desired. Whenever you make the other party work out self-justification, you run the risk of strengthening his or her attachment to an oftentimes indefensible position.

If you are going to try to argue a young person out of a position, be sure to give a balanced presentation. A study of teens and steroids at Oregon Health Sciences University showed that teenagers are much more inclined to take warnings about steroids seriously if the drugs' muscle-building benefits are acknowledged in the same presentation. Doctors lecturing high school football teams on steroids' effects found that those who heard a balanced presentation were fifty percent more likely to believe that the drugs could harm their health than those who were told just of the dangers.[4]

Sometimes a cool head is the best ally we have in trying to influence a specific person in a specific situation—especially a young person. This said, however, we need to return to our basic thesis: It is very difficult to directly and deliberately influence anyone else.

Option Three: Influence Yourself

We have seen that our first option, altering the situation, often fails to solve the problem. Our second option, trying to alter another person, may actually make the problem worse. The third option, to change ourselves, is the most difficult of the three. However, it is usually the most fruitful. Principle number one of the Law of Influence is that the first person you influence is yourself. Actor and director Rob Reiner put it perfectly: "Everybody talks about wanting to change things and help and fix," says Reiner, "but ultimately all you can do is fix yourself. And that's a lot. Because if you can fix yourself," Reiner adds, "*it has a ripple effect.*" (Italics mine).[6]

I couldn't have said it better, and it's true. Mahatma Gandhi said it this way: "You must be the change you wish to see in the world." To a disciple who was forever complaining about others, a Zen master said, "If it is peace you want, seek to change yourself, not other people. It is easier to protect your feet with slippers than to carpet the whole of the earth."

The following words were written on the tomb of an Anglican Bishop in the Crypts of Westminster Abbey:

> When I was young and free and my imagination had no limits, I dreamed of changing the world. As I grew older and wiser, I discovered the world would not change, so I shortened my sights somewhat and decided to change only my country.
>
> But it, too, seemed immovable.
>
> As I grew into my twilight years, in one last desperate attempt, I settled for changing only my family, those closest to me, but alas, they would have none of it.
>
> And now as I lie on my deathbed, I suddenly realize: If I had only changed myself first, then by example I would have changed my family.
>
> From their inspiration and encouragement, I would then have been able to better my country and, who knows, I may have even changed the world.

Here is where we discover the most promise. If we can change ourselves, we have a better chance of changing those around us.

A reader wrote to the *Ask Marilyn* column[5] with this provocative question:

"In what order of strength would you rank the following four influences on the outcome of our lives: environment, self-determination, genetics, and luck?" Marilyn Von Savant is reputedly one of the brightest people in the world. You might be surprised by her answer. She ranked genetics as the most important influence on our lives; your genes determine whether you are a human being or a bamboo tree. Environment ranks second in importance; a childhood spent on a farm in Kansas is worlds removed from a childhood spent in the slums of Calcutta. Marilyn chose luck as the next important factor in our lives; wars, social revolutions, technological changes—all these things combine to influence individuals and society. Last in importance, according to Marilyn, is self-determination. As she writes, "I believe we can influence far more in our lives than many people think, but far less than the rest of them wish." This is an interesting concept. We obviously cannot do anything about our genes. We can do a little about our luck (more about that later). But there indeed may be something we can do about our environment.

Creating New Environments

"We are the product of two forces in our lives—our heredity and our environment." I first heard that truism stated when I was at the University of Tennessee majoring in psychology thirty-five years ago. What a pessimistic doctrine, I thought. That gloomy theologian, John Calvin, was right. We are predestined, predetermined, mere robots, guided by all the past influences that have been brought to bear on us.

Then it occurred to me that each of us is continually creating a new environment for ourselves. Every time we pick up a book to read, watch a show on TV, or talk to a friend, we are creating a new environment. So you see, we are not helpless victims. We can and do choose many sources of influence in our lives. Emerson once said, " A man is known by the books he reads, by the company he keeps, by the praise he gives . . ." What books are you reading? Or, if most of your information comes from movies or television, what are you learning from them? I am amazed at how many people reach the middle years of life and quit growing intellectually, psychologically, and socially. They apparently reached a plateau when they left high school; they have the same opinions, values, and outlook they had thirty years ago. By failing to influence themselves in ways that could have helped them grow, they've missed out on a lot of life. How sad! In today's fast-changing and competitive world, the only job security we have consists of the people we know and the information we acquire.

The Reverend William Byron, S. J., president of the Catholic University of America, asks students a key question, "Which is more important to you, your credit card or your library card?" If the future is important to you, you will value the latter.

I love to go to seminars in spite of the fact (or because of the fact) that I speak and lead seminars myself. Reading makes a big difference in my life, but there is something about being in the presence of an energized and motivated presenter who has done his or her research and has a well-thought out presentation that makes information come alive for me. Such experiences advance my consciousness immeasurably. Maybe hearing a great speaker energizes you, too. The medium by which growth occurs is irrelevant; some of us will receive more from books, others from tapes, and still others from live presentations. The point is to keep growing.

Psychologists estimate that not even one person in a million lives up to the best that is in him/her. Are you making the most of your inner resources? What is it that holds you back? Fear? Complacency? When you ride the bus or stand in a crowded elevator, look into the faces of the people around you and try to imagine what life would be like if all these people should suddenly awake and become their best possible selves. Then, look in a mirror and reflect on this same thing. Can you imagine what your life would be like if you could realize your full potential?

If you want to change your life, change your family, change your world, you must begin by creating for yourself a positive environment conducive to that change. Ask yourself these critical questions:

•What am I reading?

•What visual and aural information am I taking in through media?

•What kind of physical environment do I need to be most effective? What can I do to my current physical environment to help me feel better and produce more?

•What kind of people am I around? Are they people who can help me go where I want to go, or are they people who discourage me?

Running with the Right Crowd

Casey Stengel, the successful manager of the New York Yankees, once gave Billy Martin some advice on managing a baseball team. Casey said there would be fifteen players on your team who will run through a wall for you, five who will hate you, and five who are undecided.

Then Stengel added: "When you make out your rooming list, always room your losers together. Never room a good guy with a loser. Those losers who stay together will blame the manager for everything but it won't spread if you keep them isolated."

Stengel was right. It is very difficult not to be affected by the people around us. Most of us are like tornadoes. Tornadoes turn black when they suck up topsoil, red when they suck up clay, and white when they suck up water droplets. We're no different. We take on the psychological color of the people close to us. That's why we need to put ourselves into the company of people who lift us up rather than put us down. We need to be around people who inspire us, not around those who encourage us just to get by.

This is particularly true of young people. A study of twenty thousand high school teens has concluded that the number one determinant of classroom performance is the peers with whom teens associate. According to the study, teens with "academically oriented" friends did better than kids who hung out with more delinquent types.[7] Researchers weren't sure which came first: do like-minded kids flock together, or does the flock make the kids like-minded? After holding a variety of factors constant, the authors concluded that "at least by high school, the influence of friends on school performance and drug use is more substantial than the influence of parents."

Such results are hardly surprising. We are the products of our environment. Therefore, it is critical that we choose positive, uplifting people to share our environment.

The Last Words of a Redneck

"What are a redneck's famous last words?" asks redneck expert Jeff Foxworthy. "Simple," he says. His last words are, "Y'all watch this!"[8] How many times have you said to your teenager, "Anyone who gets you in trouble is not your friend"? The kind of people we choose to be around will affect the quality of our lives.

In his book *Winning with People,* Michael G. Zey tells about a woman who grew up in Great Neck, Long Island, an affluent community populated by executives, doctors, and lawyers.[9] This woman described what Zey calls an "invisible but potent 'community standard' of excellence." "There is no one in Great Neck who doesn't do something important," said this woman. "Just to keep up with them, I went for a Ph.D." It helps if you choose the right kind of people to be around.

An outstanding example of this truth is found in a cassette presentation on teenage girls, *Reviving Ophelia* by Dr. Mary Pipher. Dr. Pipher tells of a special interview with a seventeen year-old girl named Caroline. Caroline had a rough home life, and her father was an abusive alcoholic. Moreover, her mother was too overwhelmed to provide much guidance. In spite of these problems, Caroline was an intelligent, responsible young woman. She explained that her self-esteem and positive attitude came from the kind, caring teachers at her school. But Caroline's greatest asset was a classmate named Sandra. Sandra was also a high-achieving student who came from an alcoholic home. Caroline and Sandra promised each other that they would not get pregnant or use drugs like other kids from their neighborhood. They spent hours at the library studying together, or dreaming about their future careers and families. These two girls encouraged one another to overcome the negative forces in their lives.

Everybody needs a friend like Sandra, someone to lift us up and not let us down.

Our Internal Environment

Our external environment is only one part of the story. Part of the environment we can choose for ourselves in any given situation is the one we produce internally. That is, we can adjust our internal environment. We can adjust our attitudes, prejudices, and emotional reactions. This is the fourth area Marilyn Von Savant referred to: self-determination.

I understand that Dustin Hoffman, after playing his part as the autistic character in *Rain Man,* took months to begin thinking in a normal fashion again. He had played the part so well that he essentially *became* the part. He had used the power of his mind to train himself into believing he was someone he was not.

The human brain is an amazing mechanism. To a certain extent, we can fool it into believing all kinds of things. This is the power of positive self-talk. If I tell myself daily, "I am a winner, I am confident, I am positive in all things, etc."—and if I act in accordance with the self-talk I am giving myself, I can become the kind of person I long to be. What can be better than that? *We can influence ourselves.*

Who Are You Trying to Impress?

We might begin by asking ourselves who we are trying to impress. Sometimes "who are we trying to impress?" is more important than "who are we trying to influence?"

In his book *Ambition,* Gilbert Brin tells about writer Roger Simon's research for his article "Winners, Losers—Each a Miss America."[10] Simon went to interview the 1976 Miss Wisconsin finalists during the final step before Atlantic City. The reactions of the young women who were finalists were interesting; the eight losers ran offstage and were led to a room where they could watch the victor on television. They were still in their evening gowns. "I just feel bad for my town," one said. "I feel I let them down; I feel I let all the people down." Another said, "I don't know how I will face the people who came here to see me; I am dreading the moment." These young women's experience of failure was colored by the expectations of significant people in their lives. If we can fail in private, failure might be acceptable. Unfortunately, that is rarely the case.

Who are you trying to impress? This is a question I often ask of pastors in seminars I lead on platform skills. I am convinced that many pastors are still trying to impress their old professor of Homiletics (Preaching) in seminary rather than the people who sit in front of them each week. But it is true of all of us. We carry around in our brains pictures of persons whose opinions really matter to us. Some of these people may have been dead for many years, but subconsciously we are still seeking their approval. It's time to take off the shackles that some of our experiences have clamped on us and to focus on the people who need us here and now. The time to begin is today.

In his early twenties, the influential psychologist William James fought relentlessly with severe bouts of depression. Unless you have battled clinical depression yourself, or watched someone you love battle it, you cannot know how debilitating it can be. By the age of twenty-five, James had contemplated suicide. Part of the problem was that he could not resist comparing his own lack of accomplishments to those of his very successful brother Henry. However, rather than giving up and giving in to his despair, he decided to challenge himself for thirty days, "to act as if what I do makes a difference." With that simple commitment, he created a totally new kind of life. William James became one of America's best-known psychologists and philosophers. Toward the end of his life, James offered this advice: "To change one's life: start immediately, Do it flamboyantly, no exceptions, no excuses."

We can change our lives by altering our internal environment. Now, you may be thinking to yourself that's not as easy as it sounds. It isn't, especially when you consider how much garbage—negative, destructive messages—we have accumulated. I must confess that I struggle with my own internal environment every day of my life. One reason I have dedicated my life to helping people feel good about themselves is that there is a part of me that is constantly whispering in my ear, "You can't do it. Give it up. You'll never make it. Loser, loser, loser." Usually I hear this voice when I am fatigued or when I have been disappointed. I have learned to talk back, but still the voice returns and through the years it has kept me from many of life's satisfactions.

Actress Michelle Pfeiffer, one of the most beautiful women in Hollywood, confesses that she was teased about her appearance throughout her childhood. She never really developed any confidence in her looks. In high school, Pfeiffer aspired to be like Linda, a classmate who was always poised, confident, and lovely. Years later, when Pfeiffer saw Linda at a wedding she felt those old feelings of inferiority return: "I felt my back hunch over," she says, "my hair felt greasy. It all came back." Michelle Pfeiffer claims that she wants to instill "Linda confidence" in her young daughter.[11]

Imagine that. One of Hollywood's most beautiful women feels her back hunch over and her hair grow greasy in the presence of a high school acquaintance.

Most of our problems really are within the confines of our own brains. If we could just tell ourselves in a convincing way that we are worthy, we are acceptable, we really could turn our lives around. Is that important to our influence on others? Remember, negative influence exudes from those who feel rotten about themselves. As speaker John Maxwell expresses it, "Hurting people hurt people." To exercise positive influence, we begin with a healthy image of ourselves.

CHAPTER 20

Step 2: Believe in Yourself

Dr. Sidney B. Simon wrote a powerful allegory called *The IALAC Story*. It is about a boy who wore an invisible sign around his neck that said IALAC. The letters stood for "I am Loveable and Capable." Pieces of the sign would be torn off whenever the young fellow had conflicts with his parents, peers, teachers, and even himself. Every time he lost a portion of his self-esteem, another part of the sign was ripped off.[1]

Can you identify with that young boy? Have pieces of your IALAC sign been torn away? Before you or I can make a difference in the world, we need to do a painful self-examination. Do we believe that we are truly worthy of making a difference in the world? If we cannot give a positive answer to that question, we will probably never achieve the measure of influence with others that we desire.

How we feel about ourselves colors every part of our lives.

How we feel about ourselves determines the kind of person we marry. A woman is on her second alcoholic, abusive husband. Why do some people seem to attract losers? It has something to do with the way they see themselves, doesn't it?

How we feel about ourselves determines what kind of job we have. According to psychological studies, people who feel good about themselves tend to get better paying jobs, especially if employment is based on a personal interview. People who feel good about themselves exude confidence when they walk into a room, and this favorably impresses the interviewer. An interviewee who seems confident in himself or herself will automatically seem more competent to the interviewer than someone who obviously lacks confidence. The interviewer will more likely be inclined to hire the person who ranks high in self-esteem because she knows that he will probably get along with the other members of the staff better and will have fewer problems with tardiness or excessive sick leave.

Once we have a job, how we feel about ourselves determines how well we perform in that job. Some years back there was a Peanuts cartoon that showed Charlie Brown working on a wood shop project. Lucy came by and asked, "How's the birdhouse coming along, Charlie Brown?" He replied, "Well, I'm a lousy carpenter. I can't nail straight, I can't saw straight, and I always split the wood. I'm nervous, I lack confidence, I'm stupid, I have poor taste and absolutely no sense of design." And then in the last frame he concluded, "So, all things considered, it's coming along okay."

Once a confident person obtains that better paying position, he or she is more likely than someone with low self-esteem to be successful in performing that job. Henry Ford was absolutely right when he said, "Whether you think you can or think you can't, you are probably right."

How we feel about ourselves affects how well we are paid. You say, sure, because you have a better job. Or you may say, sure, people with high self-esteem produce more and thus they are rewarded more. Those things are true, of course, but more than that is involved. When you have high self-esteem, you put higher value on your services. There are some people who, if they were allowed to set their own salary, would set it lower than their boss would.

The newspapers carried an interesting story sometime back about professional basketball player Nat "Sweetwater" Clifton, who starred with the New York Knicks and Detroit Pistons in the 1950s. This was just before the salary explosion made millionaires out of even moderately talented players. Clifton's starting salary with the Knicks was two thousand dollars a year. Like all players in those days, he did his own negotiating— and never made more thanseventy-five hundred dollars a year. After his pro basketball days, Sweetwater Clifton took a job driving a cab in Chicago. He got other offers of employment, but refused them because he wanted to stay near his invalid mother.

Looking back on his basketball career, he regrets that he never made much money. He doesn't hold it against the owners, though. He says, "The guys I negotiated with were nice guys. They gave me whatever I asked for. I just didn't ask for enough." Can you relate to that? If you don't value your work, how can you expect anybody else to?

How we feel about ourselves affects how healthy we are. People with high self-esteem are healthier than those with low self-esteem. Their positive attitudes actually help them live longer and have fewer accidents. The reasons for this are numerous.

For one thing, people with high self-esteem feel guilty less often than people with low self-esteem. Guilt is one of the major causes of depression, sleeplessness, high blood pressure, and asthma, so people with high self-esteem are not as prone to those ailments.

Another reason why people with high self-esteem are healthier is that they are much less likely to engage in self-destructive behavior. They don't feel the need to turn to chemical substances like drugs or alcohol for stimulation, and they don't have to take stupid risks to impress people. They are comfortable with themselves and their lives, and their good health and longevity are a reflection of their mental attitude toward themselves. As if that were not enough, there is accumulating evidence that, physically, our general attitude affects our ability to ward off disease. So people with high self-esteem are sick less.

How we feel about ourselves affects the quality of our personal relationships. The Bible tells us to love our neighbor as we love ourselves. We cannot love anyone if we do not ourselves feel worthy of being loved. Loving oneself is not narcissism; it is a healthy appreciation of our value as children of God.

How we feel about ourselves affects how often we are depressed. Depression and low self-esteem are forever intertwined. It has to do with the self-talk that we continually engage in. For example, a certain young woman was rejected by a young man. Instead of shrugging it off, here is what she told herself, "I couldn't go through this again. It's all over for me. Nobody will ever love me. Even when I do everything I can to make a man love me, he leaves me. I'm the worst. The lowest."

Ever hear of the self-fulfilling prophecy? What is this young woman doing to herself?

If you have devalued yourself, your situation, and your future prospects, what alternative is left but a major downer? Depression is regarded as America's number one major untreated illness, by the way. There is something about modern life that tears away at our IALACs. For example, a study reported in *Psychology Today* pointed out that the average thirty year-old American is ten times more likely to be depressed than his grandfather.

How we feel about ourselves affects how we handle decisions. "Next year I'm going to be a changed person!" Charlie Brown tells Lucy in another *Peanuts* cartoon.

"That's a laugh, Charlie Brown!" she says.

"I mean it!" he replies. "I'm going to be strong and firm!"

"Forget it," she says as she walks off. "You'll always be wishy-washy!"

"Why can't I change just a little bit?" Charlie Brown asks himself. "I'll be wishy one day," he shouts, "and washy the next!"

Do you hate to make decisions? Chances are you need to work on your feelings of self-worth.

How we feel about ourselves affects how we feel about our bodies. There is a notorious difference between the way men view their bodies and women view theirs. *People* magazine regularly publishes an issue on the fifty most beautiful people in the world. If a man saw that issue, he would probably look to see if his name was spelled correctly. That's typical of men, isn't it? Big belly, bald as an ostrich egg, ugly as sin, and a man will still think he's God's gift to women. But a woman is different.

It is interesting how women who made *People's* fifty most beautiful people list a few years back devalued their looks. Actress Jaclyn Smith complained that she had "skinny bowlegs." Singer Jody Watley felt it important to point out that her bottom teeth are crooked. And actress Vivian Wu noted that "In China, being beautiful is more than on your face—you have to be kind and good to people." My heart breaks for these women. Nevertheless, this tendency that many women have to devalue their own body is not only sad, but potentially dangerous.

In a study of one hundred and sixty West Coast college-aged women presented to the American Psychological Association, more than twenty-three percent said they had at some time engaged in bulimic behavior. Two percent could be classified as having met the strict clinical criteria for a diagnosis of bulimia nervosa. About seven and a half percent of the women had induced vomiting without binging, while an equal number binged without the vomiting. Thirteen percent practiced chronic dieting and meal-skipping.

Many people, especially women, would experience a real morale lift if they could accept their bodies.

How we feel about ourselves may even affect our physical attractiveness.

I ran across a fascinating story about a man named Boris Blum. Blum spent years in the unimaginable tortures of a concentration camp during World War II.[2] Not long after he was released, he and his friends spent the night in an abandoned German house. There were many mirrors in the house, which were fascinating to the men because they hadn't seen any in the years that they'd been in the concentration camps. When the men crowded around a mirror, Blum was horrified to discover that he didn't recognize himself. He literally didn't know which of the reflections in the mirror was his. He had to make faces at himself in the mirror before he could pick out his own reflection from the reflections of the other men. His time in the concentration camp had changed him so much that he didn't recognize the man he had become.

I wonder if, in a sense, that doesn't happen to everyone—at least for those over forty. We look in the mirror one day and are shocked at the person we have become.

A trusted advisor of President Lincoln recommended a candidate for Lincoln's cabinet. Lincoln declined. When he was asked why, he said, "I don't like the man's face."

"But the poor man is not responsible for his face," his advisor insisted.

"Every man over forty is responsible for his face," Lincoln replied.

I spent several years working with teenagers. The conventional wisdom is that attractive-looking young people are more popular with their peers. That is undoubtedly true. But I have long contended that a young person with a good personality is perceived by his/her peers as more attractive physically than a person with a less favorable personality. And now a study has come along by Leslie Zebrowitz, Ph.D., of Brandeis University that affirms that over time—for women at least—personality affects appearance.[3]

This was a follow-up study of personality tests taken by a group of women when they were in their teens. They were now in their fifties. The researchers wanted to know if a woman's personality could affect her attractiveness. And these forty year-old tests provided the perfect opportunity to answer this question. Here is what the study found: women who as teens had been rated by their friends as friendly and outgoing were seen as better-looking in their fifties by a group of objective observers than their peers who had been judged aloof and unfriendly as teens. This result held true regardless of the women's original physical appeal.

The researcher summed it up like this: "The kind of person a woman is influences the kind of appearance she develops." Think about the implications of that study, if you are a woman. It's fine to invest in exercise equipment and to eat a proper diet so that you may look your best. But, if you really want to look good, you really ought to invest in the kind of person you are. Your character can affect your appearance. Now other factors such as genetics and physical health can certainly play a role; but it is true that you can tell by looking at some people that they have had a hard life. You can see the anger, the bitterness, and the regret. You can look at other people and tell just from their faces that they are of a kind and generous nature. You can see the love and self-acceptance. There are some things about the way we look that we can't do much about—except, perhaps, with modern chemistry and plastic surgery: the shape of our nose, how much hair we have, and the color of our eyes, etc. But that is not to say that we are helpless. The love we have for others, the peacefulness within our own souls, and the delight we take in the small pleasures of life can all contribute to what we will one day see when we look in the mirror.

How we feel about ourselves affects our moral behavior. Some of the benefits of high self-esteem found by the Gallup poll commissioned by Dr. Robert Schuller: high moral and ethical sensitivity, strong sense of family, successful in interpersonal relationships, less materialistic, high productivity, low in chemical addictions, more involved in local and political causes, and more generous to charitable organizations.[4]

Improving the way we feel about ourselves means so many things. It means getting along comfortably with other people, and forming lasting, mature relationships. It means living from day to day without feelings of guilt, fear, or regret. It means courage in the face of adversity or change, and the ability to take charge when others are afraid to do so. Self-esteem means avoiding self-destructive behavior and actions that cause others pain. It results in openness and sharing, respect for others, and genuine benevolence. Self-esteem is "I can" rather than "I can't." High self-esteem is not a luxury, but a necessity in our endeavor to make a difference in the world. So, I am not overstating the case when I say that how you see yourself is the most important single factor in your life, except for perhaps your faith commitment.

If positive self-esteem is this important, why do so many people have low self-esteem? Why are we not all confident and content? It's a paradox. By the time we become aware of how our feelings about ourselves affect the way we interact with the world, it is almost too late to remedy the situation. According to psychologists, our sense of self-esteem develops in early childhood when we are very sensitive to the way in which others perceive us. We build our self-esteem upon what we hear about ourselves from others.

It happens to us the moment we are born. Excited family members press their noses against the nursery window in the hospital and begin playing the game, "Who does he look like?" After much discussion, it is decided that the red-faced, wrinkly, toothless, bald baby looks like "Uncle Harry."

The labeling of the little child increases as his personality develops. It is a normal human reaction, and we all do it. Suddenly a child is "Fatty" or "Four Eyes" at school. The last one chosen. The outsider. Parents exacerbate the problem by placing limitations on the child because he is a *C* student, a "fair" runner or a "plain" child. Unless parents exercise care, their children will grow up selling themselves short because of the box parents put them in, the expectations parents have placed upon them. Positive or negative, we believe what we hear. Unfortunately, we often hear many negative messages.

Dr. Joann Larsen, a leading family therapist, found that between birth and twenty years of age, the average person receives one hundred thousand negative messages from parents, teachers, siblings, and peers. Once we begin to believe the negative things we hear about ourselves, we start to listen for further negative input in order to confirm what we already believe about ourselves. We then ignore the positive messages given to us because they seem to oppose our perceptions of ourselves.

Another reason why some people have low self-esteem is that our society does not value the things that make them different or special. The emphasis is on conformity, on fitting in. The smartest kids in school, for example, are labeled "geeks" and become social outcasts.

Or an isolated failure might have gotten blown out of proportion. Maybe the tree we drew in elementary school looked different from everyone else's and our teacher told us that we didn't know how to draw trees. It's a simple example, but a person who takes a message like that to heart becomes inhibited about or embarrassed by his or her own unique traits. He spends his life trying to cover up the things that make him special or different, and his self-esteem suffers terribly in the process.

Some of us have some real hurts from our days as children. Some of these hurts carried over into our teenage years where they were rightly or wrongly reinforced, and some of them have become self-fulfilling prophecies drastically affecting our lives today.

Choosing the Way We View Ourselves

What is the difference between a highly paid executive and his more modestly paid employees? Let's say the executive is paid three hundred thousand dollars, and the employee, thirty thousand dollars. What is it that makes the executive worth ten times more? Is he or she ten times smarter? Chances are that in a large company there will be many people in the company who will have a much higher IQ than the boss. Does the executive work ten times harder? Sure, he works four hundred hours a week! Did she have all the advantages growing up? Could be, but it's doubtful.

A study of three hundred highly successful people—people like Franklin Delano Roosevelt, Helen Keller, Winston Churchill, Albert

Schweitzer, Mahatma Ghandi, and Albert Einstein—reveals that one fourth had handicaps like blindness, deafness, or crippled limbs. Three fourths had either been born in poverty, come from broken homes, or come from exceedingly tense or disturbed situations.

What, then, is the difference? Somewhere along the way, that executive had something happen in his or her life that increased the feeling of "can do." He or she began to believe his or her rightful place was at the top and proceeded to do those things that made success not only possible, but also almost inevitable.

There are three vantage points from which you can proceed to reach success in your life. You can choose to be successful, to believe in yourself, and to have positive images about your future. You can choose the status quo—nothing ventured, nothing lost or gained. Or, you can choose the path of failure, leading a life filled with negative images and actions that give you nothing and create dissatisfaction. The choice is yours.

Once there was a little girl who said to her mother, "Mom, I've had such a happy time today." The mother wanted to know what made it different from other days. "Well," the little girl answered, "yesterday my thoughts pushed me around—today I pushed them around." Success is primarily mental; by changing your thought processes, you can change the results you experience in life. Here are some steps you can take to raise your level of self-esteem.

Believe That You Are a Person of Destiny

Benjamin Disraeli said it best: "A consistent person believes in destiny, a capricious person believes in chance." Many people do feel that way about their lives. They believe that God has placed them here for a very special reason. Some people spend their lives searching for their destiny, their reason for being. Do you believe in the words of the old melodrama that you have a date with destiny? It's an interesting truth backed up by years of research—if you believe that your life has some ultimate purpose, you will go farther than if you believe that your life is essentially meaningless.

It reminds me of the story of the famous orchestra conductor who was driving a friend in his car. The friend noticed a rabbit's foot on the seat. "Surely you don't believe that rabbit's foot will bring you luck, do you?" The great conductor answered, "No, but I understand this particular rabbit's foot will bring you luck whether you believe in it or not."

Studies consistently show that if you believe you are lucky, you really will have more good things happen. Call it a self-fulfilling prophecy. Explain it by saying that if you feel lucky, you're apt to seek out more positive experiences. Rationalize it as you will, but the truth remains. If you feel like something good is going to happen to you, chances are it will. Believe that you are uniquely created for a special purpose that you alone can fulfill and it will amaze you how the universe will acquiesce to your actions. This truth was brought home to me by something that happened in our office.

We were setting up a series of seminars in the Midwest. I picked up fourteen thousand brochures at the printer, dropped off a few at our office for the files, and promptly took the rest to our mailing service to have mailed to the cities we had targeted. I breathed a sigh of relief. The brochures were done barely in time.

While I was at the mailing service I got the fateful call from our office. "Sit down," the voice on the phone said, "there is a typo on the brochure." "Oh, great," I thought. Here we are trying to convey a professional image and something is spelled wrong. Then I discovered that the situation was far worse than that. The typesetter had typed our toll-free number wrong. This is the number people would be using to make their reservations for the seminars. They would be calling but we would not be answering because the number was wrong. Fourteen thousand brochures. The worse possible mistake that can be made on a mailing piece. Now they were worthless.

What would you do at this point? Do you have a suggestion? I already had nearly two thousand dollars invested in typesetting, photographs, layout, paper, and printing. I had fourteen thousand mailing labels ready to attach to the brochures. I had meeting rooms reserved in nine different hotels in Chicago, Minneapolis, and seven other Midwestern cities. It was too late to reprint and too late to cancel. I had already spent several thousand dollars in promotion.

Someone in the office suggested that we take our whole five-person staff and spend two days furiously marking out the wrong number and using a rubber stamp to imprint the right number. Can you imagine what an ordeal that would be? Can you imagine how that would look to the person receiving our flyer? What do you do? Situation hopeless.

But then Patti, who was at that time in charge of our computer operations made a suggestion. Why not try calling the number that was printed on our brochure by mistake? "Maybe it hasn't been assigned," she suggested. "That's silly," I said in my all-knowing masculine boss-like manner. But it was worth a try. So we did and guess what? We got a recording, "This line is no longer in service." Well, what do you know?

Then someone else said, "Let's try AT&T and see if they will assign us that number." And so the call was made. And guess what? For approximately eighty-six dollars, we added an additional 800 number for the next two months and solved a problem that potentially could have cost us thousands of dollars.

Afterward someone in the office asked, "What are the odds that a misprinted 800 number would be available on that short notice?" Patti pointed to the ceiling and said, "Somebody up there is looking out for us."

Well, maybe so. Who knows. But I do know this, as long as people on my staff believe that, good things are likely to happen to us. That's the first path to personal power—a sense of destiny. A sense that you have been put on this earth for a special purpose that you and you alone can fulfill.

Have a clear-cut direction for your life. Do you know what you really hope to accomplish in life? Have you written it down? Only about five percent of us ever will. You know what the experts say. Your goals should be written. They should be specific. They should be realistic and yet challenging. They should include action steps. They should have deadlines.

Successful people are goal-setters for numerous reasons. For example, what happens when you set a goal for yourself and you make that goal?

You get the following:
1) A new sense of competence
2) A feeling of personal worth
3) A sense of confidence
4) A feeling of control

Be realistic in the setting of goals, of course. IBM sets their goals so that eighty percent of their workforce is guaranteed success. Don't set yourself up for failure by absurd goals. The failure will plunge your self-esteem lower than it was before. Choose attainable goals. I will never look like Tom Cruise. That would be an absurd goal. But I could lose a little fat, gain a little muscle, and improve my posture, etc.

The difference between a purpose-driven life and a reactive life is the difference between light coming through a windowpane and light passing through a magnifying glass. The rays of the sun, falling upon a piece of paper through a windowpane have little effect. Let them, however, pass through a magnifying glass to a focus and they create an intense heat that will quickly burn a hole in the paper. The person who succeeds is the person who is focused. If we are not focused, we are nothing but a "pane."

Be willing to make decisions. That's what we pay top executives for, isn't it? They don't really work any harder. They aren't really that much smarter. But they make the critical decisions that determine whether a company, a university, or an organization moves forward. How do you feel when you have to make an important decision? Nervous? Frustrated? Depressed? Join the crowd. Lots of people feel that way.

It would be easier if other people were not involved. "No man is an island," said John Donne, and he was right. We are all peninsulas—other people are involved in our decisions. Crowds of people are watching—spouses, friends, perhaps even parents or peers.

Decision-making is hard, and it requires courage. Fearful people are hindered by paralysis by analysis; they see all sides of a problem, but not a solution. Modern life, of course, complicates the matter. We have many more options which makes choosing that much more difficult. Making decisions is hard. But they have to be made. Have you ever been around someone who has difficulty making decisions? It drives me crazy.

There is a scene in an old W. C. Fields' movie in which a mother sends her young daughter to the store to buy a small item. As she is leaving, the girl asks her mother which brand she should buy. The mother says, "It makes no difference. You decide."

"Either one," says the girl, "it's all the same. Tell me which one."

"You decide," says the mother. "I don't care."

"I don't care," says the girl, "you decide."

"I don't care," the mother replies, "you decide."

W. C., listening from a porch swing where he's trying to take a nap, finally screams at the girl to get along. Most decisions are not clear-cut. Some are no-win: if I go out with Bob, I'll make Ted feel hurt; if I don't, I might miss a great time. Sometimes we have to bite the bullet and decide. The method we choose for making a decision is not as important as the fact that the decision is made.

A friend sent me a clipping from *Reader's Digest* about a flight attendant who had just returned from a vacation in the Rockies. While there, she fell in love with a very eligible bachelor. He owned and operated a cattle ranch, and lived in a log cabin. At the end of this week, Mr. Wonderful proposed. The flight attendant had never been good at making up her mind. She returned home and to her job feeling that she would somehow be guided.

The next day, in flight, she found herself wondering what to do. To perk up, she stopped in the restroom and splashed a bit of cool water on her face.

There was some turbulence and a sign lit up: PLEASE RETURN TO THE CABIN. She did—the one back in the mountains.

I wonder how her decision turned out. It troubles me when people are always looking for a sign (no pun intended). But at least she decided.

Remind yourself of your strengths. Everybody's got a few good points. Some people can work with their hands. Some people are good listeners. Take a few minutes from time to time to quietly and privately list your good personality qualities and your past successes and achievements. Be as objective as possible, and don't downplay your good points or be too modest. Use this list as a daily reference. Read your list at least twice a day, once in the morning and once in the evening, stroking yourself for these good attributes. This simple process will help you to reinforce the positive feelings you have about yourself. Again, don't worry about your areas of weakness, you can take care of these later. You need to have the attitude of the shapely young lady in the t-shirt: "I'm not perfect . . . but parts of me are excellent."

We are all different. No two of us have the same fingerprint or the same footprint. We don't even have the same voice print.

A University of Chicago professor has recorded numerous voices of certain celebrities on tape and then scrambled the words so they are unintelligible. Only the tone and the pitch are left. Yet students can identify not only the mood and the situation but also the person. The personalities are perfectly identifiable from this intangible factor, the timbre of the voice. Imagine that! A machine can positively identify you by the sound of your voice alone. No one has a voice just like yours. Rich Little cannot fool this machine.

You also have a different DNA code than anybody else who has ever lived. Police are now relying on DNA prints. If they even find a hair or a tiny fragment of skin at the scene of a crime, the criminal can be positively identified. God has given us our own little identification system from the moment we are conceived in our mothers' wombs. At the most basic level of our existence, we are all unique.

Don't be intimidated if you are not like everybody else. The Creator never intended you to be. The special way in which you express yourself on a day-to-day basis, either through your talents or hobbies, is a valuable component of your self-image. You should never try to inhibit yourself by mindless conformity. No matter how much you've tried to fit in all these years, you must come to realize that the successful person is the person who stands out from the crowd. Be a person who is different enough to be remembered. No one ever changed the world by being like everybody else.

In fact, strict conformity can be a loss in that it makes you feel more inhibited and causes you to be noticed by others less often. So take pride in your non-conforming qualities and make sure others know about them.

Picture in your mind the kind of person you would like to be. Athletes use this technique before a big competition to psyche themselves into winning. There is a famous study in which half of the members of a basketball team practiced an hour a day on free throw shooting. The other half spent the same amount of time visualizing their shots. That is, in their minds they went through the process of shooting free throws, they felt the weight of the ball, they extended their arms as if they were shooting, they watched in their minds the arc of the ball, in their ears they heard the swish of the net. They did everything except actually shoot the free throws. After several weeks, the improvement in performance between the two groups was practically the same.

Would you like to be the CEO of a large Fortune 500 company? Decide in your mind what a CEO would be like. What would he or she wear? What would this CEO talk about? How would he or she be treated? How would he or she spend spare time? You may even want to read books about prominent CEOs to give you some ideas. After you've built this mental picture of your ideal, you must act on it. If your ideal image wears a certain kind of clothing, modify your wardrobe as much as you can to imitate your ideal. If your ideal behaves in a certain way, act the way your ideal would act. The more you try to imitate your ideal image, the more like your ideal you'll become.

Sound ridiculous? Maybe so, but it works. Visualization is powerful stuff. Is there some change you would like to make in your life? Visualize yourself as having already made it. Act accordingly, and you will have taken the most crucial step in achieving it.

If it helps, cut out pictures and paste them on your refrigerator, above the sink, in the bathroom. Let the subconscious part of your brain, up to ninety percent of the brain, go to work trying to think up ways your vision can become a reality. It has worked for many, many people. It is not magic. It still involves a lot of self-discipline, but it puts to work your most valuable asset—your brain.

That means, of course, that some of us will have to give ourselves permission to dream. But as Bloody Mary sings in *South Pacific*, "If you don't have a dream, how you gonna have a dream come true?"[5]Besides, what's to lose by setting your sights a little higher in life? What's to lose? We accept it as an axiom that we are the products of our environment. We are the result of our past. Why can't we be the products of our dreams?

A newspaper cartoon shows two Eskimos sitting on chairs, fishing through the hole in the ice. One Eskimo is fishing through an opening about the size of a manhole. However, the other Eskimo has his line in a hole that looks to be an enormous crater in the shape of a whale. Visualize the kind of person that you would like to be, and the kind of lifestyle you would like to have.

Learn to talk to yourself positively. We have already noted the destructiveness of negative self-talk. "I'm no-good. I can't do anything right. There's no hope for me." You may have a tape-recorder in your brain that continually chastises you for being human—no more, no less. Usually the things your tape recorder tells you are wrong. For example, that tape recorder almost always speaks in generalities. It will tell you, "You always say the wrong thing." That's absurd. I'm certain that some-time in your life you've said the right thing at least once. In fact, you say some right things every day. Things like, "You did a good job on that . . . That's a pretty dress . . . I love you." No, the truth is that it is very rare that you say the wrong thing, but when it does happen, you blow it all out of proportion and punish yourself with all kinds of critical and completely false self-talk.

Another quick example: "I'm so clumsy." Has your tape-recorder ever told you that? Well, maybe you are a little clumsy—as a ballet dancer, a tightrope walker, or as a professional athlete. But, believe it or not, most of us can walk down the hallway without tripping over our own feet. We can make it through the cafeteria line without dropping our tray. It's been a long time since we spilled a Coke on somebody's nice carpet at a party. How dare your brain tell you you're clumsy! Besides, poise is ninety per-cent confidence. If you act clumsy every once in a while, it is that dumb tape recorder's fault. You're going to fix him. You're going to tell yourself every day for the next twenty-one days, "I am a graceful and poised per-son. I have the knack of doing the right thing in all situations."

We have all kinds of faulty beliefs about ourselves, don't we?

- We feel we are not mechanical. We can't set a digital clock.
- We can't cook. We even burn coffee.
- We can't play sports. We have the grace of an elephant on rollerblades.
- We have no sense of direction.

We need to reprogram our brains. Remember, your subconscious believes whatever it is told. It's been given all those negative messages all those years and it has believed them, regardless of how faulty they may be. Now you want to re-program your subconscious. You want to make it your ally rather than your enemy. It does work like a tape recorder. If you record new material over old material on a tape recorder, the old material is erased. That can happen with our brains. We can give our brains positive messages that will record over all those negative messages. It takes time. It will not happen the first time we tell ourselves, "I am a graceful and poised person," after thirty years of telling ourselves that we are an oaf. Usually twenty-one straight days of telling ourselves a certain message will be required before the subconscious really starts believing it.

The point is, it does work. After twenty-one days of repeating positive self-talk to yourself at least once a day, you should be able to alter your negative core beliefs about yourself.

Try to be around people who contribute to your positive self-image. In fact, it is imperative that you socialize with people who treat you positively and with respect. Many attitudes you have about yourself are reflections of what other people think about you. If you are around people who put you down, you are likely to feel down about yourself. Try to take an objective look at some of your relationships. Is there someone in your life who makes you feel bad when you're around her? If you feel that way around her, is her friendship worth having? If possible, try to avoid people who put you down, and strengthen relationships with people who build you up. Remember, in a relationship, never be a martyr to someone else's negative comments or actions; you deserve better than that.

Always enhance and emphasize your good qualities, especially those things which make you special. Begin with your appearance. Any fashion designer, makeup artist, or model will tell you that the key to looking great is to downplay your less desirable physical traits and to emphasize the good things about your appearance. An easy way to go about enhancing your appearance is simply to assess the way you look when people give you compliments. If people tell you you look sharp every time your wear your navy blue suit, you can pretty well assume that it's a suit you should continue to wear. If you feel especially good whenever you wear that red shirt, then keep wearing it. When you feel good about the way you look, you are more confident, and you make a better impression on others.

I find that working out at a gym makes all the difference in the world how I feel about myself. I have always had a problem with my posture (a sign of low self-esteem, perhaps?). By working out with weight-training equipment, I seem to be standing straighter and taller. Placebo effect? Maybe so, but I still feel better.

Master a skill. It can be any skill that requires some practice on your part. Start with things you already enjoy doing, like a sport you play on a regular basis or a hobby you've cultivated. At fifty-six, I took up playing basketball on a senior Olympics team, and I love it! I had not played a team sport since the eighth grade. The other team members have more experience than I, and some played all four years in high school, while others played in college. But they have been patient with me. They know I am committed and that I am slowly improving. At first, it was hard on my ego. I will never be quick enough, I said to myself, or shoot well enough. But I kept hanging in there. Now, each time I shoot the ball I say to myself, "I can do this." And I have come to the realization that lack of quickness can be a result of lack of aggressiveness, so I am working at being more aggressive. I will never be Kobe Bryant, of course, but I take real pride in the improvement I am showing.

Whatever hobby or sport you begin, take it seriously; make a conscious effort to perfect your skill. If you can't think of a sport or hobby you're already involved in, consider taking up a craft like wood working or needlepoint. You'll be amazed at the gratification you'll feel by displaying your finished product, whether it be a bookcase you've made or an enviable serve in tennis. By doing something that makes you feel competent in one area of your life, you'll find that other areas of your life begin to feel more successful.

Define your values and live up to them. Nothing will destroy your self-esteem as quickly or surely as betraying your most deeply held values. It is another of those self-fulfilling cycles—the higher your sense of integrity, the higher your self-esteem; the higher your self-esteem, the higher your sense of integrity.

Develop a physical exercise plan. There are few plans for feeling better about yourself that will work better than a good exercise program. Aerobics are great, jogging is wonderful, lifting weights is terrific, but for most of us, simple walking does wonders. A brisk forty-five-minute daily walk will help you keep your weight down, and it will help muscle tone. It will increase your level of energy, and it will help the release of chemicals in your brain that work as anti-depressants.

Watch your posture—look like a winner. There is a posture of failure. A *Peanuts* cartoon shows Charlie Brown with his head down, his shoulder drooping. He says to Peppermint Patty, "This is my 'depressed stance.' When you're depressed, it makes a lot of difference how you stand . . . The worst thing you can do is straighten up and hold your head high because then you'll start to feel better . . . If you're going to get any joy out of being depressed, you've got to stand like this."

As usual, Charlie Brown is right! I have a good friend, Fred Needham, who declares that it is impossible to get depressed if you will make it a rule to always keep your eyes at shoulder level or above. Fred is one of the most positive people I have ever known. His favorite Bible verse is "I will lift up mine eyes unto the hills . . "

Put your chin on your chest, let your shoulders slump, stare at the ground, and it is almost impossible to think positive thoughts about yourself. On the other hand, walk erect, breathe deeply, keep your shoulders back, look people in the eye, seek to keep a warm expression on your face, and you will begin to feel that you can take on the world.

Learn to accept compliments. Give yourself permission to excel. If somebody says, "Hey, you look great!" say thank you. Don't devalue their kindness. After all, you're calling them a liar if you dispute them.

Look for someone else whose life you can brighten. Nothing will help us feel better than the feeling that we have contributed to someone else's life. Dr. Alfred Adler said that we can be cured of depression in only fourteen days if every day we will try to think of how we can be helpful to others.

Remember, you cannot fail. If you don't succeed at something, pick yourself up and enter the race again with renewed strength. After all, there really is no such thing as failure except in your own mind. Give yourself permission to make mistakes. We all make them. Don't sit around cringing over mistakes you made five years ago; the past is past. It no longer exists. Let it go.

It does you no good to lament over things that went wrong—it's just a waste of time. If you know that you personally have made a mistake, simply acknowledge that you made it and resolve to learn from it next time. And if you did learn from it, it is just a stepping stone to your next success. Under no circumstances should you blame yourself for things over which you had no control. When things go wrong, don't always expect to find a scapegoat, because often things happen because of unforeseen circumstances. Look at every situation objectively, and keep in mind that very few mistakes are unredeemable; they can usually be corrected or compensated for. Most importantly, never be afraid to take on a new challenge because of a mistake you made in the past. Every new challenge is different, and your past mistakes will help you deal with it better.

The main thing to remember is that you cannot influence others without working on yourself first. The people who make an impact on others are people who believe in themselves, believe in their values and stride confidently into the world knowing that they are worthy of the cause which they champion.

A South African diamond miner found one of the world's largest diamonds. It was the size of a small lemon. The miner needed to get the diamond safely to the company's office in London, so he sent it in a small steel box and hired four men to carry it. Even when it was in the ship's safe en route, it was guarded day and night by at least two armed men. But when the package arrived at the company's office in London and was carefully opened, it contained no diamond. Rather it contained a lump of black coal. Three days later, the diamond arrived by ordinary parcel post in a plain package. The owner had assumed correctly that the diamond would be safer delivered in such a manner because most people would not pay attention to an ordinary cardboard box.

We are surrounded by people who come to us in ordinary cardboard boxes. We run into them every day—people who don't look or sound like they have all that much to offer. Yet, some of them are diamonds on the inside. And they don't even know it. Maybe you fall into this category. If so, then it is time to rip off the layers of ordinary wrapping and let the diamond show through. You are lovable and capable.

CHAPTER 21

Step 3: Express Yourself

"Times have changed in corporate America," says speech consultant Roger Ailes. "At one time, the most qualified person got the job. Today . . . the one with the best communications skills gets it." Adds Ailes: "This becomes a bigger consideration every year."[1]

Communication seems like a simple process. And sometimes it is.

I have had a delightful time listening to my grandson, Sebastian, who recently turned three, learn to talk. Compared to many children his age, he has been a bit slow mastering this skill. There may be a reason: his mother speaks to him in English and his Austrian father speaks to him in German. Like many children raised in bilingual homes, Sebastian is a little confused. So, beginning early in his maturation, he developed his own means of communicating by means of animal sounds, car sounds, train sounds, etc.

An example is my toy, a 1979 MGB. The leather seats are gradually deteriorating, so I ordered some seat covers. The ad in the catalogue sounded appealing. "You Can Have Looks and Comfort . . . Synthetic Sheepskin Seat Covers Give You Both," said the headline. The ad continued, "The coolest cover-up known is the synthetic sheepskin cover. This top quality, one hundred percent acrylic sheepskin seat cover has a universal slip fit . . ." Looks and comfort? Top quality? I should have known there was a catch when I saw the low price—fifty dollars. Still, "hope springs eternal."

They were the most awful things I have ever seen. Off-gold and off-white, they looked like no sheepskin that I have ever seen, synthetic or not. Still, I needed something to cover the seats of my car. As I pondered my dilemma, then eighteen month-old Sebastian happened by. He took one look at the seat covers and gave his critique in one word, "woof." He was right. It looked like a mangy mutt had been slung over my car seat. Back in the box the synthetic sheepskin seat covers went. Communication seems like it should be an easy task, but it is really one of the most difficult tasks you and I have to master.

There was a movie years ago called *Cool Hand Luke*. This Paul Newman classic was about a man in a prison in the southern part of the United States who couldn't quite get the hang of prison life.[2] A famous quote came out of that movie. After Luke had escaped twice and frustrated the warden's need for order, the warden utters this classic line: "What we got here is a failure to communicate." How many times has that line been appropriate to attempts at human dialogue? Communication is a complex process at best. The matter is further complicated by the fact that people sometimes use deceitful communication. I am fascinated by the way we use words at times not to clarify, but to obfuscate, or at least to cast things in the best possible light.

I was in the post office recently to have my passport renewed for an upcoming seminar in Europe. I asked the gentleman in charge when I could expect to receive my new passport. His response interested me. "Twenty-five working days," he replied. I am certain that this was a very carefully crafted reply. It is actually five weeks, but "twenty-five working days" sounds so much better. Our initial thought might even be: "Why, that's less than a month!"

When we want to obfuscate the truth without outright lying, we manipulate language. In our nation's capital, where it has become an art, it is called, "spin." Even more threatening to society today than manipulating language, however, is that we are rapidly devaluing language.

Is It a Sin to Cuss?

I remember when my youngest daughter who was then barely a teenager came to me one day and asked, "Daddy, is it a sin to cuss?" She said, "I'm not going to do it, but many of my friends do. And I was just wondering, is it a sin?"

Who can go to a movie today without being bombarded with what used to be considered obscenities? This is occurring not just in movies and books, but on prime-time television programs and even at the next table as we sit with our children in McDonald's. Every year the bounds of acceptable speech seem to stretch just a little farther. So, is it a sin? Well, your pastor, priest, or rabbi would be better equipped than I to answer that question.

However, the word "profane" is interesting. Taken at its base root, profane means "before the temple." In order for something to be profane, it first has to be sacred. Think about the profane words that people use. They deal with religion, they deal with the most intimate parts of our body, and they deal with our most intimate relationships. In order for something to be profane, it must deal with that which is most personal and most sacred. Now what is it that causes us to take that which is most sacred and corrupt it? Isn't it our need to distance ourselves from that which makes us uncomfortable?

It is very difficult for the average person to handle the most intimate areas of life—God, sexuality, relationships. Think how much easier it is for many people to use vulgar names for intimate body parts than it is to use their proper names. The problem is that, if we engage in the profane long enough—standing before the temple, as it were, taking that which is sacred and corrupting it—we run the danger of creating an enormous distance between ourselves and those things that are sacred and holy.

For instance, we might legitimately ask whether the constant use of crude sexual terms in everyday conversation has not served to devalue sex? Something that used to be regarded as private and special has now become just another bodily function. I personally think something has been lost in the process. Similarly, when we devalue God's name, God becomes less sacred in our lives. Even worse, it becomes a self-fulfilling prophecy; the greater the distance we create, the more profane we must become in order to make ourselves comfortable in the distance we have created.

In the introduction to this book, I mentioned the motion picture *Pay It Forward* starring Kevin Spacey, Helen Hunt, and Haley Joel Osment. This is a very idealistic movie, but someone expecting a wholesome, family movie will be decidedly jarred by the language. However, we need to consider the lives of the main characters; Kevin Spacey's character is a man whose face has been tragically disfigured. Consequently, he fears intimate relationships. Helen Hunt, on the other hand, plays an alcoholic waitress who has endured an abusive marriage. Even the young hero of the movie, portrayed by Haley Joel Osment, has been scarred by his parents' inability to forge a wholesome relationship. These flawed people live disjointed, disconnected lives. Their crude language is almost a metaphor for the distance they have built not only from one another, but from themselves. What concerns me is that the common reaction to this is, "Well, they're just words." But words are important. Language is powerful.

Studies show that vocabulary and success in society and business are positively related. Earl Nightingale, in his unforgettable tapes on success, would always begin by identifying vocabulary as the number one skill a person would want to develop if he or she wants to be successful.

In *My Fair Lady,* based on George Bernard Shaw's version of the

Pygmalion myth, Dr. Higgins turns Liza Doolittle into a lady.[3] Liza is a poor, cockney peasant who is completely unpolished. And the first thing Dr. Higgins works on is her speech and language. Do you remember, "The rain in Spain falls mainly on the plain?" Language is very important. Our self-image is related to the language we use.

Our ideas are dependent on our language. Can you think of a way we can ponder an idea without using language?

"The limits of my language," wrote the philosopher Ludwig Wittgenstein, "are the limits of my mind. All I know is what I have words for."

In George Orwell's futuristic book *1984,* the government manipulates language on a large scale in order to influence the thoughts and understanding of the people. The government was affirming this principle: we think with the amount of language available to us. So the range of our vocabulary will have some impact on the way we think. Therefore, we should worry about a generation of young people who are brought up on a diet of four letter words. What does this say to their subconscious about their own self-worth and the value of life in general?

Our language makes a powerful impact on others. In fact, the Supreme Court has a whole body of law about so-called "fighting words." We do have freedom of speech, but we cannot use words that might adversely affect people around us. The classic example is that we can't yell "Fire!" in a crowded theater. Think of the emotions we evoke when we say to another, "I love you," or conversely, "I hate you." How about "You're despicable" or "You can do it"? Just words? Hardly.

In *All I Really Need to Know I Learned in Kindergarten,* Robert Fulghum tells of villagers in the Solomon Islands who felled a tree by screaming at it for thirty days.[4] The tree died, confirming the islanders' theory that hollering kills a living thing's spirit. And it does, doesn't it? Spirits shrivel in the face of constant belittling. Confidence is destroyed when efforts are continually demeaned. Words make a frightening and lasting impact on persons to whom they are directed.

Language used poorly can cause major misunderstandings.

A teacher said: "Give me a sentence about a public servant."

A young fellow wrote: "The fireman came down the ladder pregnant."

The teacher took the lad aside to correct him. "Don't you know what pregnant means?" she asked.

"Sure," said the young student confidently. "It means carrying a child."

A Belfast newspaper once reported the launching of an aircraft carrier with this classic description: "The Duchess smashed the bottle against the bow and amid the applause of the crowd she slid on her greasy bottom into the sea." Beware: sloppy use of language may get you into trouble. Even more to the point, the proper or improper use of language can affect our happiness and our ability to influence others. That's what the evidence indicates. The language we use can affect our health and our attitude toward life.

Like most people in the motivational field, I am astounded by the power of attitude in our lives. It has always interested me that if you take the word "attitude" and assign each letter a numerical value based on its place in the alphabet (A=1, T=20, T=20, I=9, T=20, U=21, D=4, E=5), the numbers add up to one hundred. The difference in being fifty percent effective in life and being one hundred percent effective, is attitude. One way our attitude affects our life is how we talk to ourselves.

I have been helped immensely in this regard by the work of Dr. Martin Seligman, who is known for advancing the concept of "learned helplessness." Seligman wanted to know why some people are able to cope with adversity while others crumble at the first sign of distress.[5] He began doing studies on depression and why some people are not able to cope better with life. Later Seligman wrote a book called *Learned Optimism.* In that book, he sought to compare people displaying optimistic and pessimistic attitudes and to determine what caused people to develop one or the other.

It is important to note that Seligman does not believe in what is popularly called "positive thinking." His goal was to determine how we can reprogram our brains so that we can cope with life and make a lasting difference. He determined that the key ingredient in determining individual success was what he termed "Explanatory Styles." He found that whenever an optimist or a pessimist had a success or failure, he/she explained the result in very different but very specific ways.

If an optimist achieves a success, his/her first response is apt to be, "Well, of course something good happened to me. Something good always happens to me." For the optimist success is pervasive. They also see success as a personal accomplishment, "I worked hard, I deserve this." And because good things seem to happen to them all the time, they see success as a permanent situation.

Pessimists, on the other hand, will react to a success by saying, "This is a fluke. It will never happen again. I got lucky this time." For them success is an isolated event which they take no credit for and which they see as being temporary.

If something bad happens, the responses of the optimist and the pessimist are reversed. When something negative happens to an optimist, he/she will say, "It was a fluke. It'll never happen again. Besides, it wasn't anything I did. I was just at the wrong place at the wrong time." On the other hand, the pessimist will respond to a failure by saying, "I did it again. I can't get anything right. Loser, loser, loser."

Charlie Brown is the classic pessimist. One *Peanuts* cartoon has Lucy say to Charlie Brown after a baseball game, "Well, you win some and you lose some," and Charlie Brown remarks, "that would be wonderful." He assumes that losing is a permanent state.

There are important implications concerning our explanatory style. Professional speaker George Walther has expanded on Seligman's work and written his own dynamic book called *What You SAY Is What You GET: How to Master Power Talking*. From his studies of the language of optimistic, powerful people, Walther has identified some of their specific characteristics.[6] Here are a few of the concrete suggestions he makes for improving our ability to "power talk."

Project positive expectations. For example, a power talker does not say, "I will try to get back to you by next Tuesday." A power talker says, "I will get back to you by next Tuesday." Using "I will try" gives you an "out" so that you've prematurely excused yourself from performing as promised. When you eliminate the "try," you're making a commitment. Even more important than the commitment your listener hears is the one you give yourself.

Don't say "I can't" when you mean "I choose not to." For example, don't say, "I can't go to the company social next week" when you mean "I choose not to go to the social because I would rather spend that time with my family visiting from out of town." Or, "I hate my job, but I can't afford to give it up now." What you really mean is, "I hate my job, but I choose the security of it over the risk of having to find another one." Maybe you feel you don't have any other choice, but you are choosing. You will be more powerful and more honest if you change your language and admit that you do make certain choices and that you have the freedom to choose.

Say "when," not "if." For example, when you are talking to your children, don't say, "If you clean up your room, you can go out and play." Say, "When you clean up your room, you can go out and play." If you say "if" you are already allowing for the possibility that they may not clean up their room, but when you say "when," the result is expected.

Beware of self-fulfilling prophecies. The moment you tell yourself you are a klutz, you are setting yourself up to fail. That's just the way our brains operate. We tend to live up—or down—to the expectations we set for ourselves.

Don't apologize for your shortcomings, change them! If you apologize ahead of time for matters you have neglected, for example, people look for flaws. For instance, when you have unexpected visitors, don't say, "Oh, I'm sorry the place is such a mess." What is the first thing people start doing? Looking for a mess! Just say, "Welcome!"

Can you see how useful understanding the power of language can be in making an impact on the world? We can take control of our language and thus take control of our lives. I speak from experience. I mentioned earlier my battle with a low self-image. There was a time in my life when I would invariably revert to what might be called "victim language." This is the language used by people who feel they are completely out of control of their lives.

When things were going wrong, I would say, "I'm finished. This is it. It's over."

What are some problems with this kind of reaction? The first problem is that it is not true. I'm still here and I was saying I was finished twenty years ago. I have had enough ups and downs by now to know that failure is not a permanent state. In fact, failure can be very liberating, giving you a chance to start over with the lessons you've learned.

Even worse, by saying I was finished, I was creating a self-fulfilling prophecy. By telling myself that I was finished, I was closing my mind to options that would have helped me make my life better. By feeding my mind negative messages, I might even have damaged my health. Studies of personnel records show that the health of men above the age of forty-five may be affected by whether they use optimistic, positive language or pessimistic, negative language.

So I changed my language. Every time my brain would begin its old refrain, "I'm finished," I trained myself to say, "That's true. The person I used to be is finished. I'm a different person than I was a year ago, and I will be a different person next year than I am right now. I will acquire skills, new knowledge, new attitudes." I was able to rid myself of some of my old self-defeating attitudes simply by changing my language. And so can you. Never take for granted the power of language.

Year after year, Anne Sullivan spelled words into Helen Keller's hand. Finally, when Helen was seven years old, Anne Sullivan poured some water over Helen's hand and Helen spoke her first word. Years later Helen Keller described that moment in her book, *The Story of My Life*:

> Somehow the mystery of language was revealed to me. I knew then that "w-a-t-e-r" meant that wonderful cool something that was flowing over my hand. That living word awakened my soul, gave it light, hope, joy, set it free! . . . I left the well-house eager to learn. Everything had a name, and each name gave birth to a new thought.

If you are going to have an impact on the world, you will need to learn to express yourself. You will need to be able to speak powerfully with yourself and with others.

People who have changed our world have generally been great communicators. But our most important conversations are those dialogues that go on within our own heads. In order to influence others you must learn to express yourself. To be truly effective you must have a "self" worth expressing. Then, and only then, do you turn your focus on the persons whom you are seeking to influence.

CHAPTER 22

Step 4: Learn to Read People

Stephen Covey once said, "Seek first to understand; then to be understood."

At one time, the most famous circus animal in England was an elephant named Bozo. Customers loved Bozo for his gentle manner. Unfortunately, Bozo did not maintain his pleasant ways. Over time he became mean and violent, so the circus owner decided to have him shot.

On the day of the execution, a man stepped out of the crowd and asked for a chance to prove that Bozo was not a threat to anyone. The gentleman entered Bozo's cage and began speaking to him in a foreign tongue. Instantly, the animal's dark mood cleared, and he became gentle again. The gentleman explained to the owner that Bozo was an Indian elephant; his previous trainers had spoken to him in Hindustani. Once Bozo heard the familiar language, he calmed down. The owner, amazed by the elephant's transformation, agreed to spare his life and find him a Hindustani trainer. The man who saved the great elephant that day was the famous author, Rudyard Kipling.[1]

If we are going to influence others, we must speak their language. By that I do not mean the many spoken languages that grace our tiny planet—Spanish, French, German, etc.—though learning a second language might indeed increase our effectiveness. People are always impressed by someone willing to meet them on common ground. But there are other ways to speak a person's language. That is to understand where they are coming from psychologically and socially.

People are different. *The Talmud* says, "When a human government stamps out coins in the emperor's image, every one is exactly the same; when God stamps out human beings in his image, every one of them is unique."

I was in Sears sometime back in the auto department. There were two people ahead of me. One was a man who was carrying under his arm the baldest tire I've ever seen—not a tread on it. The salesman behind the counter asked, "What can I do for you?" The man reached into his pocket and pulled out an old wrinkled Sears ticket.

"Back in 1992," he said, "I bought a set of shock absorbers for my car here at Sears with a lifetime warranty. I just wanted you to see what those shock absorbers are doing to my tires." 1992! And he still had his ticket!

The next person in line was a woman. The salesman asked, "How may I help you?"

The woman said, "The *kewump* is back."

"I beg your pardon?" said the salesman.

"The *kewump* is back," she said. "I brought my car in here a few weeks ago. It was going *kewump, kewump, kewump.* The salesman said if I would put on new shocks, new struts, and new front tires, that would take care of the *kewump.* The *kewump* is back."

Do you know the salesman almost seemed relieved when I told him I just needed a new battery for my car? People are different.

Another time I was in a Waffle House in Atlanta at four o'clock in the morning. I was having trouble sleeping, so I thought I might as well get some coffee so I could get some work done. I noticed as I sat down that there were only three other people in the Waffle House at that early hour: a man was cooking at the grill, and a waitress was serving the solitary customer sitting at the counter. The customer was harassing the waitress, making all kinds of derogatory remarks. When he got up to leave, the man at the grill turned and held up his spatula and nearly screamed, "I don't want that man to ever come in this Waffle House again. If he comes into this Waffle House again, I'm calling the police. You can tell he's up to no good," he said resolutely, "He smiles too much. If anybody smiles that much, don't turn your back on him. He'll stab you in the back."

Now normally when I am interacting with someone I have a tendency to smile. That is my Southern upbringing—like Jimmy Carter. In fact, like Carter, I've been told I smile too much. But not this particular morning. I tried to see how straight I could keep my face. People are different. In fact, each of us is unique. As we noted earlier, none of us has the same fingerprints, footprints, DNA prints, or even voice prints. Physically, we are all very special people.

We are unique mentally as well. Have you been following the research on right and left functions of the brain? It is exciting. Ian Fleming in one of his James Bond adventures notes that an average person can manage without his gall bladder, spleen, tonsils, appendix, one kidney, one lung, two quarts of blood, two-fifths of his liver, most of his stomach, four feet of intestines, and half of his brain.

Isn't that amazing? We could get along with half a brain. A thousand cheap jokes come to mind. Fortunately it is not necessary for most of us to cope with having only half of a brain, but theoretically we could if we needed to. That is because the two sides of the brain are almost mirror images of one another. If you have damage on one side of the brain, the other side can take over—a fact which gives real hope to stroke victims who have experienced damage to an area of their brain. Oftentimes, if they are willing to undergo the necessary amount of therapy, they can get the undamaged side to compensate. In spite of the many similarities between the right and left sides of the brain, however, there are also some significant differences.

Research on the right and left sides of the brain began in earnest in the 1960s with the work of Roger Sperry and his associates. They were experimenting with brain surgery in an attempt to help people suffering from epileptic seizures so severe that Dilatin, Phenobarbitol, and other seizure-preventing medications were ineffective. What they discovered was that the two sides of the brain process information differently. They perform different tasks. The left hemisphere is concerned with language and logic, while the right side is said to be the creative, emotive, artistic side.

Is this important to know? Well, consider that our educational system is set up to cater to left brain aptitudes, those that require logic and language skills. Suppose, however, you happen to be a right brain dominant child trying to cope in this alien environment. You are labeled as slow, a dreamer, and an underachiever. That may be a faulty diagnosis. Maybe you are simply a right-brained person living in a left-brained dominated world.

My left-handed daughter Angela is like that. She is a bright, articulate, funny person. She is an excellent writer, but ask her to do math, and the gears in her brain come to a grinding halt. Or ask her to find her way across town in a car, and you better send a cell phone with her so that you can come to her rescue. Her brain works exceedingly well—brilliantly in some respects—at some tasks, but it does not work in the same way that the brains of other family members work. And thank God for it! Angela brings many gifts to our family.

People are different and different is good! We are all unique, valuable, and special. We all have contributions to make to the world. We all have our niche. At the same time, we live in a world of amazing diversity.

Some of us are male, some female. John Gray has made a fortune out of a little book that makes broad generalizations about gender differences titled, *Men Are From Mars And Women Are From Venus.* One of my daughters says she is going to write a book titled, *Women Are Stupid; Men Are Scum: Breaking the Cycle.* Her thesis is that many women raise their sons to be irresponsible. If women wouldn't spoil their boys, she contends, men wouldn't be scum. The title will win no awards for subtlety, but who can deny that the thesis is sound?

Some gender differences in communication are quite striking. For example, Deborah Tannen in her best-selling book, *You Just Don't Understand: Men And Women in Conversation,* points out that women tend to suggest, whereas men command.[2] Women use the word "let's" much more frequently than men. Female nurses will even say to patients, "Let's take our medicine." Yuck. You can decide for yourself whether this tendency robs women of their authority and makes it more difficult for some women to be perceived as leaders.

You'll always find exceptions to the rule, but research and experience consistently point to basic differences between the ways men and women act, think, and feel. For example, men generally base their self-esteem on achievement. They are more competitive and aggressive than women. Women, on the other hand, generally base their self-esteem on relationships. They relate to other people on a more personal level.

A University of Pennsylvania study conducted by brain researcher Ruben Gur demonstrated that women were better able to read emotion in facial expressions than men, a trait which may help women be more empathic. A survey conducted by *Glamour* magazine showed that sixty percent of conversations between women are on emotional or personal topics, compared with twenty-seven percent of similar conversations between men. Of course, these are generalizations. They may or may not refer to any particular man or woman. Nevertheless, men and women tend to see the world through different eyes. No wonder, then, that communication between genders is sometimes a challenge.

But people are different in many other ways. For example, birth order. As most of us have probably surmised from experience, studies show that the oldest child is usually more conservative than his younger siblings. The oldest child more often reflects the mores and attitudes of his parents. He is usually more responsible, but he is also more uncertain whether he measures up simply because so much was expected of him as a child.

Does the order of your birth really make that much of a difference? Listen to these statistics: Of the original twenty-three astronauts in the United States space program, twenty-one were first-born children. All of the original Mercury astronauts were first-borns. More than fifty percent of all United

States presidents have been first-born children. Finally, more than sixty percent of people listed in *Who's Who in America* are first-born children.

How do you explain that? Don't siblings grow up in the same environment? Well, yes and no. They share many of the same experiences. My sister and I shared the same parents, but she had to put up with me. It isn't easy having a brother four years your senior. Then five years later, another sibling comes along, and you're a "big sister." You're expected to help care for your little brother. So, yes, my sister and I shared the same environment, but it was really not the same at all; people are different. Unfortunately, some of these differences lead to needless conflict.

The Most Ignorant Statement in the World

Two of the most important ways we differ are national origin and the color of our skin. The whole discipline of sociology in this country traces its origins to studies that were done to explain why Jewish immigrants from Russia prospered in the early part of the twentieth-century more rapidly than did Roman Catholic immigrants from Italy. The answers, researchers postulate, are both social and cultural.

Fortunately national origin—at least European origin—is one area where we can still have a little fun. In heaven it is said:

> The cooks are all French,
> The mechanics are all Germans,
> The police are all Brits,
> The lovers are all Italian,
> And the whole thing is run by the Swiss.

In hell it is said:

> The cooks are British,
> The mechanics are all French,
> The police are Germans,
> The lovers are the Swiss,
> And the whole thing is run by Italians.

Having experienced British cuisine and Italian efficiency (both oxymorons), I have a certain affinity for these stereotypes.

Stereotypes, of course, can be cruel, especially racial stereotypes. It is true that we differ according to the color of our skin. My own feeling is that this is the most superficial difference of all, but what a mess we have created by keeping alive ancient biases and stereotypes. This brings us to the most ignorant statement in the human language, in my opinion. It's a statement that we used to hear in the South quite frequently. I learned the idiocy of this statement indirectly from that great, prototype liberal clergyman, the late Harry Emerson Fosdick.

Fosdick once noted that the more we know about any subject, the less we think in terms of the general, and the more we think in terms of the specific. For example, let's suppose my car breaks down. I open the hood and I stare at a mass of wires, rubber and metal, none of which means anything to me. I don't know anything about cars, so when I look under the hood, it is all one big blob. But a trained mechanic will look under the hood of my car and he (or she) will not see a blob or a mass; the mechanic will see the carburetor and the fuel pump, and will reach into a part of the motor that I do not even see and tighten a connecting wire. You see, the more you know about cars, the less you thing in terms of the blob, the mass, and the more you think about individual parts to the car. Let's use another analogy.

Let's imagine an illiterate person walks into a public library. What does he see in that library? A mass of books—walls and walls of them. They don't mean anything to him because they are just books. To the librarian, though, each book has its author, title, and catalogue number. And a favorite book can produce hours and hours of pleasurable reading and even more pleasurable conversation. The more you know about books, the less you think in terms of books in general and the more you think about individual volumes. The more we know about any subject, the less we think in terms of the general and the more we think in terms of the specific!

Fosdick's point was that God, who is the source of all knowledge, does not see humanity as a faceless blob, but in His infinite power can know each of us intimately. It is an argument that is most appealing.

However, let's take this principle one step further: I get off the airplane in China and make my way onto the streets of a major city. What do I see there? I see all these strange-looking Asian people, and in my ignorance, what do I say? They all look the same to me. Why do I say that? Because I don't know any Asian people. However, if I got to know them, I would realize that they are as distinctive as people back in my hometown of Knoxville, Tennessee.

Fortunately, this is no longer a common predicament, perhaps because with the walls of segregation broken down, we actually know people of other backgrounds. Maybe there is hope for us yet. It's time for us to recognize how silly racial divides are. According to the Book of Genesis, we all come from a single mother and father. There is but one race—the human race. Skin color is only skin deep. In terms of understanding why people do the things they do, race may be the least important characteristic of all.

Let's consider some differences that really do matter, though—behavioral differences. Before we look at these, you may be asking what all this has to do with influence. It has everything to do with influence. If I don't respect you, I may be less willing to learn from you. If I don't respect you, I may treat you in such a way that I actually have a negative influence on you. On a practical level, if I know more about you than you know about me, I may have a slight advantage in dealing with you. However, if I know more about you than you know about yourself, I am in a position to greatly influence your response to our interaction, and hopefully I will be able to help you find a satisfying solution to a dilemma that may be frustrating you. Again, we need to learn to speak other people's language. The more we know about one another, the more effective we will be in our relationships with each other. Let's consider some behavioral differences that affect our ability to influence others.

Neuro-Linguistic Programming (NLP)

You may be familiar with California psychologists Richard Bandler and John Grinder, and Neuro-Linguistic Programming (NLP). There is much in NLP that I cannot understand at all, but there is one area of this discipline that is both entertaining and insightful. According to NLP people have different ways of relating to their world.

For example, some people are very visually oriented. You can always discern high visual people, because when they are remembering something from the past, they will look up and to the left. When they are creating, they will look up and to the right. (This is true for most right-handed persons. These modalities may be reversed for left-handed people.)

Theoretically, you can tell by watching people's eyes whether they are telling you the truth or not. If you ask a high visual a question about something that supposedly happened in the past, and they look up and to the right, they are creating—not remembering. It means they are creating false information. Some folks call this lying.

Other people are auditory. When they are trying to remember, their eyes wander to the side—in the direction of their left ear. When they are creating, they look to the right. Sometimes an auditory person will look down and to the left. If you know a good musician or a radio broadcaster with a deep, melodic FM voice, ask them a question about the past and watch their eyes. This can be a great game, and you will impress other people that you are so interested in listening to them that you actually stare into their eyes.

A third group is kinesthetic. They want to touch their world. Feelings, both external and internal, are very important to the kinesthetic. Kinesthetics will look down and to the right when they are remembering. Have you ever heard the expression, "down-right mean?" All of us, when we are feeling something very strongly, have a tendency to look down and to the right.

Watch your family members or people in your office or your customers when they are asked a question. See if their eyes give you clues as to their communication style. Our Arab friends are supposedly very adept at reading people's eyes. It is for this reason that many politicians in the Arab world will wear sunglasses even when they are indoors. They want to hide their eyes!

Remember, moving the eyes like this is an unconscious response. Some people have trained themselves to overcome this tendency by looking directly into the eyes of the person with whom they are talking, so it is more difficult to type them. Many of us, however, cannot access our brain without moving our eyes to one of the aforementioned locations.

Even if you can't see their eyes, there are other clues about a person's primary orientation as a visual, auditory, or kinesthetic. Visuals will often say things like, "I see what you mean . . . " or "Picture this . . . " Auditory persons will often say things like "I hear what you are saying . . ." or "I like the sound of that." Kinesthetic people will say things like, "I can't get a feel for what you're saying."

Would it help you to know you are interacting with a person whether he or she is primarily visual, auditory or a kinesthetic? It might if you are a salesperson, a teacher, a parent, or a spouse. In fact, it would help you in any relationship where you want to exercise influence. Is your partner a person who values touch, or does soft music do the trick? Is your customer impressed by how the product looks, or its sound or the feel of the expensive upholstery?

NLP is a program for exercising influence. In NLP you learn how to build rapport with others through mirroring their body language, breathing patterns, etc. Neuro-Linguistic Programming can be quite manipulative. It is not the point of this book to teach you how to manipulate others. But it is helpful for us to understand people more thoroughly so that we might build a bridge to them. NLP is but one tool for reading people. There are many others.

Take, for example, one of the most remarkable literary successes of the past couple of years. Writer Spencer Johnson has proven more than once that a book does not have to be weighty to be a bestseller. Remember *The One-Minute Manager,* co-authored by Ken Blanchard? Johnson's most recent work, *Who Moved My Cheese,* is a tiny volume that spent months atop the best-seller list. It details reactions to change, as experienced by two people, named Hem and Haw, and two mice, named Sniffy and Scurry. As we watch them adjust to the sudden depletion of their supply of cheese, we are inspired to think through our reaction to loss in our own lives, whether it is the loss of a job, a dream, or a relationship. Each of us copes with change in different, but in relatively predictable ways.

Years ago the *New York Mirror* shut down its presses for the last time. The announcement caught most of its sixteen hundred employees off guard. Some calmly went about their work wrapping up the last issue, while others cleaned out their desks without a word and went home. Some raced to the phones to call loved ones with the news while others were hurriedly making calls to line up new jobs. Each employee responded to the news according to his or her natural behavioral style. Understanding these behavioral styles can open a new world of knowledge about the people who share our world.

Mommy, Do Idiots Ever Get out on the Road When Daddy's Not Driving?

Have you ever noticed how a person's basic personality is revealed when he or she gets behind the wheel of a car? See if you recognize some of these people:

The kamikaze, the demon of the highway, would pass a funeral procession going uphill. She has a bumper sticker on the back that reads, "As a matter of fact, I do own the road." Kamikazes are impatient and highly aggressive. Let's call this type driver an "assertive" driver.

Then there are the party animals, the drivers who forget all about their driving if other people are in the car. They love to talk. If you are sitting in the back seat, they will put one hand on the wheel and turn all the way around to talk to you. Have you been in Washington, D.C.? You know those little circles that they have at major intersections? They're designed to drive around. A friend of mine once drove right through the middle of a small circle in Northwest D. C.—over the grass and around a statue. Why? He hadn't been drinking and he definitely wasn't high on drugs. No, he was talking. Driving was a secondary concern to him, if there was an opportunity for a good conversation. Let's call this driver a "socializer."

Then there are those nice steady drivers, the overly cautious ones. Don't you love them? If there is a turn ahead, they will be in the proper lane a good mile before they need to turn. And if there are others of the same temperament, you will have a long line of drivers in the same lane with no one trying to pass—except for one assertive driver (kamikaze) who is going bonkers trying to beat the system. Let's call this steady, conservative driver "dependable."

Finally there is the highly conscientious driver. Her car is immaculate. She has read the owner's manual, of all things. Her tires are rotated on schedule. Nothing is left to chance. She has studied the map before she left home, folded it precisely, and returned it to its proper place. Let's call her a perfectionist personality.

Did you know that people's behaviors fall roughly into these four categories? Research shows that people usually respond to pressure-filled situations according to four predictable patterns. For purposes of this discussion, let's call these four patterns assertive, socializer, dependable, and perfectionist.

Assertive Personalities

Some people have assertive personalities. They like to be in control. They like challenges. They make decisions quickly. They are straightforward. You don't have to wonder what a person with an assertive personality thinks, because he or she will tell you. They are determined people. They are sometimes wrong, but rarely in doubt. They are direct, blunt, and outspoken. They are risk takers. They like places of leadership and they are very impatient with folks who march to a different drummer. Assertive people are better talkers than listeners. Better at giving orders than taking them. They like to play according to their own set of rules.

People who drive their way to the top of their professions are usually assertive personalities. Ted Turner is, and so is Madonna. It was she who said, "Listen, everyone is entitled to my opinion."

Tom Watson once asked Ross Perot how successful he would have been if he had stayed at IBM. "I'd be somewhere in middle management, being asked to take early retirement," said Perot. "I would not have been successful in a big corporation. I'm too direct. Too purposeful." Perot is an assertive personality.

So is Jack Welch, former chairman of General Electric. A former executive with GE said of Welch, "If you put Jack in charge of a gas station at a corner with four gas stations, he wouldn't sleep until the other guys had plywood over their windows."

One of my favorite examples of this style of behavior appeared in a psychology text I read years ago. It concerns a little fellow named Jonathan, age three. His parents took him to a fancy restaurant, where he ordered a grilled cheese sandwich. The waitress explained that grilled cheese was not on the menu.

Jonathan, determined to have his way, asked, "Do you have cheese and bread?" The waitress nodded, "We do . . . "

"Then," Jonathan asked, "do you have a pan?" Remember that this is a three-year-old.

Jonathan got his sandwich.

When it arrived, the waitress took beverage orders. Jonathan ordered a milkshake, but this time the waitress was one step ahead. "Jonathan, we don't serve chocolate milkshakes. It is true we have milk and ice cream, but I'm sorry we don't have any syrup." Jonathan then asked, "Do you have a car?"

This young man will one day run the world. Assertive people can be quite intimidating, but without them, the world would suffer.

Socializing Personalities

Some people are talkative, enthusiastic, and positive to a fault. They like being the center of attention. They wear bright clothes and drive flashy cars. They like to party. They are usually warm-hearted and friendly. That is because being around people is very important to them. If you want to involve them in a learning experience, you need to make it fun.

I think of Willard Scott and Dolly Parton as socializers, though both of them obviously have a high assertive component as well or they would never have gone as far as they have. Former President Clinton is also a socializer; the first tip-off is that people say it is difficult to get him to quit talking. The second is that he has a reputation for disregarding the clock. Time is not important to a socializer. Being with people is what gets the socializer's juices flowing. No wonder Clinton is a great campaigner. Socializers have a tendency to be disorganized and they can wreak havoc when there is a need to run a tight ship.

Dependable Personalities

Some people are just slow, steady, good-natured folks. They don't need to be the center of attention. They would rather follow than lead. They like to stay on traditional paths. They don't like change. We call them solid and reliable. They make good mates, good neighbors, good workers, and good citizens. They are peacemakers. They value tranquility. They are not risk takers. They are particularly adverse to conflict. Dependable people are patient and loyal. They're good listeners. They are harmonious, and somewhat low-keyed—especially in comparison to the other personality types.

Mr. Rogers of the PBS show *Mr. Rogers' Neighborhood* is a dependable. It is difficult to identify many celebrities who are dependables for the simple reason that dependables are not known for ambition or love of the spotlight. Thus, they are more apt to labor behind the scenes. In our culture, however, high dependables are the largest single group. They are the stabilizing influences that keep our society, our businesses, our churches, civic organizations, and our families intact.

Perfectionist Personalities

Some people are more comfortable controlling things than they are at dealing with people. The perfectionist is generally more comfortable with tasks than with interaction. They have high standards. They want to make sure things are done right whether in the lab or at home. They tend to be compulsive, at least as viewed by non-perfectionist people. Sloppiness is not to be tolerated in any area of life. Remember Tony Randall's character, Felix, on television's *The Odd Couple*? Definitely a perfectionist personality.

Personal standards are very important to the perfectionist personality, who is efficient, precise, organization-minded, and logical. He or she wants everything done right. Perfectionist people love details. If you are a manager, you don't want to come down too hard on people with this style; they are harder on themselves than you will ever be.

Coping with the Four Personalities

People are different. Everyone scores high on at least one of these personality types, while some people score high on two of these styles of behavior. Actually, each of us is a mixture of these four personality types.

If you are an assertive/socializer, you likely will make a good leader. If you are an assertive/perfectionist, you are apt to be very creative, etc. All of us, though, will score high on at least one of these styles: assertive, socializing, dependable, or perfectionist.

Now it is important for us to realize that there is no bad personality type. None of these styles of behavior is superior to the others—though each of them is advantageous in given situations. The fact that we are different is one of the Creator's great gifts to us. What if we all were assertive personalities? We would charge around looking for people to lead, but there would be no followers. What if we were all socializers? Life would be a continuous party, but who would be producing goods? If we were all dependables, we would be relatively content with the status quo. Very little progress would take place. If we were all perfectionist personality types everything would be done correctly, but no one would have much fun. We're different, and that's good. Let me give you an example.

I once led a group in which there was a classic socializer. I'm trying not to be stereotypical, but this girl was an archetypal ditzy blond. She talked very fast and was very expressive. She would cut her sentences and shift thoughts so quickly that I sometimes could not even figure out exactly what she was saying. She had lots of energy and enthusiasm, but there were times when I thought the lights were on, but nobody was home—if you know what I mean. How in the world does somebody this scatterbrained make it in the real world, I asked myself?

Then somebody told me she is one of the most popular teachers in her school. She teaches first grade. I had already noticed by watching her eyes that she is a high kinesthetic—high touch, high feeling. Suddenly I saw how valuable she was to the boys and girls in her school. I could see her bouncing into the classroom with all that positive energy and enthusiasm and greeting each of the children with a big hug. Wow! How lucky those boys and girls would be to have her. You see, each of us is different and that's good!

I was on one of these tiny commuter planes flying from Charlotte, North Carolina, to my home in Knoxville, Tennessee. I don't mind flying on big jets, but I don't like these twelve-passenger commuter planes—that's too much like flying for me. I remember the words of our Lord, "Lo, I am with you always." Here I was on this tiny commuter plane. There were storms brewing all around us. I could see them glowing red on the pilot's radar.

Then, about halfway home there was a sound like air coming in around a window across the aisle and a harsh rattling. I started thinking about that flight from Hawaii some years back where a piece of the plane peeled away and a flight attendant was sucked out of the plane. I thought to myself, what if there are major problems with this plane? What kind of pilot would I want in the cockpit—an assertive? I can hear him now: "Hold on, I'll get this baby to Knoxville, or die trying."

A socializer? "Here, Larry, you take over the controls. I want to get to know some of the passengers."

I think I would want a perfectionist person in the cockpit: "Ladies and gentlemen, I heard that strange rattling noise too and I have decided to stop in Asheville and have it checked out." That would be my kind of pilot.

Each of us would have our own preference. But people are different, and that's good! That's the way the Creator intended things to be. And we empower others when we recognize and value those differences.

There are some managers who are assertive personalities. They got to be managers because of their drive and determination. But they are terrible managers because they think everybody ought to be like they are. They don't realize that if everybody in the company was assertive, it would fold in six months. So, rather than empowering those under them, they appeal to fear and intimidation, and they actually stifle those they've been assigned to lead. If they would value the socializers, dependables, and perfectionists under them for who they are, they could watch them blossom in ways that they cannot imagine.

It's also true in the home. Imagine a couple who are both dependables. Quiet, unassuming, and responsible. But they have a socializer child, a real party animal. Can you see the possibility for conflict?

Or imagine two assertives, husband and wife both very aggressive, very goal-oriented. But they have one of these quiet, unassuming, almost passive dependable children. Can you sense that they might express a great deal of frustration with that child, rather than valuing that child and helping him/her according to his or her personality type?

I know a woman who has many difficulties in her home life. At work she is a ball of fire, but at home she has an abusive husband and an extended family that takes advantage of her. Why does she put up with it? Guess what? I tested her and she scored equally high in assertive and dependable. That is a strange combination. Can you see why she might have conflict in her life? She has a great need for control as a assertive personality and an equally strong need for loyalty to her loved ones because of her dependable component. She spends a great deal of her time in torment.

It is tremendously helpful when dealing with persons to know their personality type if you want to exercise any influence with them at all. Two of my four daughters are assertives. How they got that way I don't know. Both my wife and I are dependable/concientious. If we had only known about these four personality types when they were teenagers, it would have saved us much grief. We thought they were simply terminally obnoxious. (Just kidding, they were great kids.)

There are ways of dealing with assertive personalities; be direct and don't beat around the bush. With a socializer, be enthusiastic, positive, and supportive. Recognize the socializer's need for interpersonal interaction. With a dependable, be patient and genuinely sympathetic. With a perfectionist, understand his need for precision, and let him know exactly what is expected of him. Let me emphasize: the more you understand why people behave the way they do, the more influential you will be.

We influence people by recognizing and valuing them as they are. We treat them, not as we would like to be treated, *but as they would like to be treated.* George Bernard Shaw put it this way: "Do not do unto others as you would have them do unto you. They may have different tastes." Before we try to influence anyone, it would be helpful if we understood who they are, how they respond to varying situations and what they value.

The Seven Forms of Intelligence

People are different. Did you know that people are also smart—each in his or her own way? That is something I have long observed, but until recently had no objective evidence to support—that is until I heard of Harvard psychologist Howard Gardner and the Seven Forms of Intelligence, a concept that has revolutionized education in many areas.[3]

Gardner says that the I.Q. tests we take in school are far too narrow. Those tests identify only one or two skills or aptitudes. He has identified at least seven. Gardner acknowledges that seven is an arbitrary figure; there may be many, many more.

For example, there is *logical-mathematical* intelligence. People with this form of intelligence are good not only with numbers, but also with abstract concepts. They make good scientists and mathematicians.

Then there's *linguistic* intelligence. People with linguistic intelligence are good with language. They are likely to be poets, journalists, and speakers.

There is *spatial* intelligence. People with this form of intelligence are good at seeing shapes and forms. They would make good navigators or sculptors. I watch my three year-old grandson working complicated jigsaw puzzles with delight. My guess is that he is gifted with spatial intelligence.

There is *bodily-kinesthetic* intelligence. These people are more naturally graceful physically. They seem to have natural eye-hand coordination. They include our dancers and athletes.

There is *interpersonal* intelligence. There are some people who seem to have a gift for working with others. They always seem to know the right thing to say. They make good therapists, pastors, and salespeople.

There is *intrapersonal* intelligence. These are our wise people. They are able to look within to find answers. They have what is often referred to as horse sense. My best friend has intrapersonal intelligence. Dave and I grew up together. I made the better grades in school, but I always knew that Dave was a bright and talented person. Dave is also a speaker, and he is the leading expert in his industry. Let me illustrate how our two brains differ.

I have a large lawn. It takes me three hours each week to mow it. One day I was complaining that I am so tired by the time I finish mowing, that I sometimes neglect to trim with the weed-eater. Dave's response: trim first. I had never thought of that. But that's the way Dave's brain works. He is wise, practical, and he has "horse sense." I won't tell you how my brain operates. Sometimes it doesn't at all.

Finally, there is *musical* intelligence. Let's face it, some people are very talented musically while others cannot carry a tune.

Now here's the important point: Gardner says that everyone he has tested has scored high on at least one of these forms of intelligence. In other words, everyone is smart in his or her own way. If we will get to know people, we will discover that nearly everyone has strengths.

Sometimes these strengths are hidden. The brick layer may go home and write poetry. The engineer may go home and play jazz on the piano until late in the night. In the same way that the *One-Minute Manager* encouraged us to catch people doing something right and to praise them, so should we look for those hidden strengths in the people we work with, live with, worship with, play with. It is impossible to have much influence with people whom we do not respect or understand.

The philosopher Alain once said, "The power of a Caesar or an Alexander rested upon the fact that each had a liking for differences and did not expect pear trees to produce plums." In this chapter I have been able to give you only a brief overview of several helpful approaches to understanding people—understanding people is the first key to influencing them.

John Powell once told of a wise teacher who was speaking to a group of eager young students. He gave them the assignment to go out and find a small, unnoticed flower somewhere. He asked them to study it for a long time. He suggested using a magnifying glass to study the delicate veins, and the nuances and shades of color and the wonderful symmetry of the leaf. Then he told them to remember that this flower might have gone unnoticed and unappreciated if they had not found and admired it. After the class returned, the teacher told the class that people are like those flowers. Each one is unique and special, but many go unappreciated because no one takes the time to admire their uniqueness.

Learn to appreciate other people's strengths, and you will lay a foundation of trust that will allow some of the NPPD of your influence to make its way into their lives.

CHAPTER 23

Step 5: Reach Out to Those Closest to You

Abbie Hoffman is best remembered as a radical from the 1960s. He was arrested fifty-three times. He died at age fifty-two, but he was a rebel until the end. Of his youngest son, America, age eighteen, Hoffman said, "He's been kicked out of class seven times already. I'm very proud of him."[1]

I really don't know how Abbie Hoffman was as a father. He might have been a very loving man. But contrast Hoffman's words with those of Arun Gandhi, the grandson of Mahatma Gandhi. Arun Gandhi is the director of the M. K. Gandhi Institute for Nonviolence in Memphis, Tennessee and a sterling advocate for peace not only in the world but also in the family. Arun tells about something that happened to him when he was sixteen years old.[2]

Arun's family was living in South Africa. It was a Saturday. His father had to go to a conference in a town that was eighteen miles away and he didn't feel like driving that day. So he asked Arun to drive him into town and bring him back in the evening. Arun agreed.

Since he was going into town, his mother gave him a list of groceries she needed, and on the way into town his dad asked him to get the car serviced. When Arun dropped his father off at the conference, his father said, "I'll wait for you at this intersection at five o'clock in the evening. You come here and pick me up and we'll go home together."

Arun had the whole day to himself. So he finished his chores as quickly as possible and made a beeline for the nearest cinema, since he was very interested in Hollywood movies, especially John Wayne movies. He went in and sat and sat, not realizing that they were showing a double feature. He became so engrossed in the movie that he didn't look at the time.

By the time Arun left the cinema, it was half past five. He ran to the garage and got the car, and by the time he reached his father, it was about six o' clock in the evening. His father was pacing up and down, worried about what happened to him. The very first question he asked Arun was, "Why are you late?" For some inexplicable reason, instead of telling him the truth, Arun lied to him. He said, "The car wasn't ready and I had to wait until they finished with it," little realizing that his father had called the garage and asked them.

When he caught Arun in the lie, his father said, "There's something wrong in the way I brought you up that you didn't have the confidence to tell me the truth, and I've got to find out where I went wrong with you. In order to do that, I'm not coming in the car with you. I'm going to walk home."

At six o' clock in the evening his father started walking eighteen miles back home. Arun could do nothing to persuade him to change his mind. He realized that much of the eighteen miles would be difficult and dangerous, the path meandering through sugarcane fields and dark roads. Arun couldn't leave him, so he crawled behind him in the car for all those eighteen miles. For five hours Arun Gandhi saw his dad punishing himself for some stupid lie Arun had uttered. He decided then and there that he was never going to lie again.

Now that Arun Gandhi's grown, he wonders what his reaction would have been if his father had given him the conventional punishment that we give to our children when we catch them lying. If his father had punished Arun and yelled at him or grounded him or done any of the things we often do when children have disappointed us, would Arun have learned the lesson that his father taught him that day? Arun doesn't think so. He thinks he would have shrugged his shoulders, suffered the punishment and said, "Well, this time I was stupid enough to get caught; next time I will make sure I don't get caught."

"I think that's what happens to our children today," says Arun Gandhi. "We punish them in the hope of disciplining them. But punishment doesn't really discipline. There is a lot of rethinking needed in our relationship with people, in our relationship with our families and our relationship with our children."

According to *Psychology Today* magazine, there is empirical evidence that Gandhi is right.[3] How we discipline our children affects their perception of appropriate solutions to problems. "Physical punishment teaches that the way to solve problems is to beat up others," says Leonard Eron, a research psychologist at the University of Illinois at Chicago. He explains that having children focus on what they did wrong and why it was wrong encourages them to internalize control of their own actions. But physical punishment, while suppressing misbehavior in the short run, ultimately promotes nothing more than a determination to avoid being caught.

How we discipline our children can have an enormous effect on their values and their sense of self worth. I showed an early version of this manuscript to a friend who is of a decidedly conservative religious bent. He violently disagreed on this one issue. He thought I was bending over backward to be politically correct. He is a proponent of spanking children and maintaining strict order.

He may be right, but I don't think so. My wife and I were rather permissive in bringing up our daughters. I was a product of the thinking of the sixties. I wanted my four girls to think for themselves. I wanted them to accept our values only if they felt they were authentic—not because they were programmed to think like us. The people I knew who had been brought up with what I consider excessive discipline seemed to be guilt-ridden and afraid of out-of-the box thinking.

Was I wrong? I don't think so. Looking back, there is little I would change. Again, we were very fortunate. It is impossible to predict how any particular child will respond to his/her environment. And, if I was only speaking from my own experience, I would speak with less confidence. But social science agrees. Violence breeds violence, even if the violence only takes the form of a hard paddling.

Of course, in many homes the violence does not end with paddling, and the results are often tragic. For example, studies show that children who see physical violence between their parents are six times more likely to abuse their own spouses after they marry. If those children were also hit by their parents as teenagers, they are twelve times more likely to abuse their spouses.

Arun Gandhi's father was wise. I sometimes think we punish our children because it makes us feel better. Many parents need to rethink the ways they seek to influence their children.

Life's Most Vexing and Most Rewarding Task

It's difficult to be a family in today's world. You might remember the classic plan that Alvin Toffler outlined for the family of tomorrow in his book *Future Shock*.[4] Since few company executives stay put in one place any more, Toffler designed a scenario in which the executive not only leaves his house behind, but his family as well. The company then finds him a replacement family. This family comes complete with personality characteristics carefully selected to duplicate those of the wife and children left behind. His successor meanwhile "plugs into" the family left behind.

I trust that Toffler offered this scenario with his tongue planted firmly in his cheek, but still, it is difficult to raise a family today. We all could use help—particularly young families with small children.

According to an old African myth, one day God asked the first human couple what kind of death they wanted. They could choose the death of the moon or that of a banana. God explained that the banana puts forth shoots that take its place, but the moon itself comes back to life.

This was a major decision for the couple. If they elected the death of the moon that represented being childless, they would avoid death. Avoiding death would be most desirable, but without children, how happy would they be? If, on the other hand, they chose the death of the banana— putting forth shoots—they would die, but their lives would have meaning and purpose as they raised their children and enjoyed their company. They prayed and decided that rather than remain childless, they would ask God for the death of the banana. With that choice, according to the myth, human mortality became a fact.

Children are a very important part of our lives. What parent would not lay down his or her life for their child? But raising children is life's most difficult as well as its most rewarding task. It is a shame that children do not come with easy-to-follow instructions about how to raise them, particularly in the fast changing world in which we live today.

Gary Apple put it this way: "Parenting would be easier if my children were better at childing." Raising children is not easy, but a parent who uses loving, patient influence will reap rewards.

When Influence Begins

How soon should we start trying to influence our children? Actually, there is evidence from several studies that influence in the family begins before birth.

A group of pregnant mothers were asked to read a Dr. Seuss story to their tummies five times a day. Soon after their babies were born, the mothers were hooked to a metering machine called the Baby Watcher. The purpose was to monitor their infant's sucking pattern. Meanwhile a tape recorder played sounds of the Dr. Seuss story, as well as sounds of a story the mother had never read.

Researchers were able to determine via the Baby Watcher when the baby was hearing sounds of the Dr. Seuss story that had been read aloud to him before birth by his mother. The response to that story was stronger than to the story his mother had never read aloud.[6] I wonder, sometimes, if studies like these are ever applied to the abortion debate. I am not a zealot on the subject. But sometimes I wonder if an organism that can be affected by the reading aloud of Dr. Seuss by its mother ought to be dismissed as simply an insignificant fetus. Perhaps anti-abortionists ought to quit quoting scripture, and begin quoting science. Maybe this is an area where our society might be better off to err on the side of caution.

In some areas, our influence begins even before birth. Certainly a staggering number of influences begin the moment the baby is spanked to life.

Years ago, I remember being impressed by an experiment in which babies were fed types of juices by nurses who held them during the feeding. In a very short time, the baby's preferences for juices reflected their nurse's preferences. In other words, if the nurse disliked orange juice, it was not long until the baby disliked orange juice. When the babies were assigned to a different nurse, their preferences changed to reflect the new nurse's preferences.

Think of the implications of both of these studies and others like them. My guess is that most parents underestimate the influence they have on their children because so much of that influence is unconscious. Children pick up the subtlest of clues even when we try to disguise our true feelings. We may be communicating very strong preferences and prejudices without even being aware of it. For example, a parent says, "I treated my son and my daughter exactly alike. Any differences in their subsequent choices of toys must reflect a basic genetic predisposition." Not so quickly! The parent was probably communicating softness to the girl and toughness to the boy at a level at which he or she was not even aware. I know that, from the very beginning, I have treated my grandson and my granddaughter differently. I "rough house" with my grandson in ways I never would have dreamed of with my granddaughter.

This is not to rule out the influence of genetic differences in behavior. I am convinced that genes do play a significant role. Some behavioral patterns seem to be unexplainable based solely on environment. Still, we communicate to our children with much more than just words. And children are much more perceptive to forms of meta-communication than we may be aware.

It is during the earliest years when a child is forming perceptions about personal identity and responsibility that influences occur that forever determine how he or she relates to the world. Is the world a hostile place where I must protect myself, or is it a warm and welcome place where I can live openly and freely? It is impossible to overstate the power of parents during these earliest years in molding the basic personality of the child. Henry Ward Beecher said it best: "What a mother sings to the cradle goes all the way down to the coffin." But it is not so much what the parent *does* as what the parent *is* that counts.

Is the parent able to openly and freely express affection? Is the parent a happy and wholesome person who communicates trust? Is there an atmosphere of love and acceptance in the home, or is there conflict and resentment? Children are sensitive to such things.

How important is the overall climate in the home to the welfare of the child? It can be devastating, particularly if the primary caretaker is in emotional turmoil.

According to studies in the behavioral sciences, the factor that best predicts which children will one day attempt suicide is depression in the mother. The factor that most accurately predicts drug addiction in children is tranquilizer use by the mother. The factor that most accurately predicts high self-esteem in children is happiness in the mother. When traditional family roles are reversed, you may substitute the word father in each of these factors. This proves that children are singularly sensitive to the overall environment in the home. In fact, one researcher has discovered that even a child's physical growth can be affected by the presence or absence of conflict in the home.[7]

According to this researcher, the hypothalamus, which produces chemical changes that control children's growth, can be affected by conflict between parents. An apparently dwarfed child, when removed from the charged atmosphere of a home in turmoil, has been known to grow from five to ten inches in one year. That is quite a radical influence. And again, it is indirect. It concerns the dominant climate in the home, more than it does any one action of the parent.

For years my wife hung a sign in our home: "The most important thing a father can do for his children is to love their mother." And it's true. Children are apt to be affected by a parent's unhappiness. Is there a climate of trust, respect, love, and joy in your home? We can give our children one of life's most valuable gifts without spending a dime. All we have to do is to pay attention to how we treat our spouse.

Walking the Talk

Although a positive emotional atmosphere in the home is crucial to a child's development, we should never underestimate the power of direct example. If you want to influence your children, you must be willing to walk the talk.

Modeling behavior—whether it is for a new employee or for one's own children—is the most effective form of influence. And we should not look to football stars or Hollywood actors to provide appropriate models. Most of what children learn about appropriate and inappropriate behavior they learn at home. As Milton Berle says, "When you're a kid, you learn a lot at your mother's knee. The rest you learn at some other joint." (Sorry, I can't resist a good line.)

Ross Perot, who rose from very poor circumstances to become a billionaire, talks about his mother feeding the homeless during the Depression. Her influence caused Perot to take seriously his responsibility to give back in service what he has received from society. He recalls that during the Depression, hoboes often stopped at their house to ask for food. A certain hobo explained that earlier visitors had left a white chalk mark on the sidewalk indicating that this house was an easy mark. Young Ross offered to scrub the mark off the sidewalk, but his mother said no. He never forgot her example of compassion.[8]

The Most Important Role Models

Long before basketball star Charles Barkley made his famous statement about not wanting to be a role model, basketball icon Larry Bird said practically the same thing. He said he didn't want to be some child's hero. "His father should be his hero," Bird said. Charles Barkley was sharply criticized for his statement, but the complete text of Barkley's famous shoe ad was, "I am not a role model. Parents should be role models. Just because I can dunk a basketball doesn't mean I should raise your kids."

In 1987, John Lucas of the Milwaukee Bucks came to the humbling realization that his addiction to alcohol and drugs was having a devastating effect on his family. He discovered his four year-old daughter holding cigarette ashes to her nose, apparently mimicking the time she saw him snorting cocaine. John Lucas went on to conquer his addictions, and now he works with other NBA players to help them overcome their deadly dependence on chemicals.[9]

Lucas chose to take responsibility for his life before it was too late, but many parents are not that responsible. As someone has said, "The worst danger that confronts the younger generation is the example set by the older generation." If mom and dad can't grow up to live their lives in a positive, constructive way, there is not much hope for their children.

A child's parents should provide the role model—particularly his or her dad. I'm not being a chauvinist when I say that—nor am I consigning to failure children brought up by single mothers. Nevertheless, it is almost impossible to overstate the importance of the father's role in modeling behavior.

Paul Lewis is president of a parenting education course in San Diego called Family University. He was involved with a study of one hundred Minnesota prison inmates. They were asked to describe men whom they considered father figures. Less than twelve percent put down their own fathers; fifty-two percent named sports or entertainment heroes as their father figures. Lewis says, "I work with a number of people who work with juvenile delinquent kids. I've never had a single case worker who has ever had a kid report a healthy relationship with their dad. Not one out of hundreds." Amazing! And frightening! Where possible, kids really do need two parents.

I am not a dreamer. And I don't want to make single mothers uncomfortable. They have a tough enough battle as it is. And many are coping admirably. But we need a national initiative to encourage dads to stay involved with their kids.

I was in Atlanta recently. A newspaper from that city carried a story that broke my heart, and at the same time made me angry. It said that a researcher in Atlanta had discovered that sixty percent of the people living in poverty were single mothers and their children. Think of that. If we could solve this one problem—fatherless homes—we could wipe out nearly two-thirds of the poverty in this country! We could also make a sizeable dent in crime and drug usage. We could build a greater society for generations to come if we could just get dads to accept responsibility for their children.

Hey, Mr. President, couldn't we use some of that enormous government surplus we keep hearing about to do a little preventive care in this one area? Think of the billions of dollars we could save fighting crime, drugs, and all the negative consequences of poverty by teaching our young people about responsible living. Oh, but somebody is going to say that is a parental responsibility. Yes it is, but the families at risk here have no models for responsible parenting. Children are raising children with predictable results!

Of course, while we are talking about the role of dads in the family, we don't want to overlook the importance of Moms. The influence a mother has on her child is awesome. Thomas Edison knew that. Once he wrote:

I did not have my mother long, but she cast over me an influence that lasted all my life. The good effects of her early training I can never lose. If it had not been for her appreciation and her faith in me at a critical time in my experience, I would never likely have become an inventor. I was always a careless boy, and with a mother of different mental caliber, I would have turned out badly. But her firmness, her sweetness, her goodness, were potent powers to help me on the right path. My mother was the making of me. The memory of her will always be a blessing to me.

Les Brown is a famed businessman and motivational speaker who overcame great personal odds to achieve astounding success. He credits his mother with having instilled in him the talents and abilities to make something special out of his life. She built character into her son with strict morals and discipline, but she also loved him unconditionally.

Les likes to tell the story of when he caught diphtheria as a very young boy.[10] Another little boy in his neighborhood had been hospitalized for diphtheria and died from it. Les' mother, fearful that he might die in a hospital too, insisted on nursing him back to health at home. Just as the worst of the illness passed, Les lost his voice completely. Les' mother was devastated, and she began praying, "Lord, give the child my voice. I've talked enough in my life. I don't need my voice no more."

The next morning, Les awoke to find his voice restored, but when he called out for his mother, she didn't answer him. Her voice had diminished to a squeak. A few hours later, she also got her voice back. But ever after that, whenever Les talked back to his mother or used curse words, she would warn him, "You talk like that again, I'll take my voice back. I asked Jesus to give you my voice and he did. You use it like that, I'll take it back."

In 1987, Dr. Ben Carson led a surgical team that performed the world's first successful separation of Siamese twins joined at the back of the head.[11] Dr. Carson has had great success in the field of medicine. He credits his success in life to his mother. Ben grew up in a poor, black neighborhood in Detroit. He was labeled, "the dummy" by his classmates. Ben's mother, worried that her boys would never escape their neighborhood, assigned her sons to read two books every week and present a book report to her. Ben loved reading, and soon his grades soared. His academic success led him on to Yale, and eventually into medical school. And he claims his mother's book reports inspired his success. But here's the interesting thing: Ben's mother dropped out of school in the third grade. Ben and his brother didn't know that she couldn't read their book reports.

Lindiwe Mabuza has spent twenty years of her life working for an end to apartheid in South Africa.[12] She has been the chief representative of the African National Congress, and has brought the plight of oppressed South African blacks to the attention of businesses and opinion makers all over the world. Last May, Ms. Mabuza was named South Africa's ambassador to Germany. She is the first black person to hold this highly visible and influential post.

Ms. Mabuza is focusing most of her attention these days on promoting trade with Germany and economic investment in South Africa. Her great intelligence and diplomacy have earned her international respect.

Lindiwe Mabuza, like so many other black people in South Africa, was raised in poverty that is beyond the scope of most Americans' imaginations. But she knew from a young age that education would take her beyond her meager beginnings. Ms. Mabuza tells of a time as a young person when her mother's employer offered the young Lindiwe a job as a maid, saying that she had had enough education. Lindiwe Mabuza's mother gave her employer a hard look and replied, "I am working in your kitchen, Madam, to make sure that my daughter will never have to earn her living like that." And Lindiwe Mabuza made sure that she lived up to her mother's expectations.

Talk show host Oprah Winfrey attributes her character to her grandmother, Hattie Mae.[13] Oprah is so extremely successful today that it is easy to forget how much she had to overcome to get to where she is. Sexually abused as a child and shuttled from home to home by her mother and father, Oprah could have been lost to the world but for the powerful influence of her grandmother. Hattie Mae was a disciplinarian. Today her methods would be frowned upon as extreme. But somehow she communicated to little Oprah a sense of being loved. She bestowed upon her precocious granddaughter a sense of character and values. "I am what I am," says this much-admired star, "because of my grandmother; my strength, my sense of reasoning, everything. All of that was set by the time I was six years old. I am basically no different now from what I was when I was six."

It would be impossible, by the way, to calculate the positive influence Oprah Winfrey has exerted in our society the past several years through her television shows, book clubs, motion pictures, etc. She devoted one entire show to the theme of random acts of kindness, which 11,774,880 people watched! How do you measure the good that could come from that one exposure? There are few people in history that have positively influenced more people directly than Hattie Mae's granddaughter.

What a shame that every child does not have a strong, positive adult to emulate. Maybe you and I can fill that need for some child.

Loving, committed parents, or, in their place, dedicated guardians and grandparents, have an incredible power to affect children's lives, to shape their characters. And unloving or selfish parents have just as much power to destroy their children's lives and to warp their characters.

Counselors Gary Smalley and John Trent tell of a client of theirs, a middle-aged man, who still suffered emotional fall-out from his father's thoughtlessness when this man was a child.[14] He and his father planned to go on a father-son camping trip with the Scouts. But on the day of the trip, the father claimed he had to go to work. Then, when he thought his son wasn't looking, the father threw his golf gear in the car and drove off. Almost thirty years later, this man still hadn't come to terms with his father's actions.

The influence we have on our children is awesome. They are our first responsibility. Before we change the world, we must make every effort to help them become happy productive human beings.

Providing Inspiration

A man was walking down the street one weekend when he spied a sign advertising a cat show.[15] He went inside and was treated to the sight of many magnificent felines. He couldn't believe the prices: a Persian worth $25,000, a Manx worth $40,000, and a Calico worth $50,000.

He went home, got his old Tomcat, and brought him to the show. An official spotted him and said, "You can't enter that common cat." He replied. "I don't want to enter him, I just want to take him through the show and inspire him."

Children need someone who will inspire them.

I was inspired by the example of Faye McFadden. Do you remember Faye? She was the woman who scooped up nineteen dollars and fifty-three cents when a Brink's truck overturned in Miami, spilling its contents in the street of one of Miami's poorer neighborhoods. Quite unexpectedly, Faye returned the money. When asked why, she explained, "I have children, and I need to set a good example." I love it. Thank you, Faye!

Barbara Jordan, the charismatic former congresswoman from Texas, had a grandfather who inspired her.[16] She always carried three photographs of him with her. She recalled that he didn't want her to be like other kids. Over and over again, he instilled in her a desire to be her own person, to be something more than ordinary, to pursue her own course. Barbara Jordan lived out his philosophy and remembered him fondly as one of the major influences in her life. Today Jordan is the first and only African-America woman resting in the Texas State Cemetery.

Barbara Jordan's grandfather had the same dreams for her that an African-American dad had for his son when he took the boy to a shoe store in Atlanta. It was during a period of segregation and extreme racial prejudice in that great city. Although the store was empty, the white sales-clerk said, "If you'll move to the back, I'll be glad to help you." But the father wouldn't tolerate this. "You'll wait on us here," he said, "or we won't buy any shoes." The clerk replied that he couldn't do that, where-upon the father took his son by the hand and left the store. Outside, he explained his behavior to his son: "I don't care how long I have to live with this thing, I'll never accept it. I'll fight it till I die. Nobody can make a slave out of you if you don't think like a slave."

That man was the father of Martin Luther King, Jr.[17] The boy never for-got that incident; it was formative in his outlook. Martin Luther King, Sr., known affectionately as Daddy King, could not know as he modeled behavior for his son that day that he was setting into play forces that would affect people of every color around the world—not only for his son's generation but for generations to come.

It is impossible to overstate the positive influence of caring parents. Of course, gauging how our influence will impact any one child is difficult.[18] It is rare, but I have seen devoted parents produce children who were ingrates. And I have seen families that could be charitably described as dysfunctional produce model citizens. The factors that regulate human behavior are far too complicated for us to isolate any one or two factors and say, "Aha! This was responsible for that!" Many parents of problem children beat up on themselves and say, "Where did I go wrong?" Remember, you were not the only influence in their lives. And even if you were, it is impossible to predict how any one child will respond to a par-ticular set of circumstances.

Psychologist Alfred Fuller researched the effects that alcoholic parents have on their children. I have heard children of such parents tell horror stories about their experiences. One of the families Fuller studied had twin boys and an alcoholic father who, by most measures, was not a good father. Neither was he a good husband to his wife, a good provider, nor a contributor to his community.

Several years later, after they had grown up and left home, Fuller inter-viewed these twins separately. One had become a good father, husband, and exemplary member of the community. The other was an alcoholic like his father, with many of the same negative traits. When Fuller asked each son why he thought he was the way he was, each gave the same answer: "Because of my father."[19]

You never can tell how a child will be affected by a parent's behavior. But if you have done the best you can to be a positive role model, you will not have the guilt that comes to the parent who knows he or she let a child down. Frequently, a child who knows he or she is loved will respond to that love with responsible living.[20] Even prodigals eventually come home.

Show Lots of Affection

John Douglas worked for the FBI for twenty-five years as a member of the "elite serial crime unit," which specializes in understanding the chemistry and mechanics of the brains of serial criminals such as Charles Manson and David Berkowitz (the Son of Sam). In his book *Mindhunter,* John shares some of the things he has learned from dealing with some of the most depraved criminals on earth.[21] John writes that he has never encountered a criminal who came from a "good background and functional, supportive family." He believes that the answer for countering this kind of evil is love.

John Douglas is right. Setting a good example is important, of course, but not by itself. Parents who live exemplary lives do not always produce exemplary children; affection is also needed.

Former professional football player Bill Glass tells of visiting a prison in Florida.[22] He asked one of the prison officials there how many Jews were in prison in Florida. The official answered, thirteen. Only thirteen Jews in all the prisons in Florida! Florida has a high Jewish population, and there are forty thousand inmates in Florida prisons.

Glass began to ask the same question all over the country. He discovered that in relation to the overall Jewish population, there is an infinitesimal number of Jews in jail or prison. One reason for this, Glass feels, is that Jewish families are strong on hugging, kissing, and touching. Jewish fathers, going back to the days of Abraham, Isaac, and Jacob, have always done three things whether their sons were three or thirty years old: "Bless you, my son. I love you, son." And then they give a big hug and kiss. Glass suggests that the rest of us in the Judeo-Christian tradition should have received this heritage. Many of us have been influenced more by the Prussian-German lifestyle, and also a sort of Puritanism that says don't touch anyone or show emotions. But hugging, kissing, and touching do make a difference in many areas of our lives. Particularly when we are young, touching and being touched help us develop a sense of being loved and accepted as we are. The more I study the literature, the more I wonder if it is even possible to give a child too much affection.

Former President Clinton set as a national goal that all children should know how to read by the time they reach the third grade. One way that goal can be reached is to pour money into our schools. A more effective way, according to Harvard psychologist Linda Russek and University of Arizona psychologist Gary Schwartz might be to teach parents to spend time each day holding their child and reading to that child.

Russek and Schwartz conducted a thirty-five-year study that followed eighty-seven college men into middle age.[23] They found that what is crucial to beginning to read is the child's attachment to an adult who spends time reading to or with the child. "Show us a child who feels loved," say these researchers, "and we'll show you someone likely to grow into a healthy adult."

None of this is surprising, of course. Nevertheless, it is critical. We have a tendency to live out a life script based on our experiences. We tend to do unto others as we have been done unto. If we have been brought up in a very affectionate family, then giving affection will be easy. However, if we were brought up in a family that did not express feelings easily and openly, we may have to really work at this in our own family. Either way, demonstrating affection toward our children is important.

Of course, we show love in more ways than simply with hugs and kisses. Cathy Guisewite is the creator of the comic strip *Cathy* in the newspapers. In an interview in the humor magazine, *Laughing Matters,* she tells how her father expressed his love for her. Guisewite remembers a special family dinner when some important friends of theirs were over for dinner. Her mom was really nervous about everything. In fact, the whole family was nervous. Guisewite was a little girl, and right in the middle of the dinner she spilled a glass of milk on the table. It was going to be a disaster. Then her dad did something she would never forget. He picked up the pitcher of milk, dumped the whole thing on the floor, and said, "What the heck. It looked like fun!"

This expression of love and acceptance changed the whole situation. We can imagine other families where Dad would have reacted in an entirely different way to this event. We communicate love not only with physical affection, but with understanding, patience, our willingness to listen and a hundred other small ways of being there and being genuinely concerned.

The Power of Positive Parenting

Set the example. Show affection. And one final thing. Be positive. It has been my personal observation that positive parents have positive kids. I can think of homes that are religious homes, loving homes, where parents conscientiously care about their children. But the children rebel. They are unhappy and unruly. Something is missing. I know to many this will seem superficial, but I believe this missing ingredient is a spirit of optimism in the home.

The benefits of a positive attitude about life and about your place in the world can hardly be overstated. People with an optimistic view of life enjoy better health, make more money, excel in school and have long, happy marriages.

A spirit of optimism or pessimism is caught in the home. I can think of families in my own experience, among my own friends, and I can see the clear difference that having a parent who has a healthy, optimistic view of life makes. Do you expect the best out of life or do you always fear the worst? Parents who expect the best and communicate that to their children give them a mind-set for being responsible citizens who have a positive influence on the world.

Perhaps you saw a newspaper story recently about a man in London who placed a thirty-three dollar bet that his son,[24] now three and a half months old, will score a goal for England in the World Cup finals in the year 2018. Raham Sharpe, a spokesman for bookmaker William Hill, said the man was given odds of fifty thousand to one, meaning he stands to win $1.67 million if his son scores. "Many parents back their children to achieve sporting prominence," Sharpe said. "But this is the most adventurous bet of its type we've ever taken."

I am not certain if that is a positive move or not. However, it does gives the young man something to live up to. People have a tendency to live up to—or down to—the expectations of their parents and peers. There is value in expecting the best.

Earl Woods expected the best for his son Tiger. When Tiger was still in diapers, Earl was pegging him as a future champion. When his mother wanted to throw away Tiger's highchair, Earl stopped her. "You can't throw it away," he said. "That's going to be in the Hall of Fame someday." And she didn't. Undoubtedly one day it will be.

But Earl's dedication to Tiger didn't begin and end with golf. In his book, *Training a Tiger* (New York: Harper Collins, 1997), Earl says he did two things with Tiger as soon as he came home from the hospital: Earl played jazz music in his bedroom, and he talked to Tiger as he lay in his crib. He would stroke Tiger's left cheek and say things to him like, "Daddy loves you. I am here for you. You're my little man. Daddy is so proud of you. I want you to be happy." Wow, no wonder Tiger walks into tournaments with so much confidence and strength. He knows he is loved.

As someone has noted, "It takes only a moment to father a child. It takes a lifetime to be a dad." Earl Woods is Tiger's dad.

It will be interesting to see how Woods bears up to the responsibilities that will surely be his over the next several decades. Not since Jackie Robinson has there been an African-American athlete with more opportunities for making a difference. Already youngsters who would never have dreamed of playing golf are asking their parents for a set of clubs. Go Tiger! Go Earl!

I will admit that tidbit about Earl playing jazz beside Tiger's crib caught my attention. We played classical music with our oldest daughter each evening from the time we brought her home from the hospital. To this day, she has a real passion for good music. We meant to repeat this process with all four of our daughters, but by the time you have your second child . . . Well, if you have more than one child you know. Good intentions are lost sometimes in the battle for survival. Our fourth daughter had to settle for whatever was being played on the radio at the time. Maybe that's the reason she plays country, jazz, and rock music today.

There are no perfect parents, but the power of a parent over a young person's life simply cannot be overstated.

Neil Kurshan tells about a professional fund-raiser in a small Polish town. A wealthy and generous man had just died, so the fund-raiser paid a visit to the man's son. The son was not interested in contributing to charity, and insisted that his father's name be crossed off the list. The fund-raiser handed his pen to the son and directed him to cross off the name.[25]

Suddenly, the son's hand began to shake. He knew his father's legacy. He could not remove him from the list. Kurshan makes the point that a parent's legacy is a powerful thing. Even after our children have left home, even after we have left the world, there will always be part of us that will remain with them forever. Let's make certain that part is positive, hopeful, and trusting.

We Set the Example of Service for Our Children

One of the finest businessmen/speakers I know of is Pat Williams, the senior vice-president of the Orlando Magic. Pat is an amazing man in many ways. The most amazing of all is Pat's home situation. You see, each day Pat Williams returns home to his loving wife, Ruth, and his nineteen children. Yes, you read that right—nineteen children. Five of the Williams' brood are birth children; fourteen of the children are adopted, from as far away as Brazil and South Korea.[26]

The Williams see their family as a calling. Ruth and Pat see their children as blessings from God, and they give each child a full measure of their love and attention. But if lots of love is the first ingredient in a happy family, then Pat and Ruth believe strong discipline is the second ingredient. There is no weekday television watching in the Williams' household, all the kids are involved in some extracurricular activity, and good grades are a must. Bedtimes are early, and everyone is assigned different chores.

But occasionally, there are extra things that need to be done, and that is when Pat and Ruth rely on what they call "second milers." When one child is unable to do his chores, or when a special job pops up, Pat and Ruth alert the family that second-milers are needed. They need someone who will put forth the extra effort, someone who will give a little bit more of himself or herself. Those kids who are willing to take on the job go that extra mile, knowing that they are contributing to the family in a very special way. Without their occasional extra effort, the household would be much harder to manage for everyone.

Every family needs "second milers." Children are influenced far more by what they see than what they hear. They need to see sacrificial love at work daily. Families are under so much pressure nowadays. At the midpoint of this century, most households were still made up of a married couple supported by one worker. Today, only fourteen percent of American households have one breadwinner! But the needs of children have not changed. They still need an extraordinary amount of time and affection.

But let's do more than that. Some of us need to provide a model not only for our own children but for our neighbors' children as well. Hillary Rodham Clinton is right on target when she says that it takes a village to raise a child. Author Kurt Vonnegut said something quite profound sometime ago in *USA Today*'s "Opinion Line." Vonnegut received a letter from a pregnant woman who wanted to know if he thought it was a mistake to bring another life into such a troubled world. Vonnegut responded, saying that, "What made being alive almost worthwhile for me was the saints I met. By saints I meant people who behaved decently and honorably in societies which were so obscene." Vonnegut concludes, "Perhaps many of us . . . regardless of ages, power, or wealth, can be saints for her child to meet."[27]

CHAPTER 24

Step 6: Build a Network of Friends

Many years ago, when actor Michael Caine was making a movie at Universal Studios, he was continually irritated by a young tour guide who ran studio tours. This young man had a talent for catching various stars as they wandered about the lot. Naturally, all the tourists wanted autographs and pictures with the stars, so this kind of thing could take up a lot of time. Caine thought of registering a complaint against the young man, but he didn't want him to get fired.

Years later, this young tour guide, Michael Ovitz, worked his way up to become head of the most powerful talent agency in Hollywood, Creative Artists' Agency. He is now Michael Caine's agent, and one of the most powerful men in the movie industry. What if Michael Caine had not chosen to treat him kindly all those years ago? [1]

People who need people are the luckiest people in the world. They are lucky in business, lucky in love, lucky in discovering opportunities for self-improvement. But is it really luck?

It is said that Henry Ford kept in his workshop a small test tube that was labeled, "Thomas Edison's last breath." Why? Recently I heard an interview with James Newton, who as a young man, was close to both Edison and Ford.

Alex Dow, the head of Detroit Edison, pointed Ford out to Edison at the company's annual convention. "Over there's a young fellow," he said, "who's made a gas car." Edison, who invented the first electric car, invited Ford over to his table. He questioned Ford about his new invention. Impressed with Ford's answers, Thomas Edison's final words to Ford were, "Keep at it!" And Ford did.

"It was the turning point for me," Henry Ford would later report. "You can imagine how excited I was. The man who knew the most about electricity in the world—my boyhood idol—telling me my gas car was better than an electric car! He was the first to give me real encouragement that my dream would work!"[2]

That encounter with Tom Edison changed Henry Ford's life. And with his invention of the Model-T and its automotive ancestors, Henry Ford changed your life and mine. Just a word of heart-felt encouragement impacted the world as we know it. Wouldn't you like to have a friend like Thomas Edison? How about this: could you *be* a friend like Thomas Edison?

The esteemed scientist Sir Isaac Newton had such a friend. His name was Edmund Halley (after whom Halley's comet is named). Halley, an English mathematician and astronomer, was quite a scholar himself. For example, it was Halley who first worked out the age of the Earth based on salinity of the oceans in 1691. More importantly, it was Halley who encouraged Newton to carry on with his work when Newton was about to give up, and even paid to have Newton's book, *Mathematical Principles of Natural Philosophy,* printed. Halley was not a wealthy man, but he believed in his friend. If not for Halley's efforts, the world may never have heard of Isaac Newton.

Building Synergy

An essential ingredient in the Law of Influence is to build a network of friends. The Rule of 250 demands that we make as many friends as possible. The more lives we touch, the greater the possibility that the ripples of influence will extend beyond ourselves to the rest of the world. On a more immediate level, the best way to effect change in the world is to have allies who are working to achieve the same goals for which you are working.

Dr. Herb True tells about a conversation he had with a trainer of Clydesdale horses. According to this trainer, the average Clydesdale is able to pull about seven thousand pounds. Put two Clydesdales together and their combined pull should equal eighteen thousand pounds. However, working as a team with proper training, the two Clyesdales are capable of pulling twenty-five thousand pounds, more than three times as much as one Clydesdale by itself. [3] This, of course, is the power of synergy. Synergy refers to the phenomenon in which two or more persons working together produce far more than the sum total of them all working separately.

A friend gave me this example of synergy. Suppose you were seated around a table with some of your colleagues and each member of the group was given five pieces of Tinkertoys—and asked to construct something.

You would each probably come up with a really small, likely not very impressive "design."

But, if each of you brings your five pieces to the group and combines the pieces, you start bouncing ideas off one another, one idea "sparking" another, then you have synergy. Synergy allows us to accomplish, with the help of others, much more than each of us would have accomplished working alone. As someone has said, "One log in a fireplace won't burn; you must have at least two." Building a network of friends allows for synergy to occur.

Building a network of friends also opens doors. Networking is one of the most significant factors in the success of many people. How often we have heard the complaint: It's not what you know, but who you know that counts? Rather than sit around whining about that oftentimes accurate observation about life, why not become one of those people who knows lots of people?

That is one of the secrets of former Secretary of State Madeleine Albright's success. Those who know her well claim that she is an expert at using her influence to get things done in Washington. She has built an extensive network of professional contacts in politics and education. Upon her nomination for Secretary of State, this network of colleagues and friends were only too happy to spread the good word about her. In this way, Albright's influence won her the position. [4]

Networking is a powerful way to create influence. By developing a network, you gain access to knowledge, ideas, technical advice, encouragement, financial capital, and professional contacts.

And there has never been a better environment for networking. Thanks to the Internet there are chat rooms, newsgroups, and websites out there for just about any field of business. Today, you can brainstorm with surgeons in Brazil, get encouragement from dance instructors in Texas, or get advice from mechanics in Japan. Influence is a two-way street. As you learn from them, so do your new contacts learn from you. In such an environment, there is no telling how far any individual's circle of influence might reach.[5]

A Lesson Well Learned

Harvey Mackay is one of the nation's most successful and respected salesmen and business authors and an outstanding speaker. He lists four "guiding principles" he has used to create the success he has today: mentoring, networking, surrounding yourself with people who make you look smarter than you are, and always knowing what the competition is up to. Each one of these principles involves the use of influence. [6]

Mackay claims his father as his greatest influence. His father trained him to look out for role models and to keep a running Rolodex file on everyone he meets (the file currently holds over seventy five hundred names). As he says, "If I had to name one single attribute that defines the most successful people, it's their ability to network."

In his excellent book on networking, *Dig Your Well Before You're Thirsty* (New York: Currency, 1997), Mackay tells one of the most fascinating stories on the power of influence that I've read. [7] It's the first person testimony of boxing immortal, Muhammad Ali. Ali tells of his first encounter with one of the pioneers of professional wrestling, Gorgeous George. I'm old enough to remember seeing Gorgeous George on a primitive black and white television. His golden locks were quite an extreme statement in those days.

This encounter with the notorious wrestler took place in Ali's younger days. He and the wrestler were on the same radio program, both promoting upcoming matches. The announcer asked Ali how he expected to do in his fight and Ali answered, somewhat modestly, that he felt he could win.

Then the announcer asked Gorgeous George the same question. As Ali remembers it, Gorgeous George practically tore the microphone from the announcer's hands. He proclaimed himself the greatest wrestler in the world and started shouting about how he was going to tear the other guy from limb to limb. Gorgeous George even vowed to cut off his own beautiful blond hair if the other guy beat him.

His tirade began to excite Ali. In fact, he went to Gorgeous George's wrestling match to see for himself if the loud-mouth grappler lived up to his hype. And he found himself in the midst of thousands of screaming wrestling fans, most of them screaming for Gorgeous George. Do you suppose that Muhammad Ali learned something from his encounter with Gorgeous George? Read on.

Remember when Muhammad Ali was about to face Joe Frazier for the world heavyweight championship fight in 1971? "There seems to be so much confusion," Ali taunted. "We're going to clear up this confusion on March 8. We're going to decide once and for all who is king. There's not a man alive who can whup me." Ali then jabbed the air with half a dozen blinding lefts. "I'm too smart," he said. "I'm too pretty. I'm the king. I should be a postage stamp—that's the only way anybody can lick me." Hmmmm . . . sounds like Gorgeous George reincarnated. Ali benefited from the power of networking. He benefited from the amazing Law of Influence.

Networking and synergy are powerful tools in business, but they are also important to our quest for a better world. Influence spreads person to person. Therefore it not only makes good business sense, but it is also a moral responsibility to make friends. We need allies and we need better ideas about how to tackle the world's plethora of problems.

Unfortunately, the average American male does not have a single close friend. Here is where the quest for influence so often breaks down. Men have difficulty maintaining relationships. Women, of course, fare better. Does it make a difference if men don't have close friends? Maybe so. It could be a factor in our inferior mortality rates.

You know the grim figures regarding the death rate for men. It is estimated that between 130 to 150 males are conceived for every 100 females. (I don't know who figures things out like that or how they do it.) We do know that more males are miscarried. So it ends up being 106 males born to every 100 females. During the first year of life, the mortality rate for males is $^1/_3$ higher than for females. And it is all downhill from there.

Did you know that at the turn of the century men and women lived to about the same age? Today the difference is nearly nine years and by the turn of this century, it's expected to be around twelve. Among the elderly, there are six women to every man. Wouldn't you know that by the time we get odds like that, gents, it's too late.

It's like an elderly man who was taking a walk one evening. He was enjoying the crisp night air and the sound of the wind blowing through the trees when, suddenly, he heard a little voice calling, "Help me! Help me!" The man looked all around and saw no one, so he continued his walk. Again he heard the tiny little voice, "Help me! Help me!" This time he looked down and saw a small frog. He gently lifted the frog and looked at it intently. The frog spoke, "I'm really a beautiful young princess. If you will kiss me, I will turn back into a princess and I will love you forever." The man thought for a moment, placed the frog in his pocket, and continued walking. The little frog looked up out of the pocket and asked, "Why didn't you kiss me?" The man responded, "Frankly, at this stage in my life, I would rather have a talking frog."

Why the big difference between the life spans for the sexes? Part of it is probably the inability of men to deal with their emotions. We men are our own worst enemies. We keep our emotions all bottled up. We try to play the Lone Ranger, forgetting that even he had a faithful friend named Tonto.

A study at John Hopkins School of Public Health revealed that employees who are allowed to talk on the job have healthier hearts. They are at a lower risk for a sudden coronary. Having a close friend with whom you can share your deepest needs may be one of the healthiest things you can do for yourself.

The National Opinion Research Center at the University of Chicago asked Americans to name people with whom they discussed important matters over the past six months. Those who could list five or more friends and acquaintances were fifty-five percent more likely to feel "very happy" than those who could name none. I usually rebel against anything that is trendy. I shudder when I hear a phrase like "male bonding." But I'm smart enough to realize that having close friends is a big need in our lives.

I heard a man say that he has four really close friends—men he can go to and spill his guts about anything that is happening in his life. This man nearly went bankrupt a few years back. He called one of those friends and asked him for a loan. The friend wrote him a check for fifty thousand dollars with no questions asked. Do you have a friend like that? To tell you the truth, I don't know that many people with fifty thousand dollars sitting around unencumbered. And even if I did, it would be very difficult for me to ask any of my friends for even five hundred dollars.

Soon after Jack Benny, the famous comedian, died, George Burns was interviewed on TV about his famous friend. "We had a wonderful friendship for nearly fifty-five years," said Burns. "Jack and I laughed together, played together, worked together, and ate together. I suppose for many of those years we talked every single day." There's a friendship. Everyone needs friends like that.

In the movie *Crocodile Dundee,* Dundee is talking with some fellows in a bar. One man says that a friend of his is going to see a shrink. Dundee, from the Australian outback, doesn't understand what the fellow is talking about.

"You know . . . a shrink," the fellow explains. "A psychiatrist. A person who listens to other people's problems."

"What's the matter?" Dundee wants to know. "Don't he have any mates?" "Mates," of course, is Australian for friends.

How important are your friends to you? Lee Iacocca's father told him that when you die, if you've got five real friends, then you've had a great life.

Writer Jay Kesler has said that one of his great hopes in life is to wind up with at least eight people who will attend his funeral . . . without once checking their watches.

Papyri were uncovered at Oxyrhynchus in Egypt which contained sayings reputed to be those of Jesus. One of these pieces of papyri reads like this: "And Jesus said, 'Make a friend.'" Where do you make friends, really close friends? I like what the fox said to the little prince: "Men have no more time to understand anything. They buy things already made at the shops. But there is no shop anywhere where one can buy friendship, and so men have no friends any more."

The old adage is "to have a friend, be a friend." If we are going to widen the circle of our influence, we are going to have to learn to be a friend. Stanley Milgram has shown us what we can do if we have fifty friends. Imagine what we could do if we kept enlarging our circle of friends.

Of course, the ideal exercise of influence is to make friends of your adversaries. You really widen your circle of influence when you do that—for you not only expand your potential "downline," but you counteract the negative pull of someone who might even try to damage you or your reputation.

When Steven Spielberg, director of *E.T., Jurassic Park,* and other modern film classics, was a skinny thirteen year-old making movies at home and in school, he was tormented for months by the class bully. "This was somebody I feared," wrote Spielberg. "He was my nemesis. I dreamed about him." [8]

Young Steven decided that since he couldn't beat the bully, he should join him. "So I said to him, 'I'm making a movie about fighting the Nazis, and I want you to play this war hero.' At first he laughed in my face, but later he said yes. I made him the squad leader in the film, with helmet, fatigues, and backpack. After that he became my best friend."

Spielberg recognized that what the bully really wanted was to be accepted by his classmates. Spielberg, the self-described "skinny wimp," now had an older, stronger ally. As a result, he gained stature, or clout, among his teen-age peers.

It is a simple thought and some people are next to impossible to win over. But it is worth a try. Make a friend of someone who otherwise might make your life miserable—a boss, a co-worker, even a spouse. How?

Be a Listener

Selina, my wife, and I were attending a national convention. We were thrilled to meet a man who is reputed to be a national expert on listening skills. Selina began asking him a question. In the middle of the question, a friend of his walked up. The "expert" on listening skills turned away and began talking to his friend as if Selina wasn't even there. That really happened!

The most important part of human interactions is communication, verbal and non-verbal. In my experience, says a friend of mine who really is an expert in communications, the one trait which people invariably look for in another human being, is "someone who will listen to me—really listen. Someone who listens without judgment or expectations; without criticism or harshness; but with openness, caring, and unconditional love for me as a human being." Do you have someone in your life who is always there for you when you need someone to listen? Dennis of *Dennis the Menace* fame helps to put it in perspective when he says, "I like Mrs. Wilson. You should hear her listen to me."

Paul Tournier, the Swiss psychiatrist, explained why so many people came to him for help. They came, he said, "to find a quiet, peaceful person who knows how to listen and who isn't thinking all the time about what he has to do next."

I believe that most of us can solve our own problems. We have our answers inside of us, but sometimes it just takes someone else to listen (without judging us) so that we can "hear ourselves think out loud."

Ted Engstrom, president of the organization World Vision, once told of a friend who listened to him think things through aloud. [9] It was a critical moment in Engstrom's career. He poured out his heart to his friend. His friend would nod his head, purse his lips, perhaps shift his feet, but he said nothing. After several hours, Engstrom testifies that "an uncommon wave of peace" came over his heart. His "spirit was renewed," his "faith was rekindled, hope was restored," and he "was a new man." All because a friend listened. Everyone needs someone who will listen.

Richard B. Wilke tells about Astrid Huerter, a graduate of the University of California with a degree in sociology. [10] After graduation, Astrid chose to become a barmaid in order to conduct a study of the environment of bars and the type of people who frequent them.

After one summer of tending bar, she came to the conclusion that people do not go to a bar to drink. People came to the bar in order to be heard. They desperately needed someone to hear them and understand them. We all need someone who will listen to us. And if we want to make a difference in people's lives, we will need to listen to the people around us. As someone has said, "There's a reason why God gave us two ears and one mouth. We should listen more than we talk." In fact, most of us could profit from being trained in listening skills. That's one step toward building a network of friends. Here's another:

Be an Encourager

A study of self-made millionaires revealed that these highly successful men and women could only see the good in people. They were people builders, rather than critics.

Everybody needs an encouraging word from time to time. Sometimes that encouragement is the difference between stunning success and dismal failure.

Raymond Orteig was an encourager. Orteig was a New York hotel man who was fascinated by the possibilities of air travel and wanted to encourage it. In 1919 he offered a prize of twenty-five thousand dollars for the first nonstop flight between New York and Paris. This prize stimulated Charles Lindbergh to make his transatlantic flight eight years later. Everybody needs encouragement.

In one of his books, Fran Tarkenton, the scrappy little quarterback of the Minnesota Vikings, tells about throwing a key block in a game the Vikings won against the St. Louis Cardinals. [11] He says that during the Monday films he kept waiting for the coach to point out his contribution to that critical play. The coach praised the linemen, the runners, the water boy, and the pom-pom girls, it seemed, but he never mentioned Tarkenton and that key block. Tarkenton went to his coach after the team meeting and said, "Coach, why didn't you say anything about my block?"

"Fran," he said, "you always give a hundred and fifty percent. You're out there gung-ho all the time. So I just didn't feel that I needed to praise you for it."

"If you ever want me to do it again, you need to," Fran said.

Former UCLA basketball coach John Wooden used to tell his players that when they scored a basket, they should give a smile, wink, or nod to the player who gave them a good pass. "What if he's not looking?" asked a team member. Wooden replied, "I guarantee he'll look." Everyone values encouragement. [12]

One of the big rivalries of the 1968 Olympics was between two female track stars, America's Madeline Manning Mims and Yugoslavia's Vera Nikolic. Both women had to make it through the qualifying finals before they could meet in an Olympic race. But in the middle of the eight-hundred-meter finals, Vera Nikolic suddenly became confused. She left the track and disqualified herself. Later, Madeline would learn that Vera had planned to leave the stadium and jump off a nearby bridge. Officials from her country had put Vera under tremendous pressure. They led her to believe that she would fail her whole country if she didn't win a gold medal. The strain was too much, and Vera Nikolic suffered a nervous breakdown.

Madeline happened to see Vera the next day, escorted by bodyguards who were taking her back to Yugoslavia. On her way to compete in her first events, Madeline stopped to comfort her biggest rival. Softly, she said, "Vera, you are young and your mistakes are behind you. . . . I care about you, and God loves you, too." Later that day, Madeline Manning Mims won the gold in the eight-hundred-meter race, the race that Vera had dropped out of.

Months later, Madeline heard from a Yugoslavian coach that Vera was doing better. At first, she had been in a catatonic state, unable even to speak. But after treatment in a psychiatric hospital, Vera finally came around. Her first words to the doctors had been, "Madeline was on her way to compete in the final, and she took the time to talk to me."

Now fast-forward four years. It is 1972, and the Olympics are being held that year in Munich. Madeline Manning Mims, the gold-medal winner and world-record holder from the year before, is getting ready to run her qualifying heat. She starts out strong, but then makes a foolish mistake. She miscalculates the finish line, and stops early. Now the judges will have to decide whether she qualifies or not. As she sits in the arena in devastated silence, a young woman comes and sits beside her and offers her encouraging words. It is Vera Nikolic, fully recovered and back in competition. And when the judges announce that Madeline has been disqualified, Vera hugs her and says, "You're young and you can put this mistake behind you. Besides, you have God on your side." Madeline Manning Mims reports that those were just the words she needed at that moment. She was able to put the loss in perspective and know that she could come back from defeat. [13]

There are enough cynics out there. Don't add to their numbers. No virtue comes in dousing another person's dream. I like something Michel de Saint-Pierre once said: "An optimist may see a light where there is none, but why must the pessimist always run to blow it out?" We all need fewer critics and more people applauding us.

Some years ago one sunny Sunday afternoon, a young priest stopped to talk to a parishioner and her five year-old daughter. The little girl had a new jump rope, and the priest began to demonstrate the intricacies of jumping rope to her.

After a while the little girl began to jump, first once, then twice. Mother and priest clapped loudly for her skill. Eventually, the little girl was able to jump quite well on her own and wandered off with her newfound skill. Priest and mother chatted a few moments until the little girl, with sad eyes, returned dragging her rope. "Mommy," she lamented, "I can do it, but I need lots of clapping." That's true of most people. We need someone applauding us, encouraging us, egging us on. [14]

That is part of the enormous success of the world-famous "Suzuki Method" of teaching children to play the violin. [15] One of the first things that children are taught in the Suzuki method is how to take a bow. The instructors realize that when children bow, audiences always applaud. They say, "Applause is the best motivator we have found to make children feel good about performing and about themselves."

Now how often do you think the average child is applauded, especially after he or she heads to school? A study by the National Parent-Teacher Organization reveals that in an average American school, eighteen negatives are employed for every positive.

Zig Ziglar, in *Raising Positive Kids in a Negative World,* quotes a Wisconsin study which states that when kids enter the first grade, eighty percent feel pretty good about themselves, but by the time they get to the sixth grade, only ten percent have positive self-images. [16] No wonder. Eighteen negatives to one positive is a good way to extinguish any good feelings any young person might have about himself or herself.

I once heard someone put it this way: It takes ten "attaboys" to equal one "gotcha."

"It's amazing when you're a kid how something can alter the direction of your life," says Michelle Pfeiffer. "I had a high-school teacher who said one simple thing to me: 'I think you have talent.' And I never forgot it, partly because while growing up, I got very few compliments. Now, I didn't at that moment think, 'Oh, I'll be an actress.' Still, I came to feel very confident in that world because of that single comment."[17]

For Willie Brown, the popular mayor of San Francisco, it was a grandmother. Brown attended an all-black, segregated school in the poverty-stricken community of Mineola, Texas. "I had a grandmother who kept telling me there was nothing I could not do," the speaker says. "She said if I worked hard enough, I would find out what I could do, and I would be certain to succeed. She made me believe it!" [18]

After graduating from Mineola High School, Brown headed for San Francisco, where he worked as a janitor, shoe salesman, and playground director to put himself through San Francisco State College and Hastings College of the Law. He was admitted to the state bar in 1959 and elected to the California Assembly in 1964. In 1980, with bipartisan support, he became the first African-American elected as speaker.

Josephine Baker had that kind of grandmother as well.[19] Baker became an internationally famous entertainer back in the 1920s, when black women had few options in life. She traveled the world, earned a fortune, met famous and influential people, had a tremendous impact on the society of her day. But Josephine Baker never forgot her roots. Josephine had been raised by her grandmother, Elvira, an ex-slave from a tobacco plantation. Elvira had instilled confidence and love in little Josephine, in spite of her difficult circumstances. After she became famous, Josephine bought a beautiful chateau in France, complete with landscaped grounds and a magnificent garden. And at the entrance to the chateau, Josephine planted a row of tobacco stalks. They stood as a reminder to her of the grandmother who had such an influence on her life.

Most of us today are who we are because somewhere along the way someone offered us some much-needed encouragement.

Lawrence Linderman interviewed award-winning filmmaker Bud Greenspan for *Modern Maturity* magazine. They were discussing Greenspan's grief following the loss of his wife. Linderman asked: "What got you through it?" [20]

Greenspan told him about a man named Sammy Lee who sent him a letter. The letter told about a dream in which a man, whose wife had recently passed away, saw a bevy of angels. They all carried lighted candles—except one. The man thought, 'That's my wife. Her candle is out.' He looked up to heaven and said, 'Darling, why is your candle not lit?' She said, 'Every time I light it, your tears put it out.' It was then that the man knew it was time to stop mourning. Sammy Lee, Olympic champion platform diver in 1948 and 1952, touched Bud Greenspan's heart in a special way with this note of encouragement.

When former Yankee great Bobby Richardson first signed with New York he was sent from his home in Sumter, South Carolina, to the Yankee's farm club in Norfolk, Virginia. Bobby writes in *The Bobby Richardson Story* that he was so homesick he could scarcely perform. But a letter of encouragement came from a junior high school coach back home. That little bit of encouragement made the crucial difference. [21]

George M. Adams once said that encouragement is oxygen to the soul. And it's true! In a university experiment, students were divided into three groups. The first group was given a great deal of encouragement and praise. The second group was virtually ignored. The third group was given nothing but criticism. The ignored group progressed the least, the criticized group made some progress, but the praised group achieved outstanding results!

B. C. Forbes wrote in *Forbes* magazine: "No human being can be genuinely happy unless he or she stands well in the esteem of fellow mortals.

He who would deal successfully with us must never forget that we possess and are possessed by this ego. A word of appreciation often can accomplish what nothing else could accomplish."

The esteemed philosopher/psychologist William James put it like this: "The deepest principle in human nature is the craving to be appreciated." It is a point that cannot be overemphasized. If you want to increase your sphere of influence, make friends, people who will encourage you and bring out the best in you. Even more important, find someone— particularly a young person—and give them what we all crave the most—some heart-felt applause. Everyone needs to be listened to. Everyone needs to be encouraged. Want to make a difference in the world? It can be as simple as being a friend.

It is not easy to maintain friendships. It is like maintaining a marriage. Friendships require time. They require being there in times of heartbreak and times of celebration. They require loyalty and trust. A good friend is hard to find, but their friendship is more valuable than gold. Want to widen your sphere of influence? Increase the number of your friends.

CHAPTER 25

Step 7: Go All Out

Robert Woodruff, president of the Coca-Cola company from 1923 to 1955, had a vision and a passion for his product. "We will see that every man in uniform," he promised during World War II, "gets a bottle of Coca-Cola for five cents wherever he is and whatever it costs." After the war, he stated that in his lifetime he wanted everyone in the world to have a taste of Coca-Cola. No wonder that Coke is still the dominant soft drink worldwide.

Why is it that people can feel that passionate about a soft drink but not about world peace? Or the environment? Or dignity for all the world's people?

People usually do not make a difference in this world by accident. Most do not make their mark because of a lucky break. The majority of people who accomplish anything in the world are successful because they care more than other people care. They are people who go all out.

The year 1947 was a bloody one for that part of the world shared by Hindus and Moslems. Warring factions had turned the region into a bloodbath. Ultimately, the region had to be split into a Moslem Pakistan and a Hindu India, but even these measures could not end the fighting and the slaughter of hundreds of thousands of people. Military forces worked in vain to keep the peace, to separate the two groups, but no amount of soldiers could end the aggression. However, one spot in all of India was an oasis of peace and reconciliation—the city of Calcutta. Hindus and Moslems in that city publicly declared friendship and peace. The fighting which was destroying the rest of the region was absent there. Strangely enough, Calcutta had once been as violent and bloody an area as any other, but one man changed that.

Mahatma Gandhi lived in Calcutta and held nightly prayer meetings there. Somehow, he had brought together the Hindus and the Moslems of the city and created a nonviolent pact between them. His prayers for peace were attended by Hindus and Moslems alike. Where thousands of soldiers were futilely trying to stop the fighting in other areas, one man was praying for, and sustaining, peace in Calcutta.[1]

In time, however, the fighting eventually came to Calcutta too. Vengeance and hatred flared, and violence permeated the city. Gandhi moved from prayer to a more public spiritual discipline. He declared a fast until peace . . . or death. At the time, he was seventy-seven years-old, weak, and everyone knew that a fast would kill him. But he was willing to sacrifice his life for the cause of peace. By the third day of his fast, Gandhi's health began to fail seriously.

Many Moslems and Hindus, moved by his devotion, began to demonstrate in the street, marching for unity and peace. Men brought their weapons of death and presented them to Gandhi, giving up their campaign of hatred and murder. A group of leaders from all the different factions announced that they had agreed on a peace pact: "We shall never allow communal strife in the city again and shall strive unto death to prevent it." Only then did an ailing Gandhi end his fast. One man's life of devout faith carried so much influence that he transformed a whole city. What gave Mahatma Gandhi that kind of influence? Was it not one thing—his passion, his commitment to the cause of non-violence? His passion made him a source of worldwide influence.

Mother Teresa had that same kind of influence. Her work began with a dream in which she was convinced that God was telling her to build an orphanage. When she informed the superior at her convent that God had told her to build an orphanage, the Mother Superior asked Teresa how much money she had. When the reply was "three pennies," the superior asked her what she expected to build with three pennies. It is said that Teresa replied, "With three pennies and God, I can build anything!"[2]

Mother Teresa went to India, where she did build an orphanage, a hospice for the dying, and medical clinics in the slums of Calcutta. Later she opened a center for AIDS victims in New York. When Mother Teresa was presented the Nobel Prize in 1979, she told the press that the most insidious disease that can prey on a human being is the feeling of not being wanted. She gave her life to making certain that no one who came within her sphere of influence ever felt rejected.

Gandhi and Mother Teresa were people of influence par excellence. What did they have in common? Their passion. People who make the biggest difference in this world are people who are driven by a passion. You only have to say their name—and everybody knows.

Gandhi—mention his name anywhere in the world and people immediately think of his commitment to non-violence.

Mother Teresa. What was there about this tiny nun that gave her a worldwide influence? Her appearance? She did have a certain radiance, but I doubt that even in her younger days she was a Cindy Crawford. A spell-binding voice? I doubt it—but Mother Teresa had something more important than either physical beauty or dazzling talent; she had a passion to help the poor.

One thing we need to recognize is that neither Mother Teresa or Mahatma Gandhi were shrinking violets. These strong-minded persons were so committed to their causes that they would move earth and sky to achieve a positive result. It is said that Mother Teresa would frequently wait until the television cameras were whirring before asking local politicians to provide food, homes, and money. The embarrassed officials would have little choice but to say "Yes."

There is a great story surrounding the opening of her AIDS center in New York. While visiting in Sing Sing prison in upstate New York, she found four inmates suffering from AIDS. Without hesitation she went to Mayor Koch's office at City Hall in New York City and asked him to telephone Governor Mario Cuomo on her behalf. She told the governor about the four prisoners and asked him to release them to her so she could begin her AIDS center.

The governor replied that they had forty-three cases of AIDS in the state prisons system and that he would release them all to her. She said four was enough to begin. Then she asked the governor for the state to provide a building to house her new center. Cuomo agreed.

Then she turned to Mayor Koch and asked him to clear some permits to allow them to get the center under way immediately. The mayor shook his head back and forth and said, "As long as you don't make me wash the floors."

One day Mother Teresa went into a grocery store in India and put eight hundred dollars worth of groceries into some shopping carts. It was food that was needed for the starving people that she was caring for. But when she got up to the cashier, she said that she was not going to move out of line until the people behind her came up with the money to pay for the food.[3]

Gandhi and Mother Teresa were people who were hard to say no to.

People with a passion become so identified with a cause that you only have to mention their name and immediately their cause comes to mind.

Ralph Nader. You may not like him. He is a pain sometimes. But your car is a safer car today, your appliances are safer appliances today, your medicine is safer medicine because Ralph Nader is such a pain.

Michael Jordan. Sure he has a world of talent. Of course he has a million dollar smile. But you don't reach that level of sports without giving everything you've got on the basketball floor. Michael Jordan is a different kind of influence, but he is a man driven by a passion. People who make a difference in this world are willing to pay the price of excellence. They are respected; sometimes they are even held in awe by their colleagues because of their dedication.

Take actor Laurence Olivier, for example. He was filming a scene in *Richard III* and an arrow was shot into his calf. Everyone went quiet while he sat there motionless, the blood gushing from his wound. When the assistant director rushed over to him, Olivier said: "Did we get it in the can?" He was so totally immersed in his work, not even being shot stopped him from performing.

Benjamin Disraeli put it this way, "Nothing can resist the human will that will stake even its existence on its stated purpose." There is no substitute for passion.

"The fundamental ambivalence of our age," according to Frederica Matthews-Green, is that "we admire Mother Teresa, but we don't want to be her. We may not want to be Leona Helmsley, but we wouldn't mind being ensconced in the luxury she so cynically sells.[4]

"We long for heroism. We want a culture of giving and self-sacrifice. We want compassion and caring . . . (But) we don't want to do the caring. We want someone else to care for us." This may be the dominant attitude of our time, but it is not universal. There are many people left in this world who are not centered in themselves.

I really appreciate the fact that *Time* magazine has instituted a section titled *Local Heroes*.[5] In that section we read about such people as Joseph Femiani, age fifty-seven, a McMurray, Pennsylvania electric-company owner who developed the Watchful Shepherd, a home-monitoring device for victims of child abuse. In the past two and a half years, his organization has protected more than two hundred children in his state.

Or how about Lawrence Leritz, age forty-three, a New York City actor who, in conjunction with Hollywood Supports, has led the "Day of Compassion" project, winning commitments from local, cable and network producers to gear one day's programming toward AIDS-related topics? On one designated day, more than one hundred talk shows, daytime dramas, and news programs contained segments or story lines, like the AIDS charity ball on *General Hospital*, to promote HIV awareness.

Response magazine carried a profile of Dorothy Height, a woman who has dedicated her life to the civil rights movement. "Here I am now still working on the things I started working on sixty years ago," she said. "You can't give up. You can't say there's no need of working on social-justice issues. It isn't up to you to determine when you have succeeded." She still holds fast to the belief that her faith demands she stand up for justice, even when the potential for winning seems bleak. Ms. Height remembered working to get an anti-lynching bill passed in the 1930s. "We never did get the bill passed but the work we did for the bill reduced and practically eliminated lynching," she said.[6]

Ms. Height recalled the story of Dorothy Tilly, then known as Mrs. M. E. Tilly, who, out of her religious commitment, brought women in Atlanta together in what she called, "The Fellowship of the Concerned." Ms. Tilly and other members of the fellowship would go into courtrooms across the South where black or poor people were on trial.

Asked by courtroom officials why they were there, the women, wearing white gloves and hats, would simply answer, "We are concerned."

"Those women wanted to see that justice was assured," Ms. Height said. "Their presence often made the difference. I think we need to go back to that kind of spirit because we do not have the evidence of that depth of concern today." There have always been, and always will be, people who are willing to step back from life and see the big picture. There will always be people who are willing to reach out to others.

Maybe you remember young Trevor Ferrell who was watching television on a cold December night in 1983. The news showed Philadelphia street people huddled over steam vents to stay warm. Trevor pleaded with his father to take him downtown so that he could deliver a blanket and pillow to some of these homeless people.[7]

This single visit became a nightly mission of mercy. As word of Trevor's generosity spread, contributions from all over the country poured into what became known as Trevor's Campaign. Some two hundred and fifty volunteers now cook and deliver soup and sandwiches nightly to the homeless. A thirty-three-bedroom rooming house, anonymously donated, is being renovated as a day shelter for one hundred homeless people. Young Trevor focused attention on the needs of homeless people and showed the nation the difference one young person can make. There are people out there who care, and they care passionately.

One way to visualize this concept of passion is to consider the difference between a thermometer and a thermostat. A thermometer can only measure temperature, but a thermostat can affect the temperature. Are you a thermometer or a thermostat? The truth of the matter is that neither a thermometer nor a thermostat can affect the climate when you need heat if there's no fire in the furnace. Passion, or the fire in the furnace, is at the heart of the people who make a difference in our world.

According to *American Demographics* magazine and Roper Starch Worldwide, there is already an ordinary group of people out there in America with an extraordinary ability to influence those around them. This group is called, appropriately enough, the influentials.[8]

About one in ten Americans qualifies as an influential, according to *American Demographics.* Influentials try new things and set new trends. Their advice is sought out and highly valued. Whether we know it or not, the rest of America tends to follow the influentials' leads.

What are some characteristics of an influential?

•They are married with children. Marriage and family are priorities for influentials.

•They are more likely than average adults to place friends at the center of their lives.

•They are well educated and have middle to high incomes

•They are very active socially and politically in their community.

•Unlike many adults, they try new products, use new technology, and visit new places.

•They read a lot and possess a great deal of information of daily interest to others.

•They are between the ages of thirty and forty-nine (on average).

And one more decisive characteristic:

•They are well defined politically, not wishy-washy in their views.

Wishy-washy people can never move the world. People who make a difference are driven by a passion. They have fire in the heart. They are remarkably focused. They know what they want and go after it.

Daniel Goleman, in his book *Emotional Intelligence,* tells about an American platoon early in the Vietnam War that was hunkered down in some rice paddies, in the heat of a firefight with the Vietcong.[9] Suddenly without looking to the left or right, a line of six perfectly calm and poised monks started walking along the elevated berms that separated paddy from paddy directly toward the line of fire.

The reaction of the combatants is intriguing. They not only stopped fighting while the monks made this strange intrusion into their battle, they quit fighting altogether. The fight had somehow been drained out of them. Goleman concludes it is "a basic principle of social life: Emotions are contagious . . . we catch feelings from one another as though they were some kind of social virus." Whenever we are driven by a passion, others are affected. As we have already noted, caring is contagious; so is apathy. When we are passionate about a cause or an idea, others become caught up in our excitement.

In 1935, German conductor Franz von Hoesslin was almost exiled from Germany for marrying a Jewish woman.[10] At his last concert, he directed Schiller's "Ode to Joy," whose central theme is, "All mankind will become brothers" (*Alle Menschen werden Brueder*). One man in the audience, moved by von Hoesslin's genius and stunned by news of his exile, stood and shouted, "Alle Menschen werden Brueder." Then, he declared that he would sign a petition to keep von Hoesslin and his wife in Germany. In the presence of hostile storm troopers, hundreds of people lined up to sign the petition. The troopers stood and yelled at the audience, "*Judenfreund!*" "Jew lovers!" The crowd grew very quiet. Then the man on the stage repeated, more loudly than before, "*Alle menschen werden Brueder.*" The crowd resumed lining up in support of von Hoesslin. The troopers were ejected from the hall. The passion of one man had influenced hundreds of others to make a most courageous stand.

Loren Eiseley once described such passion like this: "In Bimini, on the old Spanish main, a black girl once said to me, 'Those as hunts treasure must go alone, at night, and when they find it they have to leave a little of their blood behind them.'" The person of passion does leave "a little of their blood behind them," but in doing so they elevate the life of us all.

And here is the amazing thing about passion: it allows ordinary people to have extraordinary influence. When an ordinary person is filled with a righteous passion, the gates of hell tremble. Indeed, an ordinary person filled with passion ceases to be ordinary.

I once began to say in a speech that passion allowed little people to do big things. I was so uncomfortable with the phrase "little people," it came out, "Big people can do little things." Embarrassing. But there are no little people. Not really.

A few years ago, a major corporation announced that it was moving its headquarters to the other side of the country. The board's chairman was quoted in the media as saying that most of the important employees would transfer, but others, among them the secretaries, would not. The enraged secretaries, learning how little they were valued by the company, decided to prove their importance by not answering any phones for one day. The resulting chaos forced the board chairman to make a public apology.[11]

There are no little people. So, I no longer say in my speeches that little people can do big things. Now I say that ordinary people can do extraordinary things.

Sometimes all it takes is for someone to get angry about a situation. Terrie Williams in her book, *The Personal Touch,* tells about a man who got so angry when New York City grocers harassed street people trying to redeem aluminum cans that he used his life savings and devoted all his time to establish a redemption center catering to, and staffed by, the homeless.[12] There is now less litter and trash in his neighborhood, and many redeemers have used the earnings to restart their lives. Sometimes all it takes is one enraged person to remedy a bad situation.

Writer Robert Fulghum tells of a tragic act of violence that occurred in the midst of the war in Bosnia, and one man's response to that tragedy.[13] One day in May 1992, mortar fire rained down on Sarajevo, killing twenty-two people who were just waiting in line to buy bread. It could have been just another forgotten tragedy within a horrible war, but one man was determined to keep the memories of the dead alive.

Vedran Smailovic was a cellist with the Sarajevo Opera Orchestra. He dressed in his finest evening clothes, and took his cello out into the street in Sarajevo where the breadline massacre had occurred. And there he sat, risking his life, playing a beautiful piece of music, Albioni's *Adagio in G Minor.* For twenty-two days straight he returned to that street each day and played the same piece.

But the story doesn't end there. Newspapers reported on Vedran's vigil. A woman in Seattle, Washington was so moved by Vedran's courage that she organized twenty-two musicians to gather in twenty-two different places in Seattle for twenty-two consecutive days to honor Vedran's spirit, and to call for an end to the war. Soon, this idea spread to other cities. On the day of the president's inauguration, twenty-two cellists gathered to play in Washington. As long as the story is told, in other places in the world, the music will keep on playing.

What are you passionate about? You can go through life without ever being passionate about anything, but life will not be as satisfying, and you will have contributed very little to the world. Those who make a difference in our world will be people who are moved by a great passion. As the young African-American girl said to Loren Eiseley, "Those as hunts treasure must go alone, at night, and when they find it they have to leave a little of their blood behind them."

CHAPTER 26

Step 8: Aspire to Leadership

There was a time not so long ago, less than fifty years in fact, when the United States controlled one-third of the total world economy. The United States manufactured half the goods sold anywhere in the world. Everyone wanted to own goods marked, "Made in America." Today the situation is reversed. Americans buy more from other countries than we can sell.

A dramatic revolution has taken place in less than half a century. It began with one man, General of the Army, Douglas A. MacArthur, Supreme Commander of the Allied Powers in Japan after World War II.

How did Gen. MacArthur accomplish this economic miracle? According to Lloyd Dobyns and Clare Crawford-Mason in their book, *Quality or Else*, it was entirely accidental.[1] MacArthur wanted reliable radios, lots of them, for his occupying army. He wanted them so his orders, as well as the various propaganda programs produced by the Allied Forces, could be heard in every Japanese town and village. When Japanese manufacturers couldn't give the general what he wanted, he sent for experts in the United States to teach them how—people like W. Edwards Deming, Jr. and Joseph Juran—fathers of the Total Quality Management movement. Moreover, the Japanese learned to produce goods superior to our own—so superior that Americans began lusting after goods "Made in Japan." The rest, as we say, is history.[2]

Think of that: one man wanted a radio that worked, and the world economic order was changed. One man wanted a better way of doing things, and humanity was forever affected. Of course, it helped that Gen. MacArthur was who he was. If you really want to make a difference in the world in a hurry, aspire to leadership.

Dismiss the thought once and for all from your mind that it is wrong to be ambitious. Ambitious people rule the world. Even more important, no one contributes anything of lasting significance to the world who is not ambitious.

Gandhi and Mother Teresa were ambitious. Merely be selective about the things for which you are ambitious, and strive always to be a leader.

After the Green Bay Packers won the 1997 Super Bowl, a photo appeared in the Milwaukee *Journal Sentinel* that showed an enthusiastic crowd welcoming the team home after their win. In one corner of the photo is a man. We can only see his back, but he is dressed in a dark hat and tan overcoat, has his hands in his pockets, and he bears a strong resemblance to Vince Lombardi, the legendary Packers coach who died on September 3, 1970. Many people like to think it is the ghost of the great coach, come back to revel in his old team's victory. Vince Lombardi was a leader extraordinaire.[3]

By definition, leaders have influence. In the last chapter we emphasized that ordinary people can accomplish extraordinary things through the power of their passion. However, leaders have more influence than non-leaders. To be a leader is to influence others to follow. If you want to have more influence in the world, aspire to leadership. The world today is hungry for leaders.

It has become a cliché, but still it is valid: leaders are people who do the right thing; managers are people who do things right. Some situations require a manager; and others call for a leader. Ideally, if you are a manager, you are a manager who leads. It may be that all managers will have to become leaders in the new, evolving workplace.

It was so much easier being a manager in the old days. You knew your place in the hierarchy. You had a boss above you and he had a boss above him and so on. When the big guy at the top gave the orders everybody fell in line. All you had to do was take orders and give orders. Simple, until somebody turned the pyramid upside down. Now, if we are a manager—or a team leader, in today's parlance—we are to empower our people. We are to encourage their suggestions. We are to be out among them coaching and mentoring. And there is no turning back.

People in business are discovering that in a knowledge-based culture you have to be more flexible. As Tom Peters notes, you could coerce a guy with a wrench on an assembly line to fasten more widgets in an hour— particularly if economic times were hard and jobs were scarce, but how do you coerce an information worker to be more creative?

Peter Drucker says that the only way to deal with knowledge workers is to treat them as volunteers. Think of that concept for just a moment. Imagine yourself to be the leader of a non-profit organization and your job is to motivate and coordinate a group of volunteers. How would you go about it?

The supervisor today is not just a supervisor. He or she must be a leader.

What would it take for you to be a leader in your company? A greater commitment to your work? More loyalty to your company's goals? A commitment to keep growing in your understanding of societal trends so that you will have your finger on the pulse of the future? If you want to make a difference in the world, aspire to a position of leadership. Here are some of the essential traits of effective leaders:

1. A high level of integrity

Lester Korn in his survey of highly successful people says that the three chief characteristics of these people were a high level of integrity, a high level of energy, and a plan for success. *Fortune* magazine asked the CEOs of many Fortune 500 companies what they considered to be the most important qualities for hiring and promoting top executives. The unanimous consensus was that integrity and trustworthiness were by far the key characteristics.

Contrary to the popular image of people at the top of the corporate pyramids as unethical sharks, the reverse is true. The higher you climb in almost any organization, the more ethical and conscientious you will find people to be. Of course, this is not always the case, and it is worrisome. There is a clear trend in our society toward an ends-justify-the-means morality. We can hardly expect the business community to be exempt.

Not everybody marches to the drumbeat of integrity. But the ultimate winners do—and thank God for them. Our society would be in trouble indeed if we could not trust people in places of responsibility.

Take, for example, Dr. Frances Kelsey. Dr. Kelsey is not a sports star or a Hollywood personality, but she made a difference. She made a difference by standing firm. A new drug, thalidomide, was being widely used in Europe when its manufacturer applied to the United States for permission to sell it here, and Dr. Kelsey was assigned to handle the application. She had reservations about thalidomide. The drug company tried to pressure her for approval, but she held her ground, insisting on more data. When some deformed European babies were traced to their mothers' taking thalidomide during pregnancy, the manufacturer dropped its application. Most of us have never heard of Dr. Frances Kelsey but we are very, very fortunate such people exist—people of character, people of diligence, people who care about doing the right thing.[5]

2. A plan for success

Successful people know where they are headed.

From the time he was eight years old, Dave Thomas wanted to own a restaurant. "That way," he says, "I'd never be hungry." Orphaned at birth, Thomas never had a stable home life, nor was he great in school. When he was twelve, though, Thomas got a job in a diner. Later, as a teenager, he was working at Regas restaurant in my hometown of Knoxville, Tennessee. Finally, he put together the necessary capital to open his own place in Columbus, Ohio. He named it after his daughter, Wendy. Today there are approximately five thousand Wendy's restaurants. Don't let that homey smile fool you. Dave Thomas knew what he wanted. He had a plan.

Lee Iaccocca is another successful person who is legendary for his focus. He had his success planned out from the time he was a young man. As you may know, his real name is not Lee, it's Lido. One of his first assignments as a sales manager was in the South. People in the southern part of the United States are a little provincial. Okay, we are more than a little provincial. We don't have too many people in the South of "Eye-tal-ian" descent—as Jimmy Carter once called them. How do you think a person named Lido Iaccocca would do in the South as a sales manager forty years ago? Not too well. So he changed his name. Started calling himself Lee. He would walk into a sales room, hold out his hand and say, "My name's Lee!" What southerner could resist an opening like that? But Iaccocca was focused, and knew where he was headed.

Zig Ziglar talks about people who are wandering generalities, instead of meaningful specifics. It makes a difference if one day you sit down and decide what you really want out of life and give yourself completely to that calling.

3. An extraordinary commitment to success

We need to eliminate forever the idea that success is a dirty word. Perhaps your experience was similar to mine. I was brought up to regard people who were overly ambitious with suspicion. I was programmed to be humble and self-effacing (I can say that I am humble with a great deal of pride). Particularly suspicious were people with money. So it seems somewhat out of character for me to say that I believe that positive people have a moral responsibility to strive to be successful. The truth of the matter is that when you are successful, you have more opportunities for doing good. More doors are open to you, and you can open more doors for others.

My favorite journalist, William Raspberry, wrote in one of his columns about the inherent disadvantages facing minority youth. He noted that they are shortchanged by not having the social background, networks, family connections, and role models that are the birthright of the privileged.

He concluded with a powerful analogy: *Life is not merely a foot race but a relay race. It matters a lot how much headway that previous runner has made when he hands you the baton."* (italics mine)

That is a powerful analogy in my estimation. There are many dangers to seeking after success, admittedly, but there are also dangers in settling for something less. We owe it to our family, we owe it to our community to strive for the best.

Successful people have more influence. In order to be a success in today's world you need to be either extraordinarily lucky or extraordinarily committed to succeeding. Since luck is not something we can program very well, we had better opt for the latter.

Dean Keith Simonton, a professor of psychology at the University of California at Davis, authored a book in 1994 titled *Greatness: Who Makes History and Why.* The great figures he focused on include Nobel Prize winners, highly-esteemed statesmen, war heroes, composers, scientists, philosophers, and artists. Though he doesn't have a formula to define how or why certain people rise above (too many factors are involved), he concluded that the most prominent characteristic of great people is an unrelenting drive to succeed. As he explains, "Greatness is built upon tremendous amounts of study, practice, and devotion."[6]

4. Vision

We said that leaders are people who do the right thing; managers are people who do things right. The difference between doing things right and knowing what are the right things to do is vision.

According to an article in the *Wall Street Journal,* when Benno Schmidt, Jr. assumed the presidency of Yale University, he expressed some fear regarding the "busyness" of the job. He said, "If I can't put my feet on the desk and look out the window and think without an agenda, I may be *managing* Yale, but I won't be *leading* it." President Schmidt was talking about acquiring vision.[7]

"Good business leaders," says Jack Welch, former president of General Electric, "create a vision, articulate the vision, passionately own the vision, and relentlessly drive it to completion."

A vision is simply a picture in your mind of something you desire. What kind of company will you have ten years from now? What kind of home will you live in? How will you look? Before you can be successful in any enterprise, you need a picture in your mind to guide you.

Several years ago World Vision developed a poster that said in big bold letters across the top, "How Do You Feed a Hungry World?" In the bottom right-hand corner was a tiny picture of a child and these words in small type: "One at a Time." That's a vision.

Bruce Larson in his book *Wind and Fire* tells about a National Football League championship game many years ago in which Dallas was playing Green Bay in Wisconsin in what came to be dubbed, "The Ice Bowl." Green Bay was behind five points, with just seconds to play. Green Bay had the ball on the Dallas one-foot line and it was fourth down. Everything hinged on that last play. In the huddle the quarterback of the Packers, Bart Starr, turned to Jerry Kramer, the offensive guard and said, "Jerry, if you can move Jethro Pugh twelve inches to the left, you will make fifteen thousand dollars." Jerry Kramer caught a vision of what he was to do. Move defensive lineman Jethro Pugh twelve inches and collect fifteen thousand dollars—the winner's share of the championship. Jerry responded, Jethro was moved, and Green Bay won.[8]

Moving Jethro Pugh twelve inches to the left may not have been a lofty vision, but it was what was needed at the moment. The point is that you do need a picture of where you want to go that you can share with others to solicit their help.

There is no substitute for vision, either professionally or personally. Very few people have a picture in their mind of where they want to be, and the net effect is lives unfulfilled and ineffective.

One of my favorite phrases when I was a young man was, "In the land of the blind, the one-eyed man is king." I had no idea where the phrase came from, but I set my mind at an early age to be that one-eyed man, to see things that other people did not, could not, or would not see. If you can do that, you are well on your way to becoming a leader.

5. Ability to communicate

One surprise among Simonton's findings is that many political and military leaders have been bright, but not overly so. Beyond a certain point, he explains, other factors, like the ability to communicate effectively, become more important than innate intelligence as measured by an IQ test. That should not surprise us. Some of our greatest leaders have become leaders because of one skill—the ability to communicate. They were perceived as brighter than they really were because they were able to organize their thoughts and express them in a forceful and winning way.

Even Sigmund Freud, according to one author, owed part of his ability to influence to his ability to communicate. This author called Freud "something of an intellectual bandit." Freud would seize the ideas of other leading thinkers and scientists of his time and give eloquent voice to them. He would publish articles and give speeches about an idea and, while he gave credit to its originator, it somehow always ended up being remembered as Freud's idea. Effective communication was part of Freud's success.[9] It is true in almost every field. It is no accident that the most popular president of our time was known as the Great Communicator.

What could you do to improve your communication skills? Purchase books or tapes on communication? Take a non-credit course at a local community college? Both would be excellent investments. I believe it would be helpful for every businessperson to involve themselves in a local Toastmasters Club. You will acquire skills there that will prove to be invaluable.

6. Perceived competence

Paul Newman once played a rather ingenious character that was a natural leader. The motion picture was titled *Hombre*. Newman's character saves a group of stagecoach passengers from murderous bandits. This does not prevent the passengers, however, from enduring a series of trials. In exasperation, one of the women passengers asks Newman, "Can you tell me why we keep trotting after you?"

Newman replies: "I can cut it, lady!"[10]

Is that how people perceive you—that you can cut it? Some persons naturally exude an air of authority. When legendary coach Vince Lombardi asserted his will on a football team, even his toughest lineman was no match. In fact, one of his linemen is quoted as saying that when Lombardi said for him to sit down, "I don't even bother to look for a chair."

Leif Erickson had that same kind of effect on his troops. According to an old Norse tale, the Vikings were willing to risk their lives following Leif Erickson, not because he was strong, courageous or smart, but because they thought he was lucky. Leif means lucky. Leif Erickson is the old Norse way of saying lucky son of Eric. (He was the son of Eric the Red, founder of the earliest Scandinavian settlements in Greenland.) Leif discovered North America by accident about 1000 A.D. He was commissioned by the King of Norway to proclaim Christianity in Greenland, but was driven far off his course by bad weather and landed in Newfoundland. I don't know if that was lucky or not, but his crew seemed to think it was.

Can you express your personality in such a way that you exude confidence? Can you walk into a room and give the impression that you own the place? People assign us a reputation of competence based partially on how we perceive ourselves.

7. A willingness to lead by example

Do you set the example in your family, in your company, in your community?

Would you be willing to go as far as Ernest "Bud" Miller, president and chief executive officer of Arvida, a real-estate company? Miller closed regional offices, reorganized departments, and cut his work force of twenty-six hundred in half. When he was finished, he resigned, giving up an "upper six-figure" salary package believing that the jobs at the top ought also to be consolidated. "I couldn't justify me to me," says Miller. "I couldn't look at the people I let go and say I applied a different standard to me. Every fiber of my person wanted to stay. But professionally this was the decision that had to be made."[11]

Do not expect to win the loyalty of today's more knowledgeable worker if you do not establish the same exacting standards for your own behavior that you do for theirs. We respect people who are willing to lead by example—people who are willing to go that extra mile, willing to pay that higher price to set themselves apart from the crowd. Leadership shines brightest when the leader does what nobody else is willing to do.

8. A commitment to excellence

Driving between Amarillo and Witchita Falls, Texas, there's not much to see. The landscape is rather bleak. You pass through a series of small towns. No McDonald's—but a Dairy Queen in each town. Covering a wall in one such Dairy Queen is a gigantic picture of the local high school football team—state champs a few years back. You get the idea.

One of those small towns between Amarillo and Witchita Falls is a place called Clarendon, Texas—population two thousand and sixty-seven. If you want to spend the night in Clarendon, you'll have to stay in a quaint little establishment named the "It'll Do" motel. That name caught my attention. "The It'll Do Motel." I didn't stay that night in Clarendon. The "It'll Do" is probably a fine establishment, but something about the name didn't inspire my confidence.

Effective leaders insist on excellence in all things. "It'll Do" simply won't do. Because these leaders' standards are high, they stand head-and-shoulders above the rest.

9. A decision to hire the best people you can find, then delegate, delegate, delegate

Good executives never put off until tomorrow what they can get someone else to do today. Effective leaders multiply their influence by hiring the best people they can find and making certain they get the best training possible. They find people who will do a better job than they would have done at the same task.

Andrew Carnegie was committed to this principle. As he once said: "I wish to have as my epitaph: 'Here lies a man who was wise enough to bring into his service men who knew more than he.'"

10. Attention to detail

General Colin Powell in his autobiography tells about a time early in his army career when he was assigned to Fort Benning, Georgia, and dispatched on a month-long course of advanced airborne training. One night he and his troops had to parachute from a helicopter after completing a day-long march. It was windy and pouring rain, and they all were exhausted.[12]

Powell was the senior officer on board. Through the roar of the helicopter engine, he shouted for everyone to double-check the static lines—the wires, hooked to a floor cable that would open the chutes when they jumped. Nearing the jump site, he yelled to check the hookups again. Finally, like an old fussbudget, Powell started pushing through the crowded bodies, checking each line himself. To his alarm, one hook was loose. He shoved the dangling line in the man's face. The soldier gasped. He would have stepped off the helicopter and dropped like a rock.

The fellow practically blubbered his gratitude. The lesson was clear: moments of stress, confusion, and fatigue are exactly when mistakes happen. When everyone else is distracted, the leader must be doubly vigilant, says Powell. "Always check the small things," became one of his rules.

Vince Lombardi took the worst team in pro football and made it the greatest team ever. One of the characteristics Lombardi's players frequently recalled was his perfectionism. There was a feeling that no mistake escaped him. He demanded the players' all on every play in every game, and even in every practice. This attention to detail was part of Lombardi's conception of "thinking like a champion."

11. A willingness to take prudent risks

Maury Wills holds the major league record for stolen bases, and the record for the number of times being caught stealing a base. An old proverb says, "You can't walk on water if you won't get out of the boat." I am convinced that this is the chief reason why many otherwise capable men and women do not achieve their dreams. Most Americans are risk-averse. We are mutual fund buyers, not go-for-broke investors. The problem is that many of us play it too safe, forgetting that fortune really does favor the bold.

Sociologist Tony Campolo tells about a study that was done wherein fifty people over the age of ninety were asked the question: "If you had it to do over again, what would you do differently?" There were multiple answers, but among them, three answers dominated. These older people said, "If we had to do it over again, first of all, we would reflect more." Secondly, "We would risk more." That was interesting. The last thing was, "We would do more things that would live on after we were dead." If you are going to do something that will live on after you are gone, somewhere along the way you are going to have to take some risks.[13]

12. Respect for all people

Thomas Watson, Jr., the former chairman of IBM, stressed the importance of the company having a philosophical backbone, a set of three basic beliefs: "respect for the individual, service to the customer, and excellence in everything we do." IBM has had its ups-and-downs in recent years, but it still maintains the loyalty of first-rate service and salespeople. Why? Because those employees are treated with respect.

When band leader Woody Herman died, Nat Pierce, a pianist and composer who worked with him off and on for many years, said, "We never felt we were working for him. We were always working with him."[14] That's a good formula for success.

It's been said so many times, but it still rings true: nobody cares how much you know until they know how much you care. In our society of personal estrangement, many persons feel that the people they work with are the only family they have. That is why the loss of a job or retirement can be so devastating for some people. The leader who can communicate sincere caring while at the same time requiring conformity to high standards will have a motivated workforce. When, as a leader, you genuinely care, your influence soars.

The *Atlanta Journal-Constitution* did an interesting study sometime back. They interviewed a wide range of persons who had bought new homes within the past five years. The first question they asked was, have you had any problems with your new home—problems that you had to call the contractor back to repair? As you might imagine, some of them had nightmare situations to report. Some of them had asked the contractor to come back several times over those five years to repair one thing or another.

Then they asked the question, would you have the same builder build your next home? What they found was that the feelings of the homeowners had nothing to do with how many problems they had incurred with their house.

The only thing that mattered was whether the contractor listened to them and came back and repaired the problem. Even those who felt they had lived through nightmares said they would use the same builder again if the builder listened to them and responded in a timely manner. People will forgive us a multitude of sins in any profession if they really believe we care.

CHAPTER 27

Step 9: Celebrate Those Who Influenced You

A quiz of unknown authorship came over the Internet. The writer suggested we name the ten wealthiest people in the world, the last ten Heisman trophy winners, the last ten Miss Americas, eight Nobel or Pulitzer Prize winners, the last ten Academy Award winners for best picture, and the last decade's worth of World Series winners.[1]

Then we were asked to name three people we enjoy being with, ten people who have taught us something worthwhile, five friends who have helped us in a difficult time, teachers who have aided our journey through school, and six heroes whose stories have inspired us. The implication was that the latter group is clearly of much more value to us than the former one.

It reminded me of the story of a young boy who awoke on his sixth birthday to a memorable surprise. His uncle took him to the kitchen where the rest of the family—parents, aunts, uncles, grandmother and grandfather—awaited. They walked him out to the garage where there was a section of a redwood tree nearly five feet tall and one foot thick waiting. Little signs were painted on the rings of the tree. One ring read, "The Emancipation Proclamation, January 1, 1863." Still another signified when the young fellow's mother and father had met and married.

As the boy studied the carefully labeled rings on that huge piece of redwood, he realized that here was a history of his family and his race. Is it any wonder that this little boy, Alex Haley, grew up to write the best-selling novel *Roots*?[2]

We live in a society that no longer cherishes its traditions. Many of us know very little about our ancestors, and that is sad. Years ago, Elton Trueblood called us a cut-flower generation, a generation cut off from its roots. That is why I was interested to read about the debut of the youngest member of the famous Wallenda family of high-wire artists.[3]

Alex Wallenda, at seven years of age was already walking a wire twenty-one feet above the ground. There was no safety net, but he did have a safety line attached to his belt to prevent him from being hurt if he fell. Alex is the youngest person ever to perform the high-wire act. He and his three sisters represent the seventh generation of Wallenda high wire performers, a tradition that was started in the eighteenth century in the Austro-Hungarian empire.

To me that is impressive—not only that Alex is the youngest high-wire artist, but that he is conscious of a family heritage that traces back that far. Most of us aren't that fortunate. We have no knowledge of the persons who lived in centuries past who are responsible for our existence today. Most of us can only look back over our own lifetimes and see more immediate influences. However, these influences are powerful and dear to us.

In fact, I suspect this is the one civilizing impulse in our lives—the memory of those parents, grandparents, teachers, friends, employers, and colleagues whose encouragement and example helped us become who we are. We stand on tall shoulders.

Writer Robert Maynard tells of a childhood incident that had a great impact on his life. While walking to school one day, Robert came across a fresh patch of cement. He bent down and scratched his name in the damp cement. Suddenly, a huge, angry stone mason grabbed Robert and began yelling at him for messing up the sidewalk. Little Robert was terrified and babbled about just wanting to put his name on something. All the anger melted from the stone mason's face. He pointed in the direction of the school and said, "If you want your name on something, you go in that school. You work hard and you become a lawyer and you hang your shingle out for all the world to see." When Robert explained that he wanted to be a writer, the stone mason smiled. "Be a writer! Be a real writer! Have your name on books, not sidewalks." Robert Maynard never forgot those words of both admonishment and encouragement.[4]

Sometimes inspiration and encouragement come from the most unlikely quarters. But as Alex Haley was fond of saying, "If you see a turtle on a fence post, it didn't get there by itself." Somebody, somewhere along the way gave a helping hand. That is one of the noblest uses we can make of our lives—to give someone else a helping hand—and we do that if we remember those who are responsible for our being who we are.

In *Making the Grass Greener on Your Side: A CEO's Journey to Leading by Serving,* Ken Melrose tells about a rabbi who came to his church to lead a discussion. "How many of you remember your grandfather?" the rabbi asked. "If you do, raise your hand." Almost everyone did.

Fewer people could recall their great-grandfather when asked, and no one remembered their great-great-grandfather.[5]

Then the rabbi dropped a bomb on his audience: "Suppose your great-great-grandchildren were in this room . . . will they remember you?" As he explained, our future descendants will only know us through the legacy of character we leave behind. Our kind or callous actions will be passed down to our future generations; what we do today may have the power to influence who our great-great-grandchildren will be someday.

We need to remind ourselves that we are who we are today because of individual acts of concern and kindness that have come to us from others. Some of those acts have come to us over the generations. They are part of our heritage. Some of these acts, however, were more recent. They are still in our memory. We can reflect on them and we can use them to spur us to make a deliberate, positive impression on the lives of others.

The Importance of Mentoring

Some of us have been fortunate enough to have had mentors who have helped shorten the learning curve in our respective vocations. The word *mentor* derives from the name of a character in Homer's *Odyssey*. When the mythological Greek hero Odysseus went off to fight the Trojan War, he asked his close friend Mentor to care for his young son, Telemachus. Mentor was a good man who taught Telemachus about wisdom and personal responsibility.

Every person would profit from having a mentor. Former President Dwight D. Eisenhower had one. His name was General Fox Conner, a senior officer whom Eisenhower greatly admired. As Eisenhower later wrote about Conner: "Life with General Connor was sort of a graduate school in military affairs . . . In a lifetime of association with great and good men, he is the one . . . figure to whom I owe an incalculable debt." It is a very fortunate person who finds a mentor.

Surveys of middle and senior managers suggest that anywhere from thirty to seventy-five percent feel they have benefited from mentor-like support from a senior colleague. Even more impressively, a recent study shows that over half of all Nobel Prize winners were once apprenticed to other Nobel laureates. Imagine that! Sure, these were brilliant folks—but still they profited from the help of those more experienced than themselves. We all need someone to show us the way. All of us can profit from having a mentor. And if we want to spread our influence in the world, there will come a time when each of us will need to be a mentor.

I have mentioned motivational speaker and author Zig Ziglar several times in this book. Obviously, he has been an important influence in my life through his books and speeches. Ziglar is possibly the most famous name in the profession of selling. In his career as a motivational speaker and author, he has been able to influence the lives of thousands, even millions, of people. Ziglar is humble enough, though, to give credit to those who have influenced his life too. One of those people is his former history teacher, Coach Joby Harris.[6]

Although Ziglar was just taking his course to fulfill a requirement, Coach Harris evinced such infectious enthusiasm that he ended up changing his major to history. But Coach Harris' influence extended beyond the classroom; he was a man of integrity, and he encouraged all his students to use their abilities to help those who are less fortunate. Ziglar learned more than history from his former teacher; he also learned character. How did Coach Joby Harris become the kind of man he was? Well, he was influenced by the first scoutmaster in Mississippi named Thomas A. Abernathy.

Mr. Abernathy made a conscientious effort to encourage and develop the skills and character of little Joby Harris. Mr. Abernathy modeled respect, responsibility, caring, and integrity to his young charges, and Joby Harris learned from his example. So, indirectly, Thomas A. Abernathy had an influence on Ziglar's life. But he also had a direct influence on Ziglar. In the Abernathy household, there were one son and three daughters. One of those daughters, Jean Abernathy, has been married to Ziglar for the past fifty-three years. The two have raised their own brood of exceptional offspring, who are going on to influence others. Moreover, Ziglar (with Jean's support and assistance) through his books, tapes, seminars, and speeches, is spreading his message of positive action. As we have noted, the chain of influence once set in motion can go on forever.

Stephen Sondheim found his mentor in Oscar Hammerstein II, famed lyricist of *Oklahoma* and *Show Boat*. At the age of fifteen, Sondheim left his divorced, angry mother and went to live with neighbors, the Hammersteins. With Oscar Hammerstein's guidance, Sondheim learned how to express his feelings in song. A driving force behind Sondheim's work was not success but rather a desire to please Oscar, to make him proud.[7]

We tend to think that great artists, scientists, and other highly creative people are different from us—born with special gifts they're destined to use, no matter what obstacles the world puts in their way. Not true, says psychologist Mihaly Csikszentmihalyi in *Creativity: Flow and the Psychology of Discovery and Invention* (Harper-Collins). The book chronicles the lives of ninety-one men and women whose exceptional achievements have earned them honors including the Nobel and Pulitzer Prizes. Some of these creative types showed special talents early on, but others didn't. Their most outstanding trait, says Dr. Csikszentmihalyi, was something most children share: a keen curiosity about the world. What made the difference, however, was a caring adult who nurtured that curiosity, let them "roam" until they found their passion, then did their best to support it, say, by taking them to concerts or museums.[8]

For instance, when astronomer Vera Rubin, who helped discover how galaxies work, fell in love with the stars at age seven, her father helped her build a telescope. Would Vera have continued her love affair with the stars without this act of encouragement? We don't know, but we do know from Dr. Csikszentmihalyi's research that a caring adult, a mentor, can make a critical difference in a young person's development.[9]

For one future Olympic star, that role was played by the great athlete Charlie Paddock. Charlie Paddock, a champion runner of the 1920s, used his fame to encourage young people. Paddock's message was simple: because you are a child of God, you can accomplish anything. One young student who heard this message and took it to heart was a scrawny little black boy by the name of Jesse Owens. He began training that very day to become a champion runner. At the 1936 Olympics, Owens set two new world records and took home four gold medals. Today Owens is memorialized in the American Hall of Athletic Fame. We cannot know how many other boys and girls were influenced by Paddock, but even if Jesse Owens was the only one, that would be quite a contribution to humanity.[10]

For gymnast Mary Lou Retton it was a coach. Under the tutelage of former Romanian Olympic coach Bela Karolyi who had fled communism to live in the United States, fifteen-year-old Retton, the West Virginia girl with the golden personality won three gold medals in gymnastic competition in the 1984 Olympics. Everyone can benefit from having a mentor. And when we mentor someone else, we are extending our influence through them.

Ron Lee Davis in his book, *Mistreated,* tells of the remarkable influence that one writer, Sherwood Anderson, had on other writers. For a time during the early twentieth century, Anderson was one of the most popular writers in America. And during those years Anderson mentored dozens of young, aspiring novelists.[11]

One of Anderson's protégés was a young man who had been wounded as an ambulance driver in World War I. Shortly after his release from the army, this young man rented an apartment near Anderson's on the Near North Side of Chicago. He spent a year talking with Anderson, sharing meals with him, writing and showing his stories to Anderson—stories that his mentor reviewed with brutal frankness. Six years later, while still in his twenties, this young man published a novel called *The Sun Also Rises.* Immediately, he became an international sensation. His name was Ernest Hemingway. Others Anderson mentored include William Faulkner, John Steinbeck, William Saroyan, and Thomas Wolfe. Wolfe said, "Sherwood Anderson is the only man in America who ever taught me anything." That is a pretty high recommendation!

"Everyone who has ever touched my life," says General Colin Powell, former chairman of the Joint Chiefs of Staff and one of the most respected men in America, "in some way was a mentor for good or bad. Life is a blend, and a person is a blend of all the influences that have touched their lives."[12]

As I look back at my life, I can think of many people whose influence touched me. Some of them, besides my parents, were neighbors, other family members, pastors, or colleagues. In addition, ever since I was three years old, I have been very fortunate to have my good friend Dave whom I have already mentioned. Dave knows me better than anyone and still is my friend. He is a person of great character. He is a speaker like me, and my life is always better when I am around him.

I've already mentioned that two of the of the most important influences in my life were teachers. Do I have a soft spot for them? You bet. No role in society is more important today than that of a teacher. More than two decades ago, President Lyndon Johnson urged Americans to stop thinking of education as a public expense, and to start thinking of it as a public investment. If we lose our young people, what will happen to us as a nation? Here is where influence really matters.

I don't know who you might consider to be the primary positive influences in your life. It might be your spouse. I can say that if my life ever produces any positive benefit for the world, it will be because of my wife, Selina. She has provided me with a steady source of strength for over thirty years and has loved me far more than I could ever deserve.

If there has been someone in your life that has provided that kind of ennobling influence, *isn't it time for you to pass that influence on to others*? That means getting outside yourself and focusing on the needs of someone else with an eye toward improving the world. That means living out those values that have been implanted in your heart and soul. That means caring enough to give your very best to your family, your friends, to the world.

Caring Enough to Be Heroic

Eighteenth-century writer Oliver Goldsmith once said, "People seldom improve when they have no other model but themselves to copy." Today's world is crying out for people who will live heroic lives, lives worthy of emulation.

Chuck Swindoll tells about a Minnesota woman who won a five-hundred-mile dogsled race a few years back. It was her third victory in this grueling competition. She and her dogs pressed on through bitter cold, blizzards, dark nights, and exhausting days. To protect the dogs' feet from the sharp ice, the woman had outfitted their paws in miniature socks. Physically and mentally, the race was a monumental challenge. The woman reported that she overcame the mental challenge by reminding herself that others had finished this race before, so it was possible for her to succeed too.[13]

Others have done it before me. Is that important to know? You bet it is. One of the by-products of the cynicism that pervades today's world is that nobody expects the heroic anymore. We need heroes because they give us the strength to be heroic too.

Amelia Earhart set the world abuzz with excitement when, in 1937, she attempted to fly around the world. She proved her credentials when, in 1930, she set the women's speed and altitude records. In 1932, Earhart was the first woman to cross the Atlantic solo. Her twenty-five-thousand-mile, round-the-world trip would have earned her a place in history. As it is, her place in history was secured by her mysterious disappearance on July 2, 1937, over Howland Island, just three thousand miles short of her destination.

Other than her love of flying, Earhart had a burning desire to demonstrate to women that they could do anything they wanted. They didn't have to settle for the limits and the boundaries of their society. Many people have been inspired by that message, but one woman, Linda Finch, is taking it personally. Finch is the pilot who successfully recreated Amelia Earhart's around-the-world flight.[14]

Finch has always loved flying. As a single mother, she used to skip lunch every day in order to save up the money for flying lessons. But when she read Earhart's books, she became fired by Earhart's vision of encouraging women to reach beyond their limits. So Finch set out to recreate Amelia Earhart's trip around the world exactly sixty years since Earhart's disappearance. She made her flight in an extremely rare breed of plane, a Lockheed Electra 10E, the same kind of plane Earhart flew. At various stops along the route, she visited schools and spoke to children about aviation, her trip, and Earhart's legacy. She also created educational packets for schools to use in teaching about her trip, and kept a journal of it to distribute on the World Wide Web. She took digital pictures on her various stops to be posted on the computer. In these ways, she hopes to educate and inspire children to reach beyond their limits too.

When Linda Finch flew over Howland Island in the Pacific, the last place where Amelia Earhart was seen alive, she dropped a memorial wreath in honor of the woman who died in pursuit of a passion and an ideal.

Where do we find the will to risk being heroic? I believe the primary motivation for being heroic ourselves is to acknowledge those who have been our heroes; we should emulate those who have gone to the trouble to make our lives better. If we can reach out to them and say "thank you," that's great. But it's like the debt we owe our parents. It is best paid by being great parents ourselves. Our primary way of saying thanks will be to pass on to others the kindness we have received. By passing on what we have received from those who influenced us, we will be ensuring that their work was not in vain. We will be building on their example.

Following His Dad's Example

In his book *Living Faith,* former President Jimmy Carter tells about visiting his father in the last few weeks before his father's death. Mr. Carter, a farmer from Plains, Georgia, was well respected in his community. He was known as a man of integrity and compassion. At one point in his life, Jimmy Carter was forced to compare his "successful" life with his father's life of service. In the end, he knew what kind of man he wanted to be. He resigned from the navy and moved back to Georgia to begin a new life as a man of integrity in his community—just like his father.[15]

In the book *Profiles in Character,* Congresswoman Barbara Cubin from Wyoming tells how her character was shaped by the moral influence of her parents, including her stepfather. Barbara's parents divorced when she was young. A few years later, Barbara's mother remarried, and her new stepfather worked hard to support the family. One particular story demonstrates his great character:

Barbara's birth father, on a visit to Wyoming, was beaten and robbed. At the hospital, a paramedic found his ex-wife's phone number on him and called the house. Barbara's stepfather went immediately to the hospital and paid her birth father's hospital bill. Then he took him to a local motel. The stepfather paid the proprietor of the motel for the father's room and meals until he had recovered enough to go home.[16]

Medieval dictionaries defined the word *exemplum* as "a clearing in the woods." Our words "example" and "exemplar" come from the root word that originally referred to taking out the trees and brush so that the sun could shine through in a clearing. In the midst of the darkness and tangle, the sun could stream in, bringing warmth and light.

There is an old Finnish proverb that even a small star shines in the darkness. Jesus said to those who followed him, "You are the light of the world." Did he not mean "you are the exemplum—the clearing in the woods"? I count myself as a follower of Jesus, but you don't have to be a Christian to be an exemplum. I have had the pleasure on two occasions to speak to groups of Jewish rabbis (conservative and reformed). They have their own light to shine and they do a splendid job. There are people of every religious persuasion and even some that have very little religious inclination who are still serving as a clearing in the woods. In one of the eastern religions, a disciple asked his master: "What's the difference between knowledge and enlightenment?" The master answered: "When you have knowledge, you've a torch to show the way. When you are enlightened, you become a torch."

The important thing is to let your light shine. You can change the world! You are changing the world whether you mean to or not. If you want to change the world in a positive way, think of all those who have been responsible for the positive influences that have brought you to this point, and determine in your own mind to transmit these positive influences to others.

If, on the other hand, we have been on the negative end, if our life has in some way been damaged by the negative influence of another, then we need to do what we can to forgive that person. We do not have to be bound by our past experiences; instead, we can choose new influences. And as we ponder the severe injustice that has been done to us, we must resolve that we will do all within our power to ensure that the tradition of pain that has impacted our life will not be perpetuated in the life of someone else. We must use it as a spur to make our life a light without equal, because we know the tragedy of a life that has been shriveled by the negative influence of another.

CHAPTER 28

Step 10: Dream of a Better World

The movie *The Elephant Man* details the sad, but true story of John Merrick, a man who suffered from a rare and horrible disease called neurofibrocytosis. Neurofibrocytosis results in a grotesquely enlarged head and disfiguring bumps all over the body. As a child, Merrick was exhibited as a freak act in a circus. He was an outcast. But a doctor bought this horribly deformed boy from the circus and began studying him. To the doctor's surprise, he discovered John Merrick to be quite brilliant. He had used his mind as an escape from the harshness of everyday life. And so an amazing metamorphosis takes place. The former outcast becomes a trusted advisor to kings and royalty around the world. As Merrick said when reflecting on his life, "Sometimes I think my head is so big because it is so full of dreams."

Isn't it wonderful to have a head full of dreams? Some people don't know how to dream.

A football coach was quizzing his players. With fire in his eyes he marched up to a seldom used third-sting offensive tackle and said, "Suppose, we are involved in a tie game. One minute to go. We are three yards from the goal line and a play was called to the left side of the line. What would you do?"

The lineman thought for a moment and then said, "Gee, coach, I don't know. I reckon I would slide down the bench where I could get a better view." That young man does not know how to dream.

I've always been a dreamer. As a small child I dreamed of being a cowboy like Gene Autry, Roy Rogers, or Hopalong Cassidy. Later I dreamed of being a great NFL quarterback like Johnny Unitas. Like millions of other young boys, I could see myself hitting Raymond Berry on the sideline as we marched down field for the winning touchdown. In my teenaged years my dreams changed. I was going to be the next Elvis. I can still do a mean version of "Heartbreak Hotel."

I still am a dreamer. I trace it back to my high school years singing in the school choir. You may remember all those great musicals of the forties and fifties.[1]

"Climb every mountain . . . "

Remember that one? Or how about,

"To dream the impossible dream . . . "[2]

One of the first items I purchased when my wife and I visited the Southwest for the first time was a Navajo dream catcher. Dream catchers often hang above the beds of infants and small children. According to the legend, you hang one over your bed and it catches your good dreams while allowing your bad dreams to pass on through.

Yogi Berra once said, "If you don't know where you're going, you might not get there." Dreams are very important for people who want to change the world. Of course, dreams come in different forms.

Night Dreams

There are, for example, the dreams we have at night. Some of these dreams can haunt us. Some of them are universal.

Let's try this one. You've been asked to give a speech, you're standing in front of an audience, and you realize that you have forgotten what you were going to say. This dream may reflect your fear of not being adequately prepared.

Or how about this dream? You're at a party. Everyone is nicely dressed except you. You're in your pajamas or your underwear or less. This dream may reveal a real fear of humiliation, we're told. You have this dream when you feel inadequate for a task you've been assigned and you fear being exposed as a fraud.

I had a recurring dream while I was in college. It was just before finals and I was hit with the sickening realization that there was one course I had signed up for but had totally forgotten about. Each time I had this dream, I would wake up in a cold sweat.

There are all kinds of common dreams—dreams of flying, or of being chased, dreams of failing as well as dreams of amazing victories.

There is a custom that the Senoi people of Malaysia have that families with small children might want to emulate. Every morning at breakfast a Senoi child dutifully reports his dreams to the other members of his family. If he has had a nightmare about being chased by a "smoke spirit," his parents don't say, "Be quiet, dear, and finish your raisin bran. There's no such thing as a smoke spirit." They encourage him to re-dream his dream, but this time to turn around and ask the spirit, "Why are you chasing me?"[3]

What a healthy approach to dreaming! Of course, the American family is far too busy in the morning to follow such a primitive practice. It makes you wonder in what ways we can call our society advanced. The simple act of listening and showing interest in one another is one of the most powerful forms of influencing.

Paying Attention to Dreams

In 1920, Dr. Frederick worked far into the night trying to solve the problem of diabetes. He fell asleep. A little before two in the morning, he awoke with a start. Grabbing a notebook, he penned three short sentences; then he collapsed again in sleep. But those three sentences later led to the discovery of insulin.[4]

A century earlier, Elias Howe was determined to invent the sewing machine, but he couldn't get it right; its stitches were jagged and uneven. One night, he dreamed that a tribe of savages had kidnapped him. They threatened to kill him if he didn't invent a sewing machine within twenty-four hours. When he was unsuccessful, spears flew at him. As they whizzed by his head, he noticed they had holes near their tips. He awoke with an idea: put the eye of the needle near the tip.[5]

In 1985, after ten years of searching, Mel Fisher found the sunken vessel *Atocha*. In the meantime, his son Dirk who was helping with the expedition drowned on a shallow underwater reef. Shortly before his death Dirk had a very vivid dream that this treasure laden ship was in the deep water where they first had searched. Mel Fisher returned to those waters and found the *Atocha*.

Friedrich Kekule dreamed one night of a ring of snakes, each trying to devour the next snake's tail. From his dream came the discovery of the structure of benzene.[6]

Daydreams

More important to our effectiveness in life than those dreams we have at night are those dreams we have during the day. Daydreams are an important part of our lives, fantasies they are sometimes called. When we are young we see ourselves throwing the winning touchdown or writing the great American novel. It's silly, of course—adolescent, perhaps. But did you know that it is also healthy?

Psychologist Burton White of Harvard's Child Development Center did some research with children. He found that about one child in thirty is both brilliant and happy. White was committed to determining what demographic or psychological characteristics distinguished those happy children. But the children came from a variety of backgrounds—rich and poor, small families and large, broken and stable homes, poorly and well-educated parents—and from all parts of the United States. Finally, through extensive questioning, he determined that the bright and happy children had only one thing in common: all of them spent noticeable amounts of time staring peacefully and wordlessly into space.[7]

How many times have you said to your child, "Quit dreaming and get busy"? Bad advice. Daydreaming is an essential part of growing up. I can remember how rich my daydreams were as a child. As a teenager, though, dreaming was sometimes detrimental. In truth, I preferred daydreaming to meeting my responsibilities.

Dreams are vital to a healthy youth. More importantly, they predict the kind of life we will find most satisfying. Denis Waitley tells about a series of remarkable studies conducted by British behavioral scientists over a twenty-eight-year period. Fifty individuals were tracked beginning at age seven. These individuals were given evaluations every seven years until each reached the age of thirty-five.

Incredibly, by the time they reached thirty-five nearly all of these individuals were doing something which was related to the daydreams they had between seven and fourteen years of age.[8] Although most of them had discarded or strayed from those interests from ages fifteen to twenty-one and beyond, virtually all found their way back to their childhood dreams by the age of thirty-five, even if only as a hobby or an avocation. Dreams are important when we are young. And sometimes those daydreams come true.

Neil Armstrong, the first man to set foot on the moon, said, "Ever since I was twelve, I dreamed I would do something important in aviation!"

Legendary actress Mary Martin dreamed of flying. She studied birds flapping their wings. She perched on fences and even tried flying from the rooftop of her home. All of this was splendid preparation to play Peter Pan on Broadway.[9]

Muhammad Ali was caught drawing in class at age twelve. He had designed a boxing jacket with "World Champion" written on it.[10]

When you're young, there is something healthy about being lost from time to time in wholesome fantasies. Of course, as we grow older, reality sets in and many of us quit dreaming. How sad. When we stop dreaming, something within us dies. A writer in the Hebrew Bible put it like this: "Where there is no vision, the people perish."

The Vision Thing

Soon after the completion of Disney World, someone said, "Isn't it too bad that Walt Disney didn't live to see this?"

Mike Vance, creative director of Disney Studios, replied, "He did see it. That's why it's here."

Every great accomplishment begins with a dream. Dreams keep us alive and growing and reaching for the stars. It's the vision thing that former President Bush couldn't quite figure out. Evidently, neither did former President Clinton. Only Ronald Reagan and John F. Kennedy among our recent presidents have.

Vision is described by Warren Bennis as the first basic ingredient of leadership, the "most pivotal" of all the characteristics that outstanding leaders possess.

John Ruskin put the point clearly:

"The greatest thing a human soul ever does in this world is *see* something, and tell what it saw in a plain way. Hundreds of people can talk for one who can think, but thousands can think for one who can see."

Henry Ford could see. He saw the need for an automobile, the Model T, that would transform the American way of life. Here is what he saw:

I will build a motor car for the great multitude. It will be large enough for the family, but small enough for the individual to run and care for it. It will be constructed of the best materials, by the best men to be hired, after the simplest designs that modern engineering can devise. But it will be so low in price that no man making a good salary will be unable to own one . . .

It would be difficult to spell out a dream any more specifically than that. Here is the key to greatness in this world. Have a dream.

When Steven Jobs (of Apple Computer fame) was asked by a reporter if he considered himself to be a driven man, Jobs replied, "No, I don't feel like I'm a driven man. I have such an exciting vision of what my team and I can accomplish that it's like I'm running towards a magnet. I have daydreams where I am literally running toward an image of our goals. I guess you'd say I'm a *pulled* man."

I like that—a pulled man. A pulled woman. The power of a dream.

We keep talking about the information age. But what happens when all the information in the world can be accessed from our desk top and everybody has access to the same information? Then we will move from the information age to the imagination age. The people who will have the advantage will be those who can see ways to use that information that nobody else has yet thought of. Those will be the winners. Actually we already live in the imagination age.

As Edward Deming once said, "No customer ever asked for the fax machine, the microwave oven, or the cellular telephone." These were born in somebody's imagination first.

Einstein put it best. He said that imagination is more important than knowledge. As if to prove his point he revolutionized the study of physics through his theory of relativity. How did he come upon this theory? He said that in his imagination he rode a ray of light around the world and back. He visualized himself facing the source of the light beam as he rode in order "to see" where it came from.

In a survey of CEOs back in 1992 the question was asked 'Which is more important for success in business?' Fifty-nine percent opted for creativity, only twenty-eight percent for intelligence.

Dreaming of a Better World

Now what has all this got to do with the Law of Influence? I am convinced that it is time for people of goodwill to start dreaming again of a better world. Before we can actually have a better world, we will have to dream of a better world. We need a consensus—a working blueprint, if you will—among persons of goodwill of what such a world would look like.

Such dreams are part of our heritage. Dr. Martin Luther King, Jr. was tapping into a very important part of our Judeo-Christian tradition when he declared, "I have a dream that one day every valley shall be exalted . . . the rough places will be made plain, and the crooked places will be made straight. And the glory of the Lord shall be revealed . . . this is our hope. This is the faith that I go back to the South with. With this faith we will be able to hew out of the mountain of despair a stone of hope."

He was citing, of course, the prophecies of the Hebrew Bible (for Christians, The Old Testament). Such dreams are part of the heritage of Christians and Jews alike. Who cannot be moved by the imagery of nations "beating their swords into plowshares and their spears into pruning hooks" or "the wolf lying down with the lamb?" We need that kind of vision today.

It is a shame that the trauma of the Holocaust cost many of our Jewish friends their dream of the Messianic age described by the prophet—that day when nations would live in harmony together. It is understandable that this doctrine would lose its appeal considering the suffering of the Jewish people in the middle of the twentieth century. Still, it is sad.

Many Christians have also discarded their dream of a better world. Part of this regrettable trend is probably due to the affluence of many modern-day Christians. Self-satisfaction is a curse to religious people. But part of it may be due to the current popularity of overly literal interpretations of the Book of Revelation. If history is to end soon in a fiery apocalypse instituted of God, as some of our conservative friends believe, there is not much use of trying to build rapport between the peoples of the world.

Sometime back I was asked to address a Sunday school class concerning the book of Revelation—that book at the end of the Christian Bible that supposedly describes in scary detail the end of time. I say "supposedly" because there are many scholars who believe that what is described in the book of Revelation is a symbolic foretelling of the fall of the Roman Empire.

In preparing for this class, I remembered that there was a very popular book about the Rapture (the dramatic account of the end of time found in Revelation) which had frightened many people a few years ago. I went into a nearby Christian bookstore to see if I could purchase a copy of this book. I could not remember the title, so I explained to the salesperson the nature of the book.

She said, "Oh, you must mean the book, *Eighty-eight Reasons Why the Rapture Will Definitely Come in 1988.*"

"That sounds like it," I said.

She said, "That also came in a 1989 edition."

I tried to keep from laughing out loud.

"We sent back our unsold copies last spring," the salesperson said apologetically. I can understand that. There are few things more out of date than a prediction that the world definitely will come to an end years after the supposed date of its demise. When the book was first published, though, impressionable people sold possessions, spent their life savings, holed up in churches, etc., on the basis of this misguided prophecy.

One positive incident occurred as a result of the prediction, however. According to the Associated Press, a North Carolina gunman who kept police at bay for thirty hours gave up after his aunt urged him to "get right" for the Rapture.

Some of the looniness that has become associated with the concept of the end of time should not prevent us from clinging to the biblical dream of an era when the nations of the world will lay down their weapons and people will live in harmony and peace together. And it should not keep us from doing our part to help that dream come true today.

God's Dream

The most haunting line in the 1989 baseball fantasy movie *Field of Dreams* has to be, "If you build it, he will come." A corn farmer, played by Kevin Costner, built it, and indeed the baseball player of his dreams came.[11]

The writer of that movie tapped into something very real and very important in our character. We can dream of a better world. And we can so align our lives with that dream that such a world becomes a reality. That is the wonderful opportunity we have been given. As a religious person, I would call it God's dream. One day every child will enjoy a nourishing diet, no one will suffer again the ravages of war, everyone will live in dignity as a child of God, and no one will know prejudice due to race, sex, economic plight, nationality, religion, or ethnic background.

It begins with a dream, a dream of a better world. In the Broadway play *The Man of La Mancha,* Don Quixote asks, "Who is crazy? Am I crazy because I see the world as it could become? Or is the world crazy because it only sees itself as it is?"[12] Good question. And then, a better one: am I living my life every hour, every day, in such a way that I am sending out positive ripples of influence so that a better world might one day be a reality?

Leonardo da Vinci's *The Last Supper,* painted over five hundred years ago, is considered one of the classic masterpieces in the history of art. According to author Michael J. Gelb, this painting was done in a circular motif. Everything on the table is round, such as the bread and the plates. Also, the disciples are arranged in a half-circle on either side of Jesus. There is a distinct purpose behind da Vinci's use of the circular theme. As Mr. Gelb writes, "Like a stone tossed into the still pond of eternity,

Leonardo conveys Christ's influence rippling out to change human destiny forever."[13]

And that is what all people of conscience and faith are called to do—let our influence ripple until God's dream of all the world's people living in dignity and harmony is fulfilled.

CHAPTER 29

A Modern Telling of an Old Tale

This amazing Law of Influence can best be summed up in a story that comes from the Hebrew Bible. It one of the most delightful stories in all of literature. Somebody ought to turn it into a Broadway musical.

The book has everything. It has comedy—almost slapstick comedy in places. It has suspense. It has a villain. It has romance. It has everything that a good Broadway musical ought to have.

The story begins with a weeklong banquet thrown by a rather pompous king by the name of Ahasuerus, a king whose empire stretched from India to Ethiopia, the greatest of its day. Ahasuerus was an interesting man. Although he was a mighty king, he was also easily influenced, and generally, he was influenced into doing stupid things. The banquet was for all the leading men of the empire. The women had a separate affair.

On the seventh day of the banquet, "when the King's heart was light with wine," he decided to display his beautiful wife, Queen Vashti, in order to impress these important men who were gathered for this celebration. We are not told what Vashti was doing at that particular moment. Perhaps she was presiding over a banquet of her own; perhaps she had her hair in curlers. We don't know, but we do know she did the unthinkable—she sent word back to Ahasuerus that she was unavailable.

These were the days when queens did not disobey kings. King Ahasuerus was distressed, but he chose to take no immediate action. Rather he waited until the banquet had ended. Then he called together his royal advisers. "Gentlemen," he said, "I have a problem. On the last day of the great banquet I sent for Queen Vashti. I wanted to show off her beauty to my guests, but she refused to come. Now what should I do?"

You will love his advisors' reply: "King Ahasuerus, this problem is greater than you realize," they said. "If word gets out throughout the empire that you gave the queen an order and she disobeyed it, all of our wives will start disobeying us. This will bring down our whole way of life."

King Ahasuerus said, "I can see that. What should I do?"

"King Ahasuerus," said his advisers, "you haven't any choice. You must banish Queen Vashti from the empire forever."

"That sounds reasonable to me," Ahasuerus replied. I told you he was easily swayed. So he issued a decree that Queen Vashti was to be banished from the empire forever.

This solved one problem but eventually created another. In all these ancient stories, it was imperative that the king have a queen. Besides, it was getting cold at night. King Ahasuerus was lonely. So he decided he must have a new queen.

His advisors decided that the best way to select a new queen was to have a Miss Media-Persia Contest. They brought in girls from all over the empire. This contest put our Miss America contest to shame. Those in charge spent six months beautifying each of these girls with oil of myrrh followed by six months with special perfumes and ointments to prepare them to spend one night with the king, for him to make his selection.

The most beautiful girl in all the empire turned out to be a young Jewish girl by the name of Esther. Ahasuerus selected her to be his new queen.

Esther's father and mother were dead, but she had an uncle named Mordecai who had adopted her and raised her as his own daughter. Mordecai was a wise and deeply devout man. When he learned that Esther had been chosen to be the new queen, he came to give her some advice. He said, "Esther, I know you're excited about moving into the palace. I know you're excited about your new clothes and all the things that go with being the Queen. But let me give you a little advice. Unless it comes up, don't tell anybody that you're Jewish. You don't have to lie about it, but unless the subject comes up, just keep quiet about your faith."

Esther saw no reason to argue. "Sure," she said. "That'll be fine."

Esther moved into the palace and became the new queen.

Mordecai was not allowed into the palace to visit Esther. Nevertheless, he stayed close by. Each day he sat for a while outside the king's gate.

One day, while Mordecai was sitting at his customary post outside the gate, he overheard two of the king's bodyguards plotting to assassinate Ahasuerus. Alarmed, he sent a message to Esther to tell the king to beware. Esther communicated this news to Ahasuerus and the plot was thwarted. Ahasuerus' life was spared. Remember that. File it in your mind. It becomes important at the end of the story. Mordecai saved Ahasuerus' life.

Esther and Ahasuerus should have lived happily ever after. But there is a villain in the story, a vain and pompous man named Haman. Picture him with a long mustache which he twirls when he is pondering mischief. Haman was the king's "Number 2 Man." More than anything else, Haman enjoyed dressing up in his royal robes and riding through the streets of the city. Because he was the king's No. 2 Man, everybody was expected to bow down to him. This was exhilarating for Haman.

Everyone bowed to Haman except one man—Esther's uncle Mordecai. As a devout Jew, Mordecai bowed to no one. Haman would pass by each day, and Mordecai would stand as tall and straight as he could. Nobody knew the agony Mordecai caused Haman, who gulped down a pack of Rolaids each time he passed this stubborn Jew.

Finally, Haman could take it no more. He went to Ahasuerus with his frustration. "King Ahasuerus," he said, "There is a group of people in this empire who refuse to obey your laws. They are a threat to our society. Something is going to have to be done about them."

Ahasuerus asked, "Well, Haman, who are these people?"

Haman said, "It's the Jews."

"Well, Haman, what do you think I ought to do?"

Haman said, "King Ahasuerus, you hardly have any choice. You need to gather all these people together and put them to death."

And Ahasuerus in his own normal, astute way replied, "Well, that sounds like a reasonable idea to me. You draw up the decree and I'll issue it. We'll set a date when all the Jews are to be gathered in one place and put to death." Hitler was not the first to have the idea of eliminating the Jews.

Somehow Mordecai learned of this decree and realized that his people were in mortal danger. He came to the palace. He was not allowed inside to see Esther, but he sent her a copy of the king's decree dooming all Jews, and told her to show it to the king and to plead for her people.

Esther sent a message back to Mordecai. She said, "Look. There is a law that nobody can go in to see the king unless he sends for them and the king hasn't sent for me for thirty days. If I go in without being requested, it could mean my death. I'm not willing to take that risk."

It is then that Mordecai sends back one of the most famous messages in history: "Think not that in the king's palace you will escape any more than all the rest of the Jews. For if you keep silent at such a time as this, then deliverance will rise for the Jews from another quarter. But you and your father's house will perish. And who knows but that you have come to the kingdom for just such a time as this."

Mordecai was asking Esther, "How do you know that God hasn't placed you in the palace for just this moment—to intervene to save your people?" Powerful question. It would be a good one for each of us. *Who knows whether you have come to this moment in time to make a difference in the world? Who knows whether the Creator of the universe has placed you just where you are for a purpose grander than you can possibly imagine? Who knows whether something you say today may be one of those significant, life-changing moments in somebody's life?*

We already know from the evidence presented thus far that we can make a difference. Perhaps God has placed a burden on our hearts at this particular moment for someone special in our lives who would be especially susceptible to a word of encouragement or instruction at a critical juncture in their lives.

"Who knows," Mordecai asked, "if God has not put you here for just such a time as this?" It's a powerful thought. But let's finish our story. The ending is hilarious.

At the risk of her life, Esther did go in to see King Ahasuerus. Fortunately he was smitten with her beauty. He raised the royal scepter, a sign of favor, and said, "Come on in, Esther, and tell me what you want. I'll give you anything you ask, even if it's half the kingdom."

Esther was somewhat tongue-tied at this point. She said, "I'd like for you and Haman to come to my quarters for dinner."

Ahasuerus replied, "We would be happy to do that."

Haman was overjoyed when he learned that he was going to dine alone with the king and queen. No one else had been given this honor. Haman was still exulting in this new honor as he headed for his home. Everyone was bowing down to him on the street, which also delighted him. And then he passed Mordecai. Mordecai stood as tall as he was able. This bothered Haman more than ever. Arriving at home he said to his wife, "Honey, we've got all this power and all this privilege, but none of it means anything as long as that stubborn Jew stands out there and won't bow to me."

His wife said, "Haman, if it bothers you that much, why don't you build an enormous gallows and hang him on it?"

Haman decided that was the thing to do. He would have an enormous gallows erected, seventy-five feet high, on which to hang Mordecai. The thought of it helped Haman feel much better.

That evening he dined with the king and queen. After the meal King Ahasuerus said to Esther, "Now what is it you want? I'll give you anything, even half the kingdom."

For some reason Esther still was not ready to divulge her secret. "Why don't you come back tomorrow evening," she said, "and we'll discuss it?"

Haman was still reveling in his new exalted status the next morning.

For the second evening in a row, he would dine with the king and queen. Outside his office window, he could see the enormous gallows that were being erected for Mordecai. Haman was feeling pretty good.

You will remember that earlier in our story Mordecai saved Ahasuerus' life. Ahasuerus suddenly recalled that he had never shown his appreciation to Mordecai. So he called Haman in and said, "Haman, there's a man in this kingdom that I would like to honor. He has done a great thing for me."

As egotistical as Haman was, he started thinking, "Now, who could the king want to honor but me?"

Ahasuerus asked, "What should I do?"

Haman said, "Well, King, I'll tell you what I'd do. I'd dress this man up in my finest robes, and I'd put him on my finest horse, and I'd send him out on the streets, and have one of my finest men lead him through the streets proclaiming, 'This is the man the king wants to honor! This is the man the king wants to honor!'"

Ahasuerus said, "That's a great idea, Haman. Well, it's that Jew, Mordecai, that stands out there by the palace gate. Haman, I'd like for you to lead him through the streets."

Haman spent the entire day leading Mordecai through the streets shouting, "This is the man the king wants to honor! This is the man the king wants to honor!" You can imagine what that did to Haman's morale.

Later that evening Esther, Ahasuerus and Haman dined in the queen's quarters. They were reclining on sofas on the floor as was the custom in those days. There had been much to eat and drink. Finally, Ahasuerus said, "Now, Esther. What is it you want? I'll give you anything, even if it is half the empire."

At long last, Esther spilled it! Ahasuerus had issued a decree that all the Jews were to be killed. If they were killed, then she would be killed, for she was a Jew. Ahasuerus couldn't believe what he was hearing. He jumped up and yelled, "Who's responsible for this?"

Esther answered quietly, "It is your wicked servant Haman."

The blood rushed out of Haman's face. He knew he was in trouble. King Ahasuerus was so angry he stomped out into the garden without saying a word. What follows is the funniest scene in the entire Bible.

Haman struggled to his feet. He had consumed too much wine. He staggered over to where Esther was reclining and hovered over her to plead for his life. Suddenly he lost his balance and fell right on top of Queen Esther, just as King Ahasuerus came back into the room.

King Ahasuerus yelled, "Haman, would you assault the queen right here in my own palace?"

One version of the Scriptures says, "And the veil of death passed across Haman's face." He knew he had committed a fatal error. To make a long story short, Haman died on the gallows he had built for Mordecai. Esther was given all his lands and property, and Mordecai became the new No. 2 Man in all the empire.

Can't you see them singing and dancing at the end of the Broadway musical? It is a perfect musical comedy. But the important thing to remember are those words in the middle of this little story, "Who knows but that you have come to the kingdom for just such a time as this?" Something you say, something you do for somebody else, might be used by God in a wonderful way. The entire purpose of this book is to sensitize us that any moment may be God's moment through the application of the Law of Influence.

CHAPTER 30

Rosa Parks and the Fall of Communism

It is time for one more trip back to the days of the Cold War. One of the most important figures in the conclusion of that war was Boris Yeltsin. Yeltsin was such a sad and pitiable figure when he finally gave up power as president that we might be tempted to forget the role he played in usurping the power of the Communist Party in his country.

You may remember that famous incident when Gorbachev was still president. Military leaders loyal to the Communist Party were holding Gorbachev hostage in his dacha far from Moscow. Next on their list was Yeltsin. They sent tanks into Moscow for the sole purpose of capturing him and thereby consolidating their power. A tank rumbled into Red Square. When Yeltsin saw the tank coming toward him, he did something extraordinary. He jumped on the tank, extended his hand to the tank commander, and welcomed him over to the cause of democracy. The startled commander responded not by taking Yeltsin prisoner, but by joining his cause.

Not long after this amazing incident, a reporter interviewed Yeltsin. He asked him what gave him the courage to stand firm and help ensure the fall of communism in the former U.S.S.R. Yeltsin credited reading the story of Lech Walesa, the electrician who helped bring democracy to Poland several years before.

Lech Walesa has said that he was inspired to his acts of sacrifice and courage by reading accounts of the civil rights movement in this country, led by the late Dr. Martin Luther King, Jr. Dr. King indicated that he was spurred to action when he learned of the courage of one woman, Rosa Parks.

Rosa Parks began the 1955 Montgomery, Alabama bus boycott. She had finished a hard day's work and had paid her fare to ride the Cleveland Avenue bus home. She took her place at the rear of the bus, in the front part of the section reserved for non-whites. (It sounds like I'm talking about a different world, doesn't it? It was.) As the white section filled, Rosa would be expected to stand so a white person could sit. But when that time came, she refused. The bus driver swore at her and threatened to have her arrested, all to no avail. She was arrested, and thus the bus boycott in Montgomery, Alabama began—and so did the ripples of influence through Dr. King, to Lech Walesa, to Boris Yeltsin, and indirectly, to millions of other persons touched by their lives. Not only did Rosa Parks' act of civil disobedience sound the death knell for Jim Crow laws, but also, perhaps, for international communism. Rosa Parks paid it forward not only for a generation of African Americans, but for the entire world community.

One person can make a difference. Through the Law of Influence, one person can change the world.

According to Harvard professor Edward O. Wilson, it is a basic principle of sociobiology that a small change in the behavior of the individual makes a huge change in the behavior of society. And if the amount of individual greatness in a given society could be increased by even one percent across the board, Wilson goes on to say, the beneficial effects on the entire society would be astonishing. If you and I increased our positive influence by just one percent, who knows where it might lead?

Dr. Everett Rogers of the University of Southern California offers a similar perspective. He concludes that 5 percent of a population needs to change before the established leaders begin to take notice that something new is happening. Once that intrepid 5 percent convinces another 15 percent, then a rapid and unstoppable momentum shifts the other 80 percent. To be more precise, he demonstrated that when 13 percent of a population accepts a new idea it is only a matter of time before at least 84 percent accept the idea. "Once the critical mass is achieved, the rate of adoption of an innovation becomes self-sustaining," says Rogers.[1]

You and I can be among that one per cent, that five percent, that fifteen percent, and finally we can experience the peace and the wholeness of a changed world. Random acts of kindness, words of encouragement, a life of integrity and purpose, and a commitment to a better world are all it takes to change the world. "Never doubt that a small group of thoughtful, committed citizens can change the world," said anthropologist Margaret Mead. "Indeed, it's the only thing that ever has."

When Good Moves In

A few years ago, ambulance service to New York's Bedford-Stuyvesant neighborhood was inefficient at best, dangerously negligent at worst.

Bedford-Stuy residents in need of medical care often died before an ambulance reached them. But, according to a story by Brad Darrach in *Life* magazine that changed the day Rocky Robinson came on the scene. Robinson, a supervisor in New York City's Emergency Medical Service, set up a trailer in a run-down parking lot and declared it to be the new site of the Bedford-Stuyvesant Volunteer Ambulance Corps. Local drug dealers and junkies tried to scare him off, but he hung in there. Robinson trained local residents in CPR and other life-saving techniques. Today, the volunteer ambulance corps cruises the neighborhood, looking for someone to help. Robinson, noting the turnaround in his neighborhood, says, "When good moves in, evil gotta move out."[2]

George Eliot put it like this many years ago:

> May every soul that touches mine—
> Be it the slightest contact—
> Get there from some good;
> Some little grace; one kindly thought;
> One aspiration yet unfelt;
> One bit of courage
> For the darkening sky;
> One gleam of faith
> To brave the thickening ills of life;
> One glimpse of brighter skies
> Beyond the gathering mists—
> To make this life worth while.

Epilogue

It seemed like a good idea at the time. Have you ever noticed that most idiotic ideas seem good at the time? We had just landed at the airport in Madrid, Spain, planning to find a hotel for the night before boarding a train to take us to the beautiful Costa del Sol.

When a man in the plane terminal turned up and told us he knew of a *manifico* hotel at a really *cheapo* price, we should have headed for the hills. But we didn't. Perhaps we were too tired from our flight to put up an argument. In any event, we dragged ourselves into his taxi and began a journey we would soon regret—though not as much as we'd originally feared.

It was a compliment to say that the hotel was past its prime. Paint peeled from the walls, and the carpet, which even in better days was not expensive, was now worn. When I turned on the light in the bathroom, a roach scampered under the sink. Still, it was not too terrible. After all, we were inexperienced travelers. What did we know about hotel standards in Madrid? It could have been worse, much worse.

While my wife was checking us in, I had my brilliant idea. Outside the hotel was the entrance to a subway stop. I noticed on the map that was posted on the wall that we were only two stops from the central railroad station. "Why don't I hop on down to the central station and see about buying tickets for tomorrow's trip?" I said to my wife, "We're only two stops away. It's four o'clock now, and when I get back, we can catch a bite for supper."

The central train station in Madrid is large, and in the daytime hours, milling with humanity. After paying the young woman for our tickets, I thought what a brilliant move on my part. We had wanted to get an early start tomorrow and now we could. Plus, I now had some familiarity with the station which would help us find our train much faster. Smiling, I walked back toward my gate. I'd be back at the hotel by half past four with tickets in hand. My wife would be so proud.

Then a terrifying thought entered my mind. What hotel? The driver had parked at the side and hustled us in (yes, hustled is a good word for it) so quickly that I had not even seen a name. And I had been in such haste to get to the central station that I'd failed to ask where we were staying. No problem. All I had to do was get back on the train that brought me into the station and get off at the second stop, and there it would be. But which train would that be? I made my way back to the boarding area for the various subway trains. It was then that I realized that in my haste to transact the business at hand, I hadn't noticed a number on the train or the name of my stop or even which track I had exited on.

Are you starting to get the picture? Absolutely nothing was making sense to me. I imagine I was experiencing more fatigue from the long flight than I realized. Anyway, there I stood in Madrid's central railroad station confused beyond belief.

My memory was that I had disembarked the train in a small area on the third of three tracks, but now as I surveyed the scene in the Madrid central station there were several times that many tracks. Which one was mine? I couldn't remember. Surely, if I thought about it for a moment, the name of the subway stop would come to me. Surely I'd noticed something that stayed with me.

No such luck. On the verge of panicking, I tried to find some official person who spoke enough English for me to explain my predicament. But the lines at each of the counters were long, and by the time I reached the agent, I really didn't know what to ask. Even the police would be no help. Maybe tomorrow morning when my poor frantic wife reported me missing, they could help, but not now. For one of the few times in my life I felt absolutely helpless. The only thing I knew for sure was that I needed to call my wife. The bad news was that I didn't know the number.

Prospects for the Twenty-first Century

Can you feel the desperation I felt that afternoon in Madrid? In this first part of the twenty-first century, there are people in our society who are lost and confused like I was in that train station. We see this confusion reflected in families that are coming apart; the rising tide of juvenile crime and suicides; the increasing numbers of people who are wasting away in a fog of drug and alcohol addiction; the decline of the influence of traditional institutions like churches, universities, and government; and the increasing dependence on materialism as a philosophy of life not only in this country but also around the world. There are people who are searching for values that are real, heroes who stand tall and true, a lifestyle that is both satisfying, yet purposeful, and each of these longings seems increasingly elusive.

Most of us want to believe that our lives make a difference, but we see little evidence of it. More and more people are singing a variation of the old Peggy Lee tune: "Is this all there is . . . to life? Does it matter that I am here?"

I believe it does matter that we are here, and I believe that by exercising our influence, you and I can improve our lives and the lives of those we love, and ultimately improve the world. The situation is far from hopeless. In fact, due in no small part to the dynamic nature of our universe, there is much cause for optimism. One person can set in motion ripples that can change the world. But allow me to finish my story.

There I was in the central train station with no idea where my hotel was, what my stop was or which train to take. I had no telephone number, no hotel name, no way of contacting my wife to let her know of my predicament. What could I do?

Would you be surprised if I were to tell you this was one of the longest evenings in my life? I knew only one solution. Starting with Line One, I began riding each of the subway lines. At the second stop I would exit the train and look around frantically for my hotel. Then I would await the next train back in to the central station. I rode every train in that station, exited at the appropriate stop, and each time saw absolutely nothing that I recognized. Meanwhile, the evening was disappearing. I knew by this time my wife was beginning to be alarmed. It was ten o'clock. The last train would run at half past ten. That didn't concern me too much. After all, I had already ridden them all in vain. I slumped over in a corner of the railroad station. I planned on staying there until my wife sent the police to find me. And then something nearly miraculous happened.

Maybe it was a payoff to the prayers I had been praying under my breath all this time. You know the drill: "Lord, if you will just help me out this time . . . " I felt like Burt Reynolds bargaining with God in the movie *The End*. Suddenly I noticed a sign posted on the back of a door near where I was sitting. I could read just enough Spanish to realize that the sign was describing another part of the station that had totally escaped my attention. Evidently I had been so intent on finding the ticket agent to buy our tickets for the coast that I had wandered into another part of the station quite far removed from the train from which I had disembarked.

There they were. Three sets of tracks, and the last train of the evening was just about ready to pull out on track number three. So I boarded this one last train, exited at the second stop, made my way up to the street and ran into my frantic wife who was certain I had been captured by terrorists. What I learned later was that the central train station in Madrid serves two separate rail systems—a metropolitan system and a federal system. The train I had boarded was one of only three federal trains that serve the city. Nevertheless, all was well. We lived happily ever after. And really that is the way I feel about our world.

I am basically optimistic about our future as a species. Part of this derives from my belief in a divine Creator who has purposed great things for our world. But also it is because I believe in the power of the Law of Influence. I believe that it is not too late for humanity to find its way in this confused and confusing world. All it takes is enough people who truly care about one another and about our common future. All it takes is people who are willing to pay the price of change and are willing to exercise their influence in this dynamic universe. As Charles Kingsley once put it, "Make it a rule, and pray to God to help you to keep it, never, if possible, to lie down at night without being able to say: 'I have made one human being at least a little wiser, or a little happier, or at least a little better this day.'"

Notes

INTRODUCTION

1. "Time's 25 Most Influential Americans," *Time* (April 21, 1997): 59.

CHAPTER 1

1. J. Sig Paulsen, *How to Love Your Neighbor* (Garden City, N.Y.: Doubleday, 1974).

2. George Land and Beth Jarman, "Breakpoint and Beyond," *Harper Business* (1992): 104.

CHAPTER 2

1. Sam Llewellyn, *Small Parts in History* (N.Y.: Barnes and Noble, 1985).

CHAPTER 3

1. Dr. Ward Williams, *The United Christian Church of Caracas, Venezuela.*

CHAPTER 4

1. William Poundstone, *Bigger Secrets* (Boston, Mass.: Houghton Mifflin Company, 1986).

CHAPTER 5

1. Erica E. Goode, "Victims in the Company of Cults," *U.S. News & World Report* (March 15, 1993).

2. Dale Dauten, *Taking Chances* (N.Y.: Newmarket Press, 1986), 174.

3. Don Voorhees, *The Book of Totally Useless Information* (N.Y.: MJF Books, 1993), 89.

CHAPTER 6

1. Lawrence Elliott, "Where Elvis Lives," *Reader's Digest* (August 1993): 48.

2. Steve Jurvetson and Tim Draper, "Viral Marketing" *Netscape M-Files* (1997)

and Christopher John Farley and David E. Thigpen, "Christina Aguilera: Building a Twenty-first Century Star," *Time* (March 6, 2000): 71, and *The Futurist* (January/February 1996). Used with permission from The World Future Society.

CHAPTER 7

1. Max De Pree, *Leadership Jazz* (N.Y.: Dell Publishing, 1992), 127-28.

2. Fred Race, "Arizona Highways," *Humor* (September 1999).

3. Alvin Toffler, *Future Shock,* (Amereon Ltd., 1970).

4. *The Washington Post* (August 15, 1989): A18.

5. Charles R. Swindoll, *Hope Again* (Dallas, Tex.: Word Publishing, 1996), 121.

6. Robert D. Dale, *Leading Edge* (Nashville, Tenn.: Abingdon, 1996).

CHAPTER 9

1. Chuck Neighbors, "The Story of In His Steps," *Guideposts* (September 1996): 52-55.

2. *Augsburg Sermons 2* (Minneapolis, Minn.: Augsburg Publishing House, 1983).

CHAPTER 10

1. Interview by Vicki Quade, *Salt of the Earth* (January/February 1997): 8-9.

CHAPTER 11

1. David McCullough, *Truman* (N.Y.: Simon and Schuster, 1992).

2. Ira Flatow, *They All Laughed* (N.Y.: Harper Perennial, 1992), 119-21.

3. Andor Foldes, "Beethoven's Kiss," *Reader's Digest* (November 1986).

4. Norman Cousins, *Albert Schweitzer's Mission* (N.Y.: W. W. Norton & Co., 1984), 303-04.

CHAPTER 12

1. Henry Steele Commager, *Crusaders For Freedom* (Garden City, N.Y.: Doubleday, 1962), 29-35.

2. C. Everett Koop, *Koop: The Memoirs of America's Family Doctor* (N.Y.: Random House, 1991), 52.

CHAPTER 13

1. William H. Hinson, *The Power of Holy Habits* (Nashville, Tenn.: Abingdon Press, 1991).

2. Donald F. Ackland and Robert Dean, *52 Ready-to-Teach . . .* (Nashville, Tenn.: Broadman, 1994).

3. William Kilpatrick, Gregory Wolfe, and Suzanne M. Wolfe, *Books That Build Character* (N.Y.: Simon & Schuster, Inc. 1994), 20.

4. *Selling Power*, (October 1999): 189.

5. Scott Raab, "What It Cost," *Esquire* (November 1998): 140-43.

6. Anthony Robbins, *Awaken the Giant Within* (N.Y.: Fireside, 1991), 90.

7. Robert L. Dilenschneider, *Power and Influence* (N.Y.: Prentice Hall, 1990), 86 and A. S. Doc Young, "Jackie Robinson Remembered," *Ebony* (February 1997).

8. Kathy McWorter, *The War* (screenplay).

9. Todd Gold, ed., *Comic Relief* (N.Y.: Avon Books, 1996), 6-7.

10. Em Griffin, *The Mindchangers* (Tyndale House, 1976), 179.

CHAPTER 14

1. Ben Kinchlow, *You Don't Have To If You Don't Want To* (Nashville, Tenn.: Thomas Nelson, 1995).

2. *The Executive Speechwriters Newsletter.*

3. Dotson Rader, "Sorrow Made Me What I Am," *Parade* (August 4, 1996): 16.

4. John Bradshaw, *Creating Love* (N.Y.: Bantam Books, 1992), 179-81.

5. Harold Willens, *The Trimtab Factor* (N.Y.: William Morrow & Company, 1984), 27.

6. *Trained Men*

7. Randy Scott, *Country Music Revealed* (N.Y.: MetroBooks, 1995), 26-7.

8. Jack Canfield and Mark Victor Hansen, *A 2nd Helping of Chicken Soup* (Deerfield Beach, Fla.: Health Communications, Inc., 1995), 208-10.

CHAPTER 15

1. "Post People," *The Saturday Evening Post* (May/June 1996): 10.

2. Jane Bluestein, Ph. D., *Mentors* (Deerfield Beach, Fla.: Health Communications, Inc.,1995), 147-50.

3. John Calis, "True Colors," *Philip Morris* (Summer 1988).

4. Jean Ollis Honeycutt, *Growing Up Country And Liking It!* (Johnson City, Tenn.: The Overmountain Press, 1996), 35-6.

5. Carl Rowan, *Breaking Barriers* (Boston, Mass.: Little Brown and Company, 1991).

6. James W. Moore, *Some Things Are Too Good* (Nashville, Tenn.: Dimensions for Living, 1994).

7. Edward Sussman, "Secrets of a Life Well Lived," *Reader's Digest* (April 2000): 101.

8. Jim Stovall, *You Don't Have To Be Blind To See* (Nashville, Tenn.: Thomas Nelson Publishers, 1996), 43-5.

9. Patty Perrin, "Cable from Kabul: Spartan Samaritan At Large!" *Modern Maturity* (March/ April 1997): 16, 18.

CHAPTER 16

1. Jacques Billeaud, et al, "Love bug infests e-mail," *The Knoxville News-Sentinel* (May 5, 2000): A1, A12.

2. US Airways *Attache* (September 2000).

3. John F. Wukovits, "Destroying Angel," *American History Illustrated* (March/April 1990): 68-72.

4. F. H. Edgecombe, *Quote* (January 1993, Vol. 53, No. 1): 25.

5. Linda Shudy, *Daily Guideposts* (Carmel, N.Y.: Guideposts, 1990), 107.

6. Max Depree, *Leadership is an Art* (N.Y.: Doubleday, 1989), 99-100.

7. *Lectionaid,* (Kamuela, HI: LectionAid, July/August/September 1994): 31.

8. Paul Grigase, "The Notion of Health," *The Courier* (August 1987).

9. Yale University, Office of Public Affairs, P.O. Box 208279, New Haven, Conn.

CHAPTER 17

1. David A. Seamands, *God's Blueprint for Living* (Wilmore, Ky.: Bristol Books, 1988).

2. James Robert Parish, *Rosie: Rosie O'Donnell's Biography* (N.Y.: Carroll & Graf Publishers, 1997), 23-5.

3. Mary Murphy, *TV Guide,* (June 15, 1996): 28.

4. *Parade,* (January 1, 1995): 6.

5. David Granger, "Boy, Do We Ever Need A Hero," *Esquire* (November 1998): 26.

6. Lorraine Lelis, "Looking Up Can Bring You Down," *Psychology Today* (November/ December 1997): 10.

7. Mark Moring, "Campus Life Sports: Olympic Edition," *Campus Life* (July/August 1996): 45.

CHAPTER 18

1. Lori Teresa Yearwood, "Archie Against the Odds," *Reader's Digest* (October 1999): 101-06.

2. *World Press Review* (February 1997).

3. Juliet B. Schor, *The Overspent American* (N.Y.: Basic Books, 1998), 82.

4. Kathleen Kelly Reardon, *Persuasion in Practice* (Newberry Park, Calif.: Sage Publications, 1991).

5. Victor M. Parachin and Mary Hopkins, "Ch—Ch—Changes," *Aspire* (December 1994/January 1995): 77.

6. Molly Ivens, *You've Got to Dance with Them What Brung You* (N.Y.: Random House, 1998).

7. Robert Persig, *Compton Encyclopedia from Aardvark to Zygote*

8. *Selling Power,* (May 1999), 115.

9. Cynthia Kersey, *Unstoppable* (Naperville, Ill.: Sourcebooks, Inc., 1998).

CHAPTER 19

1. *The Houston Chronicle* (February 18, 1993): 8A.

2. Robert B. Cialdini, *Influence* (N.Y.: William Morrow and Company, Inc., 1984).

3. Geoff Burch, *The Art And Science of Business Persuasion* (N.Y.: Carol Publishing Group, 1994).

4. *Spokesman Review,* (November, 1991): C1.

5. Marilyn Vos Savant, *Ask Marilyn, Parade* (March 19, 2000): 28.

6. Joe Griffith, *Speakers Library of Business* (N.Y.: Prentice-Hall, 1990).

7. Connie Leslie, "Will Johnny Get A's?" *Newsweek* (July 8, 1996): 72.

8. Jeff Foxworthy, *No Shirt. No Shoes . . . No Problem* (N.Y.: Hyperion, 1996), 21-2.

9. Michael G. Zey, *Winning with People* (Berkley Publishers, 1995).

10. Gilbert Brin, *Ambition* (N.Y.: Basic Books, 1992).

11. Melna Gerosa, "Michelle: Up Close and Personal," *Ladies Home Journal* (March 1996): 206.

CHAPTER 20

1. Sidney B. Simon, *I Am Loveable and Capable: A Modern Allegory on the Classical Put-Down* (Values Press, 1990).

2. Steve Zeitlin, ed., *Because God Loves Stories: An Anthology of Jewish Storytelling* (N.Y.: Simon & Schuster, 1997), 248.

3. Leslie Zebrowitz, Ph. D., "A Reason to Smile," *Psychology Today,* (March/April 1999): 18.

4. Dr. Robert Schuller, *Self Esteem: The New Reformation* (Waco, Tex.: Word Books, 1982).

5. Richard Rodgers and Oscar Hammerstein II, *South Pacific* (Hal Leonard Productions, 1980).

CHAPTER 21

1. Roger Ailes, *You Are The Message* (N.Y.: Doubleday/Currency, 1988).

2. Mark Littleton, *When They Invited* (Camp Hill, Pa.: Christian Publications, 1992).

3. Frederick Loewe and Alan Jay Lerner, *My Fair Lady* (N.Y.: Chappell, 1956).

4. Robert Fulghum, *All I Really Need to Know I Learned in Kindergarten,* (N.Y.: Villard Books, 1988).

5. Martin E.P. Seligman, Ph.D., *Learned Optimism* (N.Y.: Alfred A. Knopf, 1991).

6. George R. Walther, *What You SAY Is What You GET* (SFE Publishing, 2000). Used with permission of the author.

CHAPTER 22

1. Dr. R. H. Schuller, *Reach Out For New Life* (Garden Grove, Calif.: Cathedral Press, 1991), 151-52.

2. Deborah Tannen, *You Just Don't Understand* (N.Y.: Ballantine, 1991).

3. Howard Gardner, *Frames of Mind: The Theory of Multiple Intelligences* (N.Y.: Basic Books, 1993).

CHAPTER 23

1. *U.S. News & World Report* (April 24, 1989).

2. Arun Gandhi, (a speech given to The National Speakers Association, Orlando, Fla., 1996). Used with Dr. Gandhi's permission.

3. Alfie Kohn, "You Know What They Say," *Psychology Today,* (April 1988): 36.

4. Alvin Toffler, *Future Shock* (Ameron Ltd., 1970).

5. Sam Keen and Anne Valley-Fox, *Your Mythic Journey* (Los Angeles, Calif.: Jeremy P. Tarcher, Inc., 1989).

6. Nancy Friday, *Jealousy* (N.Y.: Bantam Books, 1991), 59.

7. Morton T. Kelsey, *Transcend* (N.Y.: The Crossroad Publishing Co., 1981), 194.

8. *Washington Post Magazine* (April 12 and 19, 1987).

9. Elliot Johnson and Al Schierbaum, *Our Great and Awesome Savior* (Brentwood, Tenn.: Wolgemuth & Hyatt, Publishers Inc., 1991), 55.

10. Les Brown, *Live Your Dreams* (N.Y.: Avon Books, 1992).

11. Walter Anderson, *The Confidence Course* (N.Y.: Harper Perennial, 1997), 203-4.

12. Hans J. Massaquoi, "Lindiwe Mabuza, South Africa's First Black Ambassador to Germany," *Ebony* (May 1996).

13. Bill Adler, ed., *The Uncommon Wisdom of Oprah Winfrey* (Seacaucus, N.J.: Carol Publishing Group, 1997).

14. D. Larry Miller, *God's Vitamin "C" for Men* (Lancaster, Pa.: Starburst Publishing, 1996), 60-1.

15. William R. Lampkin, *Minute Devotions* (Lima, Ohio: Fairway Press, 1990).

16. Robert and Jeanette Lauer, *Watersheds* (Boston, Mass.: Little, Brown and Company, 1988).

17. Doug Sherman and William Hendricks, *How to Succeed Where it Really Counts* (Colorado Springs, Colo.: NavPress, 1989), 151-2.

18. J. Peter Zane, "How I learned responsibility," *Parents* (March 1996): 82.

19. Ron L. Fronk, Ph.D, *Creating a Lifestyle* (Springdale, Pa.: Whitaker House, 1988).

20. "Caring parents produce healthier children," *McCall's* (July 1996): 90.

21. John E. Douglas and Mark Olshaker, *Mindhunter: Inside the FBI's Elite Serial Crime Unit* (N.Y.: Simon & Schuster, 1996).

22. Bill Glass, *Moving Beyond Belief* (Nashville, Tenn.: Thomas Nelson Publishers, 1993), 151-152.

23. Linda Russek and Gary Schwartz, "Why Are We Not Surprised?" *Aspire* (August/September 1996): 10.

24. Raham Sharpe, *Lexington Herald-Leader* (January 16, 1997).

25. Neil Kurshan, *Raising Your Child to Be a Mensch* (N.Y.: Atheneum, 1987), 77.

26. Pat Williams, *The Magic of Teamwork* (Nashville, Tenn.: Thomas Nelson, 1997). Used with permission of the author.

27. *USA Today* (June 8, 1994).

CHAPTER 24

1. Michael Caine, *What's It All About?* (N.Y.: Turtle Bay Books, 1992), 250-1.

2. Harold Ivan Smith, *No Fear of Trying* (Nashville, Tenn.: Thomas Nelson Publishers, 1988).

3. David Newton, *Bringing Total Quality Management to . . .* (Hackettstown, N.J.: NKBA, 1996).

4. "Time's 25 Most Influential Americans," *Time* (April 21, 1997): 42.

5. Lorie Parch, "Cyber Schmoozing," *Working Woman* (March 1998): 20.

6. Charles Pappas, "Harvey Mackay," *Success* (February 1999): 51-4.

7. Harvey Mackay, *Dig Your Well Before You're Thirsty* (N.Y.: Currency, 1997). Used with permission of the author.

8. Joyce Brothers, "How to Get Clout," *Reader's Digest* (April 1994): 185.

9. Ted W. Engstrom, *The Fine Art of Friendship* (Nashville, Tenn.: Thomas Nelson Publishers, 1985).

10. Richard B. Wilke, *Tell Me Again, I'm Listening* (Nashville, Tenn. and N.Y.: Abingdon Press, 1973), 50.

11. Fran Tarkenton, *Playing to Win* (Toronto, N.Y.: Bantam Books, 1984).

12. John C. Maxwell, *Developing The Leaders Around You* (Nashville, Tenn.: Thomas Nelson, Inc., 1947), 70.

13. Nancy Thies Marshall and Pam Vredevelt, *Women Who Compete* (Old Tappan, N.J.: Fleming H. Revell, 1988), 142-4.

14. Ernest Kurtz and Katherine Ketcham, *The Spirituality of Imperfection* (N.Y.: Bantam, 1992).

15. Jay Strack, *Good Kids Who Do Bad Things* (Dallas, Tex.: Word Publishing, 1993).

16. Zig Ziglar, *Raising Positive Kids in a Negative World* (Ballantine, 1996).

17. Stephen Rebello, "Personal Glimpses," *Reader's Digest* (February 1996): 125-6.

18. Willie Brown and Dennis Conner, *The Art of Winning* (N.Y.: St. Martin's Press, 1988), 8.

19. Jean-Claude Baker, Jennifer Gates Hayes, ed., *Pearls of Wisdom from Grandma* (N.Y.: Regan Books, 1997), 48-9.

20. Bud Greenspan, *Modern Maturity* (July/August 1996).

21. Bruce Larson, *Living Out the Book of Acts* (Dallas, Tex.: Word Publishing, 1984), 64.

CHAPTER 25

1. Steven R. Mosley, *Glimpses of God* (Sisters, Ore.: Questar Publishers, Inc., 1990), 83-5.

2. John E. Fellers, *Secrets For Successful Living* (Nashville, Tenn.: Dimensions for Living, 1993), 15.

3. C. Edward Bowen, *Emphasis* (March/April 2000): 4.

4. "Etcetera," *Salt of the Earth* (July/August 1996): 34.

5. "Local Heroes," *Time* (June 24, 1996): 21.

6. A. Victoria Hunter, "Leaving No One Behind," *Response* (March 1996): 15.

7. Douglas M. Lawson, *Give to Live* (Calif.: ALTI Publishing, 1991), 112.

8. Rebecca Piirto, "The Influentials," *American Demographics* (October 1992): 30-8.

9. Daniel Goleman, *Emotional Intelligence* (N.Y.: Bantam Books, 1995), 114-5.

10. Dr. Ernst G. Beier and Evans G. Valens, *People Reading* (N.Y.: Stein and Day, 1975).

11. William E. Diehl, *Thank God, It's Monday* (Philadelphia, Pa.: Fortress Press, 1982).

12. Terrie Williams, *The Personal Touch* (N.Y.: Warner Books, 1994).

13. Robert Fulghum, *Maybe (Maybe Not)* (N.Y.: Villard Books, 1993).

CHAPTER 26

1. Lloyd Dobyns and Clare Crawford Mason, *Quality or Else,* (N.Y.: Houghton Mifflin Company, 1991).

2. *Bits & Pieces,* (January 5, 1995).

3. "St. Vince," *Lexington Herald-Leader,* (January 30, 1997): B2.

4. Don Martin, *Team Think* (N.Y.: Penguin Books Ltd: 1993), 34.

5. B. J. Connor *Daily Guideposts* (Carmel, N.Y.: Guideposts, 1990), 28.

6. Michael Ryan, "Who Is Great?" *Parade* (June 16, 1996): 4-5.

7. *Wall Street Journal,* date unknown.

8. Bruce Larson, *Wind and Fire* (Waco, Tex.: Word Books, 1984).

9. Dale Dauten, *Taking Chances* (N.Y.: Newmarket Press, 1986), 112.

10. Daryl G. Mitton and Betty Lilligren-Mitton, *Clout* (N.J.: Prentice-Hall, Inc., 1980), 1.

11. Emory Thomas, Jr., "Re-engineer Cut Corporate Fat, Then Fell on His Own Budget Ax," *Wall Street Journal* (March 21, 1995) :B1.

12. Colin Powell with Joseph E. Perisco, *My American Journey.*

13. Tony Campolo, *Following Jesus Without Embarrassing God* (Dallas, Tex.: Word Publishing, 1997), 35.

14. Burt Nanus, *The Leader's Edge* (Chicago, Ill.: Contemporary Books, Inc., 1989), 95.

CHAPTER 27

1. ktodd@vci.net (Keith Todd).

2. Dennis and Barbara Rainey, *Moments Together for Couples* (Ventura, Calif.: Regal Books, 1995).

3. *Quote,* (August 1996): 8.

4. Jeffrey Holland, *Vital Speeches.*

5. Ken Melrose, *Making the Grass Greener on Your Side* (Berrett-Koehler Publishers, Inc., 1994).

6. Zig Ziglar, *Ziglar on Selling* (Nashville, Tenn.: Oliver Nelson, 1991), 49-52.

7. Robert J. Sternberg and Todd I. Lubart, *Defying the Crowd* (N.Y.: The Free Press, 1995), 266.

8. Mihaly Csikszentmihalyi, *Creativity: Flow and the Psychology of Discovery and Invention* (Harper-Collins, 1996).

9. Gini Kopecky, *American Health* (June 1996): 46.

10. Norman Vincent Peale, *Powerful Results* (N.Y.: Foundation for Christian Living, 1982).

11. Ron Lee Davis and James D. Denney, *Mistreated* (Portland, Ore.: Multnomah, 1989).

12. Richard G. Capen, Jr., *Finish Strong* (N.Y.: Harper San Francisco, 1992).

13. Charles R.Swindoll, *The Bride* (Grand Rapids, Mich.: Zondervan Publishing House, 1994), 150-1.

14. Peg Roen, "The Sky's the Limit" *Aspire* (February/ March 1997): 33-34.

15. Jimmy Carter, *Living Faith* (N.Y.: Random House, Inc., 1996).

16. Barbara Cubin, *Profiles in Character* (Nashville, Tenn.: Thomas Nelson, 1996), 68-9.

CHAPTER 28

1. Richard Rodgers and Oscar Hammerstein II, *The Sound of Music*.

2. Mitch Leigh and Joe Darlon, "To Dream the Impossible Dream" from *Man of La Mancha.*. Judith Hooper and Dick Teresi, *Would the Buddha Wear a Walkman?* (N.Y.: Simon & Schuster Inc., 1990).

4. Robert J. Morgan, "The Well-Fed Imagination," *Leadership* (Summer 1993): 33.

5. Michael Michalko, "How Would da Vinci Make A Sale?" *Personal Selling Power* (October 1993): 61.

6. F. Albert Cotton, *Chemistry: An Investigative Approach* (Boston, Mass.: Houghton Mifflin, 1973), 454-5.

7. Michael Ray, *Creativity in Business* (N.Y.: Dell Publishing, 1989), 142.

8. Denis Waitley, *Timing Is Everything* (Nashville, Tenn.: Thomas Nelson Publishers, 1992).

9. Florence Littauer, *Dare to Dream* (Dallas, Tex.: Word Publishing, 1991).

10. Desmond Morris, *The Book of Ages* (N.Y.: The Viking Press, 1983).

11. *Field of Dreams,* (Universal Studios, 1989).

12. Mitch Leigh and Joe Darlon, *The Man of La Mancha* (Cherry Lane Books, 1965).

13. Michael J. Gelb, *How to Think Like Leonardo da Vinci* (N.Y.: Dell Publishing, 1998), 29.

CHAPTER 30

1. Everett Rogers, *The Diffusion of Innovations* (N.Y.: Simon & Schuster, 1996).

2. Brad Darrach, "A New Birth of Freedom," *Life* (October 1995): 87.